REVIVING RURAL AMERICA

We often hear that there is no way out of the modern economic and political tensions that fall along geographic lines. Media commentary regularly declares that rural America is dying and that rural voters are driven only by anger. This narrative of hopelessness centers on the role that markets have played in abandoning rural regions and populations. In *Reviving Rural America*, Ann M. Eisenberg makes the case for hope by analyzing the role our society's laws and policies play in the urban/rural divide. She demonstrates how law and policy, as well as decision-makers acting on their own subjective values, have contributed to modern rural challenges. Each chapter debunks a common myth about rural people, places, and policies, helping reveal how we got to where we are now. Ultimately calling for our laws and policies to steward rural America holistically, as a collective resource for all, this book envisions an alternative, more resilient and more just future.

Ann M. Eisenberg is Professor of Law at West Virginia University College of Law and Research Director at the Center for Energy and Sustainable Development. Her research examines how law shapes rural communities.

Reviving Rural America

TOWARD POLICIES FOR RESILIENCE

ANN M. EISENBERG
West Virginia University College of Law

Shaftesbury Road, Cambridge CB2 8EA, United Kingdom

One Liberty Plaza, 20th Floor, New York, NY 10006, USA

477 Williamstown Road, Port Melbourne, VIC 3207, Australia

314–321, 3rd Floor, Plot 3, Splendor Forum, Jasola District Centre, New Delhi – 110025, India

103 Penang Road, #05–06/07, Visioncrest Commercial, Singapore 238467

Cambridge University Press is part of Cambridge University Press & Assessment, a department of the University of Cambridge.

We share the University's mission to contribute to society through the pursuit of education, learning and research at the highest international levels of excellence.

www.cambridge.org
Information on this title: www.cambridge.org/9781108834018

DOI: 10.1017/9781108989022

First published 2024

A catalogue record for this publication is available from the British Library

Library of Congress Cataloging-in-Publication Data
NAMES: Eisenberg, Ann M., author.
TITLE: Reviving rural America : toward policies for resilience / Ann M. Eisenberg, West Virginia University College of Law.
DESCRIPTION: Cambridge, United Kindgom ; New York, NY : Cambridge University Press, 2024. | Includes bibliographical references and index.
IDENTIFIERS: LCCN 2024000027 | ISBN 9781108834018 (hardback) | ISBN 9781108989022 (ebook)
SUBJECTS: LCSH: Rural development – Law and legislation – United States. | Agricultural laborers – Legal status, laws, etc. – United States. | Rural-urban relations – United States. | Resilience – United States. | United States – Rural conditions.
CLASSIFICATION: LCC KF1682 .E37 2024 | DDC 307.1/4120973–dc23/eng/20240129
LC record available at https://lccn.loc.gov/2024000027

ISBN 978-1-108-83401-8 Hardback
ISBN 978-1-108-98440-9 Paperback

Contents

Figures

Acknowledgments

This project is the culmination of nearly a decade of lived experience, hands-on work, and scholarly research. It would not have been possible without a diverse set of supporters, collaborators, and readers over the course of that decade. I am grateful to the faculty and staff of the West Virginia University College of Law Land Use and Sustainable Development Clinic for taking a chance on hiring me as a young attorney and offering invaluable lessons about West Virginia, Appalachia, and being a good lawyer. My thanks goes to Kat Garvey especially for her mentorship. I am similarly grateful that my colleagues at the University of South Carolina School of Law saw my potential as a scholar and practitioner and for their feedback and encouragement on my research agenda over the years. Most recently, I am grateful to the Kluge Center at the Library of Congress and their generous support of my research on the Rural Electrification Act of 1936; to the West Virginia University College of Law and Arthur B. Hodges College of Law Fund for their support of this project in its final stages; and to the West Virginia University College of Law for the opportunity to return to West Virginia to join their faculty.

This book also would not have taken shape were it not for the literature, encouragement, and scholarly community in the Law and Rurality movement. The work, feedback, support, and organizing efforts of Lisa Pruitt, Jessica Shoemaker, Hannah Haksgaard, and many others have helped motivate and inform this project substantially. The same goes for the generosity of time and feedback from many of my colleagues in South Carolina and beyond, especially the ever-reliable readers Claire Raj, Emily Suski, and Shelley Welton.

This project benefited substantially from the incisive review of South Carolina's Ashley Alvarado, Vanessa McQuinn, and Inge Lewis. Law student research assistants over the course of several years also contributed to this book. My thanks especially to Madison Chapel, Michael Crump, India Whaley, and Destinee Wilson.

Finally, I thank my family for their support, feedback, and sense of humor over the years. I especially thank my uncle, economic historian Gavin Wright, for his encouragement and feedback. My late father, Ted Eisenberg, mentioned on this book's first page, did not live to see me follow in his footsteps as a law professor, but I think he would have been proud. I dedicate this book to his memory.

1

Introduction

The year 2014, when I first ended up living in West Virginia, was one of the worst years of my life. My father died, my relationship ended, my short-term postgraduate job in St. Louis ended, my housing was in flux, and I could not seem to find a new job as a young attorney in one of the east coast cities where I wanted to settle. Having just turned thirty, grieving and disoriented, I found myself for the first time in Morgantown, West Virginia, like Dorothy in Oz.

Foreign and unplanned as it was, taking a job in West Virginia made some sense because it got me back within driving distance to my distraught family in Upstate New York. I had interviewed for my new position, a two-year academic fellowship with West Virginia University (WVU) College of Law, over Skype. I accepted the fellowship sight unseen, taking a $44,000 pay cut to do so. Getting there was a whirlwind: I found an online listing for a studio apartment above a WVU professor's garage in Morgantown for $420 per month, sold all of my furniture on Craigslist because it would not fit in said garage apartment, and got into my parents' old Volvo to drive back east.

I had no idea what I was getting into. But I was grateful to West Virginia for catching me as my life fell apart. I was nervous about being hired for a fellowship focused on land use law, in which I had no background whatsoever. Apparently there hadn't been that much competition for the job, I presumed.

I started this new position, called the Land Use and Sustainable Development Law Fellowship, in the summer of 2014. I would spend half of my time pursuing a funded master's degree in Energy and Sustainable Development Law, which meant taking courses on environmental, agricultural, and energy law. I would spend the other half of my time working in a program called the Land Use and Sustainable Development Law Clinic.[1]

I had been involved in law school clinics as a law student and liked them quite a bit. Clinics let law students gain practice experience while providing pro bono legal

---

[1] *Land Use and Sustainable Development Law Clinic*, W. Va. Univ.: Land Use & Sustainable Dev. L. Clinic (March 1, 2023), https://landuse.law.wvu.edu/ [https://perma.cc/D5PL-AJ8K].

services to those in need before graduating. But I did not initially grasp in full what this program did.

Housed in a set of offices in WVU Law's basement, the Clinic was made up of one director (Kat), several attorneys (Jesse, Nathan, Jason, and Jared), a planner (Christie), and an office administrator (first Sarah when I started, then Erica). Each new academic year, a cohort of law students joined the team as well in exchange for academic credit. Half of the program's mission was to work with local governments throughout West Virginia on land use planning. The other half of the Clinic's work involved helping land trusts acquire conservation easements on natural space, particularly where it meant protecting drinking water sources.[2] When I was hired, the Clinic was also doing a special project on dilapidated properties.

I harbored some new-attorney fantasies about what a glamorous public interest career looked like. These daydreams involved passionate courtroom speeches, class action lawsuits, civil rights, and criminal law. They did not include drafting small municipalities' comprehensive land use plans and zoning ordinances, investigating property titles, or sorting out the law on derelict old buildings. They also did not involve the large spiders I discovered happily living in my new home above the professor's garage, one of which I awoke to find nestled in bed with me during my first week there. But I had a job, at least, and it was close to home.

When I drove my parents' old Volvo back east to West Virginia that summer (accompanied by my indefatigable mother), I did not know that living and working there would change my life and plant the seeds for various obsessions that would ultimately drive my work and fill my days as a law professor. Living in West Virginia turned out to be radicalizing. I became preoccupied with the socioeconomic, physical, and legal aspects of energy production, the business practices of fossil fuel companies, the struggles of small-town local governments, and the ways property and wealth seemed to systematically flow away from poor people. I observed the ways in which geographic and cultural distance from population centers shielded exploitative practices from scrutiny and reform and how policymakers – and even broader society as a whole – either enabled these practices or turned a blind eye to them.

While some people in my life would act like moving to West Virginia was akin to moving to the moon, West Virginia is not actually that far removed from cities and power centers. Figure 1.1 shows the state's layout. Monongalia County, where Morgantown sits, is less than a four-hour drive from Washington, DC.

I ended up enjoying life in Morgantown. I frequented the quaint downtown, shown in Figure 1.2. I ate the best scones I had ever tasted at the Phoenix Bakery,

---

[2]   Landowners can place a restriction on their land known as a conservation easement, which means they give up development rights and restrict the land's development in perpetuity. A land trust is a nonprofit organization authorized to hold and enforce the easement's restriction on development. *See Frequently Asked Questions*, LAND TR. ALL., www.landtrustalliance.org/what-you-can-do/conserve-your-land/questions [https://perma.cc/56A6-EAHA].

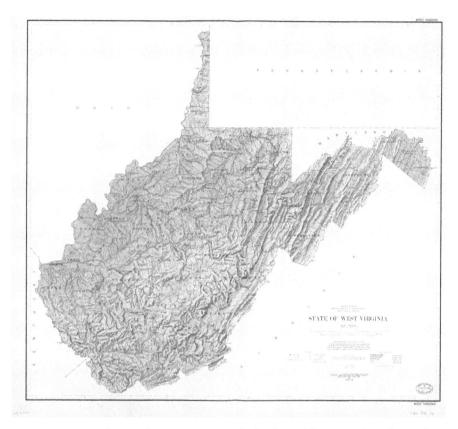

FIGURE 1.1 Map of State of West Virginia, U.S. Geological Survey, 1984, Library of Congress

jogged along the Monongahela River, and rode around town for free in a system of small, driverless trams elevated on a track that made me look like one of the Jetsons (the "Personal Rapid Transit" or "PRT," shown in Figure 1.3). I started a book club with people I met on Craigslist, met the guy who founded the Appalachian Queer Film Festival, and drank local beer with my two co-fellows and their boyfriends. I spider-proofed my little apartment. I grew to love the rest of the state, too – Coopers Rock, the New River Gorge, the Secret Sandwich Society, Point Pleasant with its stories of the Moth Man, and many breweries became favorite destinations. People were generally welcoming. There was a lack of affectation that I was accustomed to in my world of wealthy progressives.

But I also had moments, much like Dorothy in Oz or Alice in Wonderland, of wondering where the hell I had just landed. Did they really, literally blow up mountains here? Seeing the world of fossil fuels up close was like going through the looking glass. After my initial shock at the things coal and gas companies did in West Virginia, I became more and more angry.

FIGURE 1.2 Old Coca Cola and local restaurant signs on a wall in downtown Morgantown, West Virginia, 2015, Carol M. Highsmith Archive, Library of Congress

FIGURE 1.3 Downtown Personal Rapid Transit station in Morgantown, West Virginia, 2015, Carol M. Highsmith Archive, Library of Congress

People's stories about coal and gas were often visceral and emotional. Life or death. The most heartbreaking moment I remember was an otherwise stoic friend choking up as he told me about bodies of people he knew being laid out on a lawn next to his house after a mine explosion.

Locals I met did not drink the Morgantown tap water because it seemed to make people sick and because investigations revealed that water quality reports throughout the state were regularly falsified.[3] I had arrived in West Virginia six months after the massive Elk River coal-processing chemical spill had left much of the region southwest of Morgantown without potable water.[4]

Driving around town, I occasionally followed a truck with an open bed full of some kind of coal waste and a sign hanging on the back that said, "Not responsible for broken windows" – which did not add up, if I recalled my law school torts class. But it was a lie nonlawyers may well have believed. One local road's pothole from truck traffic was so wide and deep I could have driven the Volvo into it – like the opening of a cave – if I hadn't learned to swerve around it.

It quickly became clear that the fossil fuel companies expected total domination of local life, even in a college town such as Morgantown. In one series of events, the City of Morgantown tried and failed to limit massive trucks' ability to navigate loudly over Morgantown's narrow, historic streets at all hours, contributing to the dangerous road conditions I had experienced. The dispute involved someone's dog getting poisoned, I was told.[5] I heard from a colleague that a local law firm pulled its funding for a conference at WVU Law because of a report a professor published endorsing renewable energy policies. We took a graduate program field trip to a natural gas drill site, where a residential landowner had to live alongside development by the company that owned the mineral rights under his home. We heard there about the homeowner's daughter with special needs being called a bitch by a gas company employee and nearly getting driven off the road on her father's property.

The more I learned about West Virginia's story, the more a sense of guilt grew. How had I not thought more before this about where my energy came from? Figure 1.4 depicts the West Virginia coalfields, lying under much of the state like organs in a body, slated to be harvested. The themes, again, were not subtle. Blown-up mountains. Mine wars. Company towns. Black lung. Land agents. Man camps. Gas flares. Opioids. "They would never do this to other mountain

---

3 Press Release, U.S. Att'y's Off., S. Dist. of W. Va., *McDowell County Woman Sentence [sic] in Federal Court for Filing Fraudulent Water Quality Reports* (March 26, 2015), www.justice.gov/usao-sdwv/pr/mcdowell-county-woman-sentence-federal-court-filing-fraudulent-water-quality-reports [https://perma.cc/K5SS-EFB4]; *Former Appalachian Laboratories Manager Sentenced for Falsifying Water Quality Data*, STATE J. (January 19, 2017), www.wvnews.com/statejournal/former-appalachian-laboratories-manager-sentenced-for-falsifying-water-quality-data/article_99b442f1-479f-508c-b645-ebc1b03a01ac.html [https://perma.cc/9CKS-Y7C9].

4 Omar Ghabra, *After the Spill: Life in West Virginia's Coal Country*, ATLANTIC (January 9, 2015), www.theatlantic.com/national/archive/2015/01/life-in-west-virginias-coal-country/384316/ [https://perma.cc/Y4K6-LR7N].

5 This was a rumor I heard associated with the case of *City of Morgantown v. Nuzum Trucking Co.*, 786 S.E.2d 486 (W. Va. 2016), in which the West Virginia Supreme Court held that Morgantown lacked the authority to regulate the weight and size of trucks traveling on portions of state road that went through the city limits.

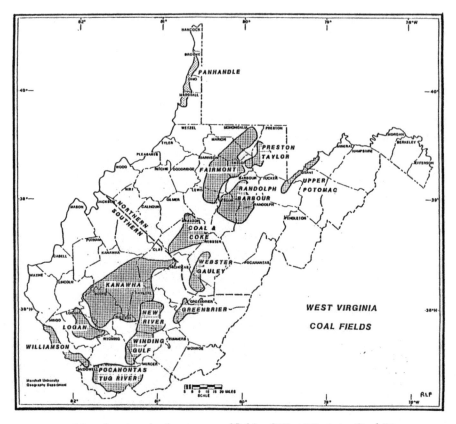

FIGURE 1.4 Map showing the fourteen coalfields of West Virginia, Coal River
Folklife Collection, 1993, Library of Congress; Marshall University, Department
of Geography

chains," a friend once commented. "Can you imagine someone blowing up
one of the Rocky Mountains? But people want to flip a switch to turn on their
blenders."

And again, there were beautiful things, too. Things that made me fall in love with
the region in all its complexity. Music. Pepperoni rolls. Jokes. Families. Sheetz.
Mountains, valleys, lakes, hollers, and gorges. Beer. Scones. Stories about uprisings.

Yet, as I settled into life in West Virginia and traveled with the Clinic team around
the state, the violent stories that surrounded me did not match the stories I heard
in the national conversation. I was taken aback by op-eds in national news outlets,
dismissive views expressed in my social circle outside the region, limited concern in
academic legal literature, and a simple lack of acknowledgment as to what Central
Appalachia continued to endure. *Hillbilly Elegy*, a 2016 memoir by a lawyer who
grew up in Middletown, OH – not then an obvious striver for the spotlight of the
political right – was eagerly consumed by the public, the author's diagnosis of a

problematic regional culture of laziness earnestly accepted.[6] But if I had not moved to Morgantown, I might not have known better either.

The legal Clinic I was highly privileged to be a part of, I came to appreciate, was doing radical work. It was, in fact, part of a long tradition of radical Appalachian and rural progressive movements that I would come to learn about. I came to call the Clinic's work "quietly revolutionary."

Doing any kind of environmental or economic development work in the heart of Appalachian coal country was, and remains, fraught with challenges. There was a reason for the Clinic's focus on transactional work – meaning work that did not involve the typical bread and butter of a law school's environmental law clinic, such as filing lawsuits, challenging permits, and pursuing other kinds of adversarial proceedings at the heart of my early public interest lawyer fantasies.

Initial funding for the Clinic came from a 2011 settlement decree after Appalachian Mountain Advocates, a nonprofit environmental law firm based in Lewisburg, sued Arch Coal, Inc., for Clean Water Act violations based on selenium pollution from six coal mines throughout West Virginia. The consent decree overseen by the U.S. Department of Justice and the Environmental Protection Agency provided that the funding would go toward a law school clinic that could help move the region in more sustainable directions – but not a clinic that would be in the business of suing coal companies, which Arch Coal would not agree to fund in the settlement.[7] So the clinic got to exist because of a win over coal, but coal's reach still tied their hands.

And so the Clinic's focus on land-use planning and natural conservation was born. The program was not set up to take down fossil fuels. It was there to mitigate some of the environmental and economic damage already done, to guard against further harm in the future, and to help the region prosper in new ways. Local governments sought the Clinic out for assistance in strategizing for a future beyond coal by way of creating locally driven community development visions that could attract new life, opportunities, and populations.[8] Or they just wanted to figure out how to

---

[6] J. D. Vance, HILLBILLY ELEGY: A MEMOIR OF A FAMILY AND CULTURE IN CRISIS (2016); *'Hillbilly Elegy' Is No. 1; New Oprah Pick Is a Best Seller*, USA TODAY (July 5, 2017, 2:44 PM), www.usatoday.com/story/life/books/2017/07/05/hillbilly-elegy-jd-vance-behold-the-dreamers-oprah-winfrey-usa-today-best-selling-books/103398062/ [https://perma.cc/36GK-4XQ8] (describing popularity and widespread sales of *Hillbilly Elegy* memoir).

[7] Vicki Smith, *Arch Agrees to Pay $2M to Settle Pollution Lawsuit*, CHARLESTON GAZETTE-MAIL (October 3, 2011), www.wvgazettemail.com/news/arch-agrees-to-pay-2m-to-settle-pollution-lawsuit/article_a2fd76a3-2b05-545d-bd2a-8eaf4a2f43fb.html [https://perma.cc/WN8V-N87B]; Manuel Quiñones, *Activist Appalachian Law Firm Wages War on Coal*, E&E NEWS: GREENWIRE (July 15, 2015, 1:09 PM), www.eenews.net/articles/activist-appalachian-law-firm-wages-war-on-coal/ [https://perma.cc/V6T6-9DXE]; Consent Decree, *United States et al. v. Arch Coal, Inc., et al.*, No. 2:11-0133 (S.D. W.Va. June 22, 2011), www.epa.gov/sites/default/files/documents/arch-cd.pdf [https://perma.cc/R4BP-ANUQ].

[8] Since it began, the Clinic has assisted dozens of communities throughout West Virginia with developing comprehensive plans, drafting ordinances, navigating floodplain management, and identifying owners of vacant and dilapidated properties, in addition to the Clinic's conservation activities.

meet basic needs that had been neglected, such as getting wastewater treatment to households that still lacked it.[9] Land trusts sought the Clinic out to preserve those places that had not yet been destroyed or contaminated.

Entering this world inspired me to learn more about it, write about it, and share with others what I was learning in an effort to help bridge the disconnect between the truth that was apparent within the region and the shallower narratives outside it. But what might have become a research agenda focused solely on environmental injustice, energy policy, and rural poverty quickly became more complicated in the fall of 2016, just after I was hired as a law professor at the University of South Carolina. When Manhattanite Donald Trump was elected to the presidency that November, West Virginia – the focal point and inspiration for my scholarship on the exploitative, extractive rural economy – was suddenly "Trump country." Suddenly, just as much as I was writing about those whose communities had been devastated by the predations of ruthless corporations enabled by our legal system, I was also writing about Trump voters. Like me before I moved there, people from my world of wealthy urban progressives had not seemed to know or care all that much about West Virginia or its struggles before 2016. But now they actively hated it.

Trump was indeed relatively popular in West Virginia. Yet, the "Trump country" characterization of the region also felt like a warped version of the truth. As Priya Baskaran describes, "No shortage of recent prestige publications has popularized the narrative of West Virginia as 'Trump Country' – evoking an image of West Virginia as exclusively white, working-class, drug-addicted, poor, and angry in the wake of cultural reforms that place their personal values at odds with modern progressive politics."[10] Baskaran critiques the Trump-country narrative for its erasure of "people of color from the coalfields, both in the present day and historically."[11] Many Black Southerners, for instance, migrated to West Virginia in the early twentieth century for a chance at better opportunities in the coal mines.[12] Modern commentary often overlooks that hard-hit places in West Virginia, such as the small town of Keystone, are in fact majority Black.[13]

The Trump-country narrative also struck me as incomplete, missing something about West Virginia's political diversity and complexity. To my knowledge, my

---

Projects, W. Va. Univ. Land Use & Sustainable Dev. L. Clinic (February 24, 2023), https://landuse.law.wvu.edu/projects [https://perma.cc/HYR9-XEF5].

[9] Glynis Board, *Part II: Is There Something in the Water, Southern W.Va.?*, W. Va. Pub. Broad. (January 15, 2015, 2:20 PM), www.wvpublic.org/news/2015-01-15/part-ii-is-there-something-in-the-water-southern-w-va [https://perma.cc/9S3P-MEYV].

[10] Priya Baskaran, *Thirsty Places*, 2021 Utah L. Rev. 501, 528.

[11] *Id.*

[12] *Id.* at 529.

[13] *See id.; Keystone, WV*, Census Rep. (2021), https://censusreporter.org/profiles/16000US5443516-keystone-wv/ [https://perma.cc/PGK2-987C] (Keystone population 74 percent Black). *See also* Maybell Romero, *Rural Spaces, Communities of Color, and the Progressive Prosecutor*, 110 J. Crim. L. & Criminology 803, 810 (2020) (critiquing "whitewashing" of rural America).

friends and colleagues, a mix of locals and transients like myself, mostly voted for Bernie Sanders in the May 2016 West Virginia Democratic primary, a couple of months before I moved to South Carolina. Sanders appealed because of his ambitious policy ideas, which seemed acutely relevant in a place that needed ambitious change. In fact, 123,860 West Virginia residents voted for Bernie Sanders in the 2016 West Virginia primary, compared to 86,354 who voted for Hillary Clinton and 156,245 who voted for Trump in the Republican primary.[14]

Few journalists would be interested in the fact that only 35 percent of West Virginia primary voters voted for Trump, while 28 percent voted for Sanders and 19 percent went for Clinton. In the 2016 general election, 489,371 West Virginia residents voted for Trump.[15] But an entire third of the state's voters – 231,860 people, or the rough equivalent of the population of Fremont, California – ultimately voted for someone other than Trump.[16] Roughly 680,000 of the eligible adult population did not vote at all.[17] So almost one million West Virginians – about half of the state's population – did something other than vote for Donald Trump in 2016.

I include this information not to suggest that Trump voters have not warranted attention or to apologize for Trumpism or the broader rise of the extreme political right in recent decades.[18] I am personally fearful about the rise of the political right in the United States and elsewhere, and I don't have the answers to fix it. I personally lost a constitutional right during the course of writing this book.[19]

And obviously, Trump did win handily in West Virginia. Some of the reasons why – trade liberalization, coal's decline, Democrats' aloofness, rural regions losing young people, misinformation campaigns, social media, a society long ago constructed on violent racial hierarchies, xenophobic rhetoric, and other fascist recruitment techniques – will emerge throughout this book. Part of why rural regions are disproportionately conservative, I will argue, is that our laws and policies make it difficult for other kinds of people to live there.

In any case, this nonuniform support for Trump is meant to illustrate that West Virginia's politics are more complex than is often portrayed. The national discourse left little room for the idea that Sanders and his more ambitious vision for redistributive policies may have appealed to the region's residents more than Clinton for

---

[14] *West Virginia Primary Results*, N.Y. Times (September 29, 2016, 10:38 AM), www.nytimes.com/elections/2016/results/primaries/west-virginia [https://perma.cc/8DRJ-K65M].

[15] *West Virginia Results: President*, N.Y. Times (June 15, 2018, 11:40 AM), www.nytimes.com/elections/2016/results/west-virginia [https://perma.cc/MX9M-2PKA].

[16] *Id.*

[17] This estimate is based on West Virginia's population of roughly 1.8 million in 2016, minus 20 percent of the population under eighteen, minus an estimated 3 percent of the population as nonvoting felons, and minus those who voted.

[18] *Cf.* Michael J. Klarman, *Foreword: The Degradation of American Democracy – and the Court*, 134 Harv. L. Rev. 1, 7 (2020) (describing weakening of Western democracies and rise of authoritarianism after 1970s).

[19] *See Dobbs v. Jackson Women's Health Org.*, 142 S. Ct. 2228 (2022).

reasons other than sexism.[20] And the national discourse left little room for the more than 900,000 West Virginia residents – almost the population of Austin, Texas – who did something other than vote for Trump.

And Trump country was, we were told, beyond hope. Most wealthier, left-leaning urbanites hadn't cared *that* much about your black lung, your kid who had died from an overdose, or your town's closing hospital or grocery store before. But if you voted for Trump? Or, say, your neighbor did? Now you and everyone around you deserved these things, and you brought them on yourselves.

I think urban/rural dynamics have evolved somewhat as of this writing, but just after the 2016 election, urban progressives seemed happy to throw out the region's substantial populations of non-whites and nonconservatives along with their Trump-country enemies. Talking about West Virginia outside of West Virginia post-2016 was confusing and disheartening. I was asking, "Why and how is our society able to do these things to these people?" And the questions I was often asked in response were, "Why should we care about them?" and "What is wrong with them?"

In 2018, I heard historian Elizabeth Catte, the author of *What You Are Getting Wrong about Appalachia*, speak at WVU. Catte's insights offered a compelling counternarrative to the Trump-country story, rebutting stereotypes about the region and the idea that Appalachians brought their own fate on themselves.[21] Catte described herself as a "debt collector."[22] I took this label to mean that she hunted for accountability for those historical and modern actors and institutions that have been let off the hook for harm they have caused. By bringing new scrutiny to bear on those connections, a "debt collector" can declare that it's time for those accounts to be paid, or at the very least, acknowledged.

Catte's impulse to collect on debts resonated with me. We are often told that things have simply been done. Stories in the passive voice are offered up as grand explanations for unfortunate events. Coal declined. Natural gas went bust. The school closed. The plant closed. The bus stopped service. The population dropped. Bad things just happened.

But to get to the truth, we need to know who did those things. And I came to believe that the truth about West Virginia went further and cut more deeply into the story of the United States than the supposed moral flaws of the region's residents.

And indeed, quite a bit of literature explains the cultural "othering" of Appalachia in service of the region's exploitation. Judah Schept describes a "century-and-a-half old script" about backward hillbillies, depraved mountain people whose cultural

---

[20] *Cf.* Alan Rappeport, *Gloria Steinem and Madeleine Albright Rebuke Young Women Backing Bernie Sanders*, N.Y. TIMES (February 7, 2016), www.nytimes.com/2016/02/08/us/politics/gloria-steinem-madeleine-albright-hillary-clinton-bernie-sanders.html [https://perma.cc/2565-2QYN].

[21] ELIZABETH CATTE, WHAT YOU ARE GETTING WRONG ABOUT APPALACHIA (2018).

[22] *See* Kim Kelly, *On Writing History in the Present Tense: An Interview with Writer and Historian Elizabeth Catte*, THE CREATIVE INDEPENDENT (May 11, 2018), https://thecreativeindependent.com/people/writer-and-historian-elizabeth-catte-on-writing-history-in-the-present-tense/.

defects "portend their own demise."[23] Like Elizabeth Catte, he observes that "'Trump country' pieces ... add a veneer of contemporary – if shallow – political analysis to an otherwise predictable adherence" to the longstanding narrative about a culture of poverty that justifies the region's struggles.[24]

Yet, while Appalachia is surrounded by a particularized and harmful mystique, West Virginia is not, in fact, entirely unique in the broader story of rural America.[25] Appalachia was not the only "Trump country" post-2016.[26] The "urban/rural divide" writ large has been in the national spotlight for years.[27] The same stereotypes that help urbanites believe Appalachians deserve their fate are applied to remote communities elsewhere. As I learned more about these patterns, it eventually seemed important to look beyond Appalachia to understand the structural nature of its exploitation.

The forces that have made West Virginia into West Virginia are observable throughout the country in one variation or another. Like in West Virginia, the name of the game in urban–rural dynamics has often been "extraction."[28] If you're not in coal country, you might be in timber country. Or hog country. Or uranium country. Or gas country.

A common theme across distressed rural communities in different regions has struck me: Those regions are often staging grounds for hazardous extractive or industrial activity that primarily benefits people in distant places, beneficiaries who also remain ignorant of how and where the resources they use were actually produced. That rural economic activity might provide some kind of lifeline, even a source of identity and pride, to the locals engaged in it. But it is often not a quality lifeline, or a sustainable or resilient lifeline, in terms of worker safety, wages, benefits, uncertainty, quality of life, environmental impacts, and regional capacity to bounce back if something with the sector goes off course. Even outdoor recreation, which offers a tamer, glossier image than energy and agricultural work, can be seasonal and

---

[23] Judah Schept, Coal, Cages, Crisis: The Rise of the Prison Economy in Central Appalachia 24, 28 (2022).

[24] *Id.*; *see also* Elizabeth Catte, What You Are Getting Wrong about Appalachia (2018); Steven Stoll, Ramp Hollow: The Ordeal of Appalachia (2017); Nancy Isenberg, White Trash: The 400-Year Untold History of Class in America (2017).

[25] Schept, *supra* note 23, at 28 (describing Appalachia as part of "the broader story about the dialectal relationships between urban and rural America ... and its location as one regional geography among many hinterlands that can be characterized by exploitation, expropriation, survival, reproduction, and resistance").

[26] *See, e.g.*, Thomas Kaplan, *This Is Trump Country*, N.Y. Times (March 4, 2016), www.nytimes.com/interactive/2016/03/04/us/politics/donald-trump-voters.html [https://perma.cc/3H5T-Q943] (including rural Massachusetts as "Trump country").

[27] *See, e.g.*, Josh Kron, *Red State, Blue City: How the Urban-Rural Divide Is Splitting America*, Atlantic (November 30, 2012), www.theatlantic.com/politics/archive/2012/11/red-state-blue-city-how-the-urban-rural-divide-is-splitting-america/265686/ [https://perma.cc/FR3Q-F8HU].

[28] *See generally* Loka Ashwood & Kate MacTavish, *Tyranny of the Majority and Rural Environmental Injustice*, 47 J. Rural Stud. 271 (2016).

precarious, a difficult economy for a community or workers to rely on.[29] Meanwhile, while outsiders consume rural resources and labor, ignorant of the full effects of that work, they simultaneously look down on rural residents. This disdain helps justify both the ignorance of the rural and the consumption of it.

Noting the widespread shock about rural anger after the 2016 presidential election, Loka Ashwood observed, "The gap between urban prosperity and rural burden is largely old news for rural scholars. Consolidation of ownership over the means of production and the metabolic rift cultivated by rural resource extraction for largely urban consumption has left many rural communities depopulated and poor."[30] In other words, rural communities have often been used for resources and materials: coal, oil, gas, crops, meat, timber, copper, uranium, nuclear power, wind power.[31] Or something else local might be consumed by outsiders: skiing, hiking, water play, nostalgia, a sense of bucolic peace.[32] But somehow, the wealth generated from these consumptive activities rarely stays local. The hog waste, the nuclear waste, the drained soil, and the coal ash often do.[33]

In general, the data on rural populations' marginalization within our society are not particularly subtle. Those figures are often worse for the Appalachian region, but there are national trends, too. Rural populations face significant barriers to accessing critical infrastructure such as broadband internet, affordable energy, public transportation, and quality schools.[34] Rural regions face shortages of doctors and a recent wave of devastating hospital closures.[35] Health outcomes for rural residents

---

[29] *See, e.g., Rural Outdoor Recreation Economies: Challenges and Opportunities,* Aspen Institute Community Strategies Group (February 16, 2023), https://extension.usu.edu/gnar/gnarly_blog/rural_rec_economies_aspencsg [https://perma.cc/V8JT-TK8Y].

[30] Loka Ashwood, *Rural Conservatism or Anarchism? The Pro-state, Stateless, and Anti-state Positions,* 83 Rural Socio. 717, 717 (2018).

[31] Jeanne Marie Zokovitch Paben, *Green Power & Environmental Justice-Does Green Discriminate?* 46 Tex. Tech L. Rev. 1067, 1079 (2014) (discussing raw material development in rural areas as environmental justice issue).

[32] *See, e.g.,* Lisa R. Pruitt, *Consuming the Rural, This Time in West Virginia,* Legal Ruralism Blog (October 14, 2018), http://legalruralism.blogspot.com/2018/10/consuming-rural-this-time-in-west.html [https://perma.cc/Z799-CF2Q] (describing tourism to rural places as form of consumption).

[33] Lisa R. Pruitt & Bradley E. Showman, *Law Stretched Thin: Access to Justice in Rural America,* 59 S.D. L. Rev. 466, 488 (2014) (describing rural communities as "increasingly the dumping ground for externalities associated with extractive industries and with all sorts of environmental hazards cast off by metropolitan areas").

[34] Ganesh Sitaraman et al., *Regulation and the Geography of Inequality,* 70 Duke L.J. 1763, 1797 (2021) (discussing "profound regional disparities in service quality and availability" of cell-phone service and high-speed broadband internet); Press Release, ACEEE, *Rural Households Spend Much More of Their Income on Energy Bills than Others* (September 26, 2019), www.aceee.org/press/2019/07/rural-households-spend-much-more [https://perma.cc/8EEW-2WZZ]; Pruitt & Showman, *supra* note 33, at 486 (discussing "dearth of public transportation in rural America" and associated challenges); John Dayton, *Rural Children, Rural Schools, and Public School Funding Litigation: A Real Problem in Search of a Real Solution,* 82 Neb. L. Rev. 99, 100 (2003).

[35] *See generally* Nicole Huberfeld, *Rural Health, Universality, and Legislative Targeting,* 13 Harv. L. & Pol'y Rev. 241 (2018).

are consistently worse than for urban and suburban residents.[36] Rural populations, especially rural populations of color, bear disproportionately high rates of chronic poverty.[37] Many rural regions are "justice deserts" in which residents can't find affordable legal assistance when they need it.[38]

Highlighting these geographic disparities is not meant to diminish disparities viewed through other lenses; I am not trying to say, "Rural people have it worse than anyone else." In fact, underinvested and exploited urban communities share many of the same challenges as struggling rural regions.[39] Overlaying additional factors, such as race, gender, and class, onto geography also changes the picture that emerges. But "rural" – a term which I use to refer to a type of geographic area that is relatively population-sparse and remote from a major population center[40] – is an axis of *potentially* severe disadvantage alongside other relevant axes, such as race, class, gender, and national origin.[41] This book refers to rural as a type of place, not a type of person, which means there is vast diversity across, and inequality within, rural regions and populations.

My attempts to "debt collect" – to unearth truth and accountability in a sea of competing, murky narratives – have involved investigating the way law treats the rural and the use of rural resources and people for societal advancement. But these inquiries have often led to more questions with broader contours, ultimately motivating the writing of this book.

Questions that arose when I lived in West Virginia included: How has so much natural resource wealth been funneled away from West Virginia and other Appalachian states? Whose fault is the prevalence of misinformation on the effects of hydraulic fracturing? What factors explain the rise and fall of coal, and where does responsibility lie for both?

Broader questions borne of these initial questions include: Is rural depopulation as natural, inevitable, and desirable as I've been told, especially vis-à-vis the

---

[36] Public health scholars refer to this as "the rural mortality penalty." Although white rural Americans experience the penalty, its effects are more egregious for rural populations of color. Laura Richman et al., *Addressing Health Inequalities in Diverse, Rural Communities: An Unmet Need*, 7 SSM–POPULATION HEALTH 1 (2019).

[37] Mark H. Harvey & Rosalind P. Harris, *Racial Inequalities and Poverty in Rural America*, in RURAL POVERTY IN THE UNITED STATES 141–42 (Ann R. Tickamyer et al. eds., 2017) (explaining that rates of poverty among racial minorities living in rural America are two and sometimes three times higher than for rural whites).

[38] *See generally* Lisa R. Pruitt et al., *Legal Deserts: A Multi-State Perspective on Rural Access to Justice*, 13 HARV. L. & POL'Y REV. 15, 16 (2018).

[39] *See, e.g.*, Baskaran, *supra* note 10 (comparing barriers to accessing clean, potable water in Flint, Michigan, and southern West Virginia).

[40] Lisa R. Pruitt, *Rural Rhetoric*, 39 CONN. L. REV. 159, 177–84 (2006) (discussing competing definitions of rural and noting the lack of a single, simple definition "from legislation or case law." *Id.* at 178).

[41] Hannah Haksgaard, *Rural Women and Developments in the Undue Burden Analysis: The Effect of Whole Woman's Health v. Hellerstedt*, 65 DRAKE L. REV. 663, 686 (2017) (discussing relevance of intersectionality theory, in which axes of disadvantage are understood as interacting, rather than independent, to questions of rurality).

waning of extractive industries like coal? How much of rural marginalization and challenges with rural service provision are natural, insurmountable outgrowths of remoteness and population sparseness? Do rural residents really destine themselves for poor infrastructure because of their relatively conservative voting patterns? How did some rural regions become so disproportionately white? Why is there so much poverty and vulnerability on Native American reservations, in Black communities in the South, and among predominantly Hispanic farmworkers?

These questions, too, led to more questions: What kinds of public programs and legal reforms would best address rural poverty and related economic struggles? How can unsustainable, isolated, hazardous mono-economies be phased out and replaced with new, more sustainable, more equitable economic and environmental practices? What can be done with a built environment that no longer matches its population? How are different geographic regions interdependent? Can societal use of rural resources be made equitable and sustainable? How do our broken, unhealthy food and energy systems fit into this story? What does racial justice in rural America look like? And, of course, the overarching question: What role does law play in all of this?

A common answer to these questions has something to do with corporations and capital. And it has something to do with government. It may be what Loka Ashwood calls "for-profit democracy," which she defines as a state of affairs "in which the utilitarian rule of the most people and the greatest profit defines the government's purpose … in a world of laws and markets deliberately designed to give the most protection to property that enables the centralization of revenue, at the expense of values that may matter more to us, like the love of family land or the security of a home."[42]

My diagnosis – an answer that sheds light on many of the questions listed earlier – turns on the widespread embrace of market supremacy in law and beyond.[43] That is, so long as our laws, policies, and collective ethos prioritize some fantasy version of "free markets" to the neglect of other, more important ideals, we are doomed to continue to exacerbate economic, racial, and geographic inequality and to feel the dire societal consequences of doing so.

Like many scholars today, I find myself returning to the programs and policies of the New Deal era as an apparently obvious antidote to the egregious inequalities that plague our modern society, as imperfect and even harmful as the New Deal often was.[44] Traditions of utilities and common carrier regulation, public infrastructure investments, government prioritization of the public interest, and efforts to rein in the power and the whims of the private sector all hold great promise

---

[42] Loka Ashwood, For-Profit Democracy: Why the Government Is Losing the Trust of Rural America 24–25 (2018).

[43] Jedediah Britton-Purdy et al., *Building a Law-and-Political-Economy Framework: Beyond the Twentieth-Century Synthesis*, 129 Yale L.J. 1784, 1796 (2020) (defining market supremacy as the perceived "necessary subordination of the political to the economic").

[44] *See* Sitaraman et al., *supra* note 34.

for redistributing wealth and opportunity from the predominantly white, urban and suburban superelite and upper middle class back to everyone else, including neglected and exploited rural regions.

But obviously, getting to reform is not a simple task, politically or culturally. The questions earlier are largely informed by questions and arguments I have heard from those who are more skeptical of rural America's prospects as a viable part of society. I have often been asked: Why do they vote against their interests? Why should we care about people who have so much disproportionate voting power and who wield it so irresponsibly? Why don't they just move to places with more opportunities and infrastructure? Why should we subsidize their expensive and inefficient way of life? Wouldn't they all just think you're a coastal, urban, liberal elite and disagree with everything you think anyway?

Some skeptics also have simpler explanations and solutions for rural challenges. The cause of rural decline? Markets. Markets have systematically disadvantaged rural regions due to those regions' inherent inefficiency. Or due to the progress of technological developments. Or due to an innate human yearning for urban vitality and opportunity. These are natural, desirable developments. And the solution for rural decline? Markets. Remove barriers to mobility, such as by building more urban housing, so that the populations in struggling regions can relocate to more prosperous urban areas and join more efficient and productive agglomeration economies.[45]

The conversation does not go much further if markets are both the explanation and the solution for today's rural conditions. Market supremacy means the phenomena I've described are no one's fault but Mother Nature's. Or the fault of inevitable, desirable progress. And if something is natural, or the result of progress, it is benign. We can all rest easy.

The growing field of Law and Political Economy (LPE) offers a helpful set of methodological tools for answering my own questions and addressing the skeptics' concerns, which are, of course, not entirely irrelevant. LPE, a relatively recent scholarly movement in legal academia, has many predecessors that still occupy similar spaces today. The critical legal studies movements, various "law and" methodologies, and feminist legal theory, for instance, all offer visions for law and society that are based in principles such as justice and equality rather than market supremacy.

A 2020 *Yale Law Journal* article by Britton-Purdy, Grewal, Kapczynski, and Rahman laid out some basic tenets of LPE.[46] The authors use the term "market supremacy" to refer to the philosophy of the "rule of the market."[47] They explain that the lens of market supremacy turns on three theories, embraced most prominently in the law and economics movement: (1) elevation of efficiency and aggregate

---

[45] *See, e.g.,* David Schleicher, *Surreply: How and Why We Should Become Un-Stuck!* 127 YALE L.J. F. 571 (2017).

[46] Britton-Purdy et al., *supra* note 43, at 1796.

[47] *Id.*

wealth maximization as ultimate priorities for society; (2) reduction of transaction costs to enhance market operations; and (3) identifying transactions' externalized costs and optimizing markets to internalize them.[48]

LPE has helped illuminate the ubiquitous-seeming market talk as merely another value-laden approach to the world. And LPE offers an alternative that seems far more intuitive, fundamental, and fair. Centrally, as articulated in the article mentioned earlier, "'the economy' is neither self-defining nor self-justifying."[49] Rather, the authors explain, "law is perennially involved in creating and enforcing the terms of economic ordering, most particularly through the creation and maintenance of markets."[50]

I appreciate this article, and LPE's emergence more broadly, because I have been trying to articulate for years – largely in response to the idea that Appalachia's struggles stemmed from naturally shrinking markets for coal – that markets are made, they are not forces of nature, and they can be changed, especially in the realms of energy and agriculture, with their heavy public policy involvement and outsized implications for rural welfare. The Yale article's authors propose that the LPE lens rejects market supremacy and instead centers on democracy, equality, and just distributions of power. They also observe that, for LPE to succeed, it must transcend beyond critique and offer something positive as an agenda.[51] This book takes on part of that task by connecting rural America to something that we don't often hear associated with it: hope and resilience.

LPE bears unique relevance to the story of rural America.[52] Rural communities are often framed as the ultimate victims of well-functioning markets that know innately to direct resources and opportunities to denser urban centers that provide more returns per capita on investments. But the LPE lens reveals the market-centric narrative of the rural, while not entirely baseless, as a red herring. This lens illuminates how human beings have made decisions, implemented through laws and institutions, that have disadvantaged rural communities on varying intersectional axes – undercutting the premise of markets as forces of nature.

It helps to name those decisions because in revealing the human agency that has shaped outcomes such as geographic inequality, we can see that alternative decisions remain within our collective control. Some examples of decisions that hurt rural communities and others, explored in more depth in the pages that follow, include President Reagan's and Congress's decision to deregulate intercity bus service in 1982; President Clinton's and Congress's decision to approve the North Atlantic Free Trade Agreement in 1993; a more recent Congress's decision to

---

[48] *Id.* at 1796–97.

[49] *Id.* at 1833.

[50] *Id.*

[51] *Id.* at 1834.

[52] Portions of this chapter appeared previously in a blog post: Annie Eisenberg, *Applying the Lens of Law and Political Economy to Rural America*, Rural Reconciliation Project (October 20, 2020), www.ruralreconcile.org/ruralreview/lpe-as-lens [https://perma.cc/L4F2-FXHP].

exclude high-volume hydraulic fracturing from major environmental statutes; and many state legislatures' decisions over the past several decades to pass so-called right-to-farm laws shielding agribusiness from nuisance lawsuits.

These decisions reveal that transportation markets, energy markets, trade markets, and agricultural markets are creatures of law and policy. And while this emphasis on decisions' consequences is geared toward accountability – debt collection – this analytical process also aims to offer a greater basis for hope than the discourse that often predominates. Laws and policies can be changed, and need to be changed radically, if crises of climate change, racial injustice, and economic and geographic inequality are to be addressed. Revealing markets for what they are – policy-driven manifestations of our collective values – helps reveal a path forward toward a more hopeful and equitable future.

LPE does not address the question of my own credibility, which arises sometimes with various audiences because I do not have a decidedly rural identity, yet have picked up a mantle of indignation about rural exploitation. I grew up in the college town of Ithaca, New York, the daughter of a law professor and a writer, and I regularly need to check my own privileged perspective as I write about rural communities. I am writing this book in the first person so that I may include my firsthand experiences as a practitioner and human being, interwoven with a more traditional scholarly discussion.

With this book, I aim to invite the reader to come along with me on the journey, part professional but also personal, that has led to my current understanding of an admittedly complex set of issues. I don't think it's a coincidence that I grew up in the backyard of Cornell University, a land-grant school whose contributions to food and agricultural sciences I'm only beginning to understand. But importantly, I am not attempting to speak for rural America or to present myself as an authentic rural voice. My goal is rather to amplify the voices of the scholars, practitioners, activists, and residents who know and care about rural regions but are too often drowned out by louder, more nefarious forces in our society. The goals of this book are to tell a fuller truth about rural places and people, to offer insights into possible ways to better address geographic inequality through law, and to persuade skeptics that addressing geographic inequality is both worthwhile and possible.

This book is designed to both amplify and advance the existing work of those who know and care about rural communities in order to address the skeptic's narrative that rural communities are beyond hope – that they are a vestige of the past and cannot be revitalized, but even if they could be, we as a society should not seek to revitalize them.[53] In other words, the book is meant to debunk the narrative, as

---

[53] Elizabeth Weeks, *One Child Town: The Health Care Exceptionalism Case against Agglomeration Economies*, 2021 UTAH L. REV. 319, 321 (critiquing the narrative that "[s]mall town America is dying and ... not worth saving" and instead, rural residents must be freed to relocate "to enjoy the benefits of 'agglomeration economies'").

Elizabeth Weeks describes it, that "[a]ny arguments for keeping [rural] residents in place and saving places like Wiota[, Iowa,] are intangible and economically irrational, the stuff of sentimental classic rock or modern country lyrics."[54] The book could be read from start to finish in narrative form. But it is also intended as a reference for those interested in particular subtopics related to the law's relationship with rural communities.

One pressing reason for non-rural people to investigate rural topics is that questions about rural life are not merely niche issues. How rural populations, lands, and resources are woven into American life is a question with broad relevance to everyone. Rural regions are still responsible for providing the bulk of the nation's food, water, energy, fibers, outdoor recreation, cultural and natural heritage sites, and wildlife conservation activities.[55] Ultimately, the rural story is a significant piece of the story of the United States. Where can people live and have a decent quality of life? Should we, as a society, expect people to relocate multiple times in their lives to pursue livelihoods? How burdensome should that be? Do we value emotional and familial attachments to neighborhoods, towns, regions, and states? How are we managing vast swaths of land, dramatic economic transitions, inequality, climate change, and crumbling infrastructure? What must we do about unsustainable, inequitable food and energy systems? What are the ongoing legacies of centuries of slavery and its deep connection to agriculture, and of ongoing occupation of Native lands? Who gets to have what in our messy society?

The overarching question here is not solely, "What should be done about rural poverty and economic decline?" It is also, "How did we arrive at such an inequitable, unsustainable way of life, and how can we do better?" Or more specifically, "How have our laws and policies done such a poor job of spreading wealth and opportunity out across populations and physical space, to the detriment of our very lifespans?" The simple answer to these questions involves the widespread embrace of market supremacy. The solutions, then, involve competing priorities: the pursuit of geographic equity, restorative racial justice, economic fairness, ecological resilience, and other principles that do not stand to make corporations much money, but on which our very survival depends. Reasons of morality, pragmatism, and collective survival all point toward trying to do better, and to think differently.

Overall, this book seeks to advance two main arguments. First, the limited stories so often told about rural communities are central to the fatalism and hopelessness that tend to surround the prospect of pursuing a different future in rural America. These limited stories stem from a dangerous alchemy of stereotypes, misunderstandings, short memories, assumptions based in market supremacy, and a simple lack of

---

[54] *Id.* at 323.

[55] Cf. Laurie Ristino, *Surviving Climate Change in America: Toward a Rural Resilience Framework*, 41 W. NEW ENG. L. REV. 521, 522–23 (2019) (noting centrality of rural America to national resilience because "it is the locus of our nation's ecosystem services, including food and fiber provisioning").

imagination. If we accept that Mother Nature created the status quo, our hands are tied until Mother Nature fixes it.

But an in-depth inquiry into the older and more recent legal history of rural communities reveals that rural America is a creature of public creation. In the rural story this book tells, legal and institutional forces – and human beings making decisions through those avenues based on their subjective values and priorities – have shaped life in small towns, throughout the countryside, and on tribal lands, challenging the idea that benign markets have organically "left them behind." In this book's alternative narrative, rural residents are often reacting rationally to circumstances beyond their control and to things that have been done to them, including our laws and policies embracing market supremacy over rural residents' well-being.[56]

Second, with a more balanced understanding of how modern rural America came to be, the prospect of a better future emerges. Since man-made laws and policies helped create the current mess of inequality and precarity that we're in, we – human beings – have the power to change those laws and policies for the better. In fact, as of this writing, many of the interventions rural scholars have been advocating for years are reflected in current policies of the Biden administration. This suggests that the prospect of a more hopeful, sustainable rural future is not simply idealism, but within reach now through federal initiatives and other efforts. By telling a fuller version of the rural story, this book seeks to help revive rural communities' path to prosperity by reimagining a rural America – and with it, the country as a whole – equipped for the challenges of the modern era.

To advance these arguments, the book is organized around three main themes. The first theme is myth-busting. Specifically, each chapter focuses on tackling a common myth or half-story surrounding rural communities, law and policy in rural communities, or the so-called urban–rural divide. The theme of my scholarship to date has been the skewed narratives about rural communities and the role of law and policy in shaping rural economic opportunity, or lack thereof. This book draws on this body of work to address the ways in which these narratives rely on mythology, and the more humanized, productive ways in which we could come to understand them.

The second theme revolves around my firsthand experiences as a legal practitioner in the field of community economic development. My career as a legal academic to date has involved a combination of practice and scholarship. As discussed earlier, my fellowship at WVU was half study through the pursuit of a master's degree, and half practice through a law clinic, the work of which this book will return to. The University of South Carolina School of Law hired me in 2016 to

---

[56] *Cf.* Alexander R. Thomas & Gregory M. Fulkerson, City and Country: The Historical Evolution of Urban-Rural Systems 8 (2021) (suggesting that the literature on urbanormativity "points not to culture influencing structure, but structure and culture in a dialogical dance as capitalism both depends upon and defines the urban–rural dynamics at its core").

start a clinic modeled on the one in West Virginia, recognizing that a transactional environmental law clinic has better prospects for surviving Southern politics than a litigation-oriented one. The stories and anecdotes that I have lived and observed as a practitioner have been key drivers of my scholarship. I think they are important data points in and of themselves, so I include many of them here, ensuring to protect any client confidences as necessary.

Finally, the third theme involves a key moment in the legal history of rural development in the United States. This book project benefited from my seven-month residency in 2022 as a Kluge Fellow in Digital Studies at the Library of Congress, during which I conducted original archival research on the legal history of rural development. I centered this research on a focal point for this book: the Rural Electrification Act of 1936 (the REA).[57]

In learning about the role of law in rural communities, it often seems that all roads lead back to the REA, one of the crown jewels of the New Deal. How do we pay for rural infrastructure? The REA provides an example. How do we pursue geographic equity in opportunity and prosperity? The REA provides an example. How is the political will to pursue massive infrastructure investments secured? The REA is illustrative. How can we implement universalist approaches at the federal level while taking advantage of and accounting for unique localities' conditions? The REA took this on.

Of course, the REA was not perfect. Far from it. Navajo Nation, for instance, was entirely excluded from the REA. As a result, tens of thousands of residents of Navajo Nation are only now being connected to the electricity grid. Black homeowners were systematically deprived of the REA's benefits through racist aid distribution schemes. In many ways, the REA represents the best and worst of what U.S. law and policy is capable of.

A focus on the REA helps round out a discussion of myth-busting and anecdotal accounts of the rural with a prominent piece of (partially) effective rural development policy that can inform what is considered possible and what cautionary tales to avoid, especially in the ongoing conversation on rural broadband deployment – the electrification task of today, it is often said. We have been living in a time of political deadlock, when all infrastructure is considered "too expensive." Yet, the tides may be turning, and Congress's ambitious recent infrastructure investments may portend a new window of opportunity. To advance a broader vision for the rural future, this book looks back to a time when people believed big things were possible and took aggressive, non-market-supremacist steps – imperfect all the same – to make them happen.

---

[57] Rural Electrification Act of 1936, Pub. L. No. 74-605, 49 Stat. 1363 (codified as amended at 7 U.S.C. §§ 901–918c (2012)). Scholars in diverse fields have recognized the ongoing importance of the REA to modern questions, including energy justice, economic development, and, in particular, broadband deployment. *See* Alexandra B. Klass & Gabriel Chan, *Cooperative Clean Energy*, 100 N.C. L. Rev. 1 (2021); Anthony E. Varona, *Toward A Broadband Public Interest Standard*, 61 Admin. L. Rev. 1 (2009).

Chapter 2 of this book begins by addressing what I call the "basic myths" about rural. These are the myths that turn on misunderstandings about definitions, data, or characterizations about rural America that lead people to believe that rural is not worth investigation in the first place. The main point of this chapter is to show that, yes, "rural" is a salient and important lens through which to understand the issues this book addresses. Rural has legal meanings. Those meanings are contested, and that contestation influences outcomes. Rural has special characteristics that affect law's reach into rural regions, including greater distances to travel and population sparseness. Rural is often forgotten altogether or mischaracterized in law and policy.

Urbanormative policymaking, scholars have shown, assumes universal urban conditions not consistent with the rural experience. Rural places are facing unique trends, such as depopulation and shrinking economic opportunities. Yet, rural regions remain necessary to a thriving and resilient society, especially in the face of climate change. Far-reaching stereotypes about rural affect all of these factors, again suggesting that the rural lens is worth looking through.

Chapter 3 turns to the myth of rural empowerment. Many tend to only think about rural populations during election season, when they see an angry sea of conservative, rural red seeming to dominate electoral maps. During that season, discourse inevitably turns to the disproportionate voting power of rural residents. Chapter 3 argues that, while this disproportionate voting power exists and is highly problematic for representative democracy, this one form of power does not somehow neutralize the other forms of disadvantage that rural populations face.

Those disadvantages include barriers to accessing infrastructure of all kinds, barriers to accessing essential service providers, patterns of chronic poverty alongside more novel trends in socioeconomic and population decline, and the effects of these trends on rural local governments' ability to meet residents' needs. Although many commentators' response to these trends is to argue that predominantly conservative rural residents "vote against their interests" – by voting for Republicans instead of the Democrats who promise to ameliorate these trends – and thereby make their own beds, subsequent chapters will illustrate how Democrats' policies have often not served rural regions well either.

Chapter 4 then challenges the myth that rural communities are unsustainable. The skeptic's narrative turns on the idea that rural communities are inefficient. Higher costs per capita for service provision inevitably dictate as much. Therefore, rural communities cannot justifiably be sustained because public and private resources will be put to much better use in cities. The chapter challenges this myth by highlighting the ongoing necessity of rural regions in our complex national ecosystem of urban–rural interdependence.

Assuming that rural communities and their many contributions to national welfare are necessary, the chapter highlights robust legal traditions of utilities and infrastructure regulation, such as the Rural Electrification Act, that helped mold markets to the public interest, including by serving disadvantaged regions that would otherwise be less appealing to private service providers. That system of economic regulation operated in service of geographic equity for decades. Although the system had its detractors from the outset, it illustrated an approach premised on the notion that rural communities were worth sustaining and possible to sustain, even in the face of unique challenges.

Chapter 5 addresses the myth embedded in the most prominent narrative about rural socioeconomic decline. Specifically, this chapter questions the ubiquitous use of the word "decline" to describe struggling rural regions' current situation. "Decline" implies a certain passive loss of vitality and does not ascribe agency to any causal factor. This chapter debunks the idea that rural regions have "declined" through the benign evolution of forces of nature by highlighting the contributing agents of federal and state laws and policies that have helped create modern rural conditions characterized by depopulation, shrinking opportunities, and reduced quality of life. The chapter proposes that rural America has not "declined," but has rather been undermined, sacrificed, or destroyed, to our collective detriment, often through policy measures where decision-makers knew the likely consequences of their actions. Modern rural America is a creature of public creation.

Chapter 6 turns to the myth that rural regions are populated only by white conservatives. The chapter takes on specifically the myth of ubiquitous rural whiteness and how that myth obfuscates rural racial and ethnic minorities' experiences and relationships with government. Much like the idea that rural voters vote against their interests, the idea of ubiquitous rural whiteness inspires some progressives to advocate nonintervention into distressed rural regions. Although this book's story of rural economic marginalization illustrates how rural white populations may well face severe challenges themselves, this chapter highlights the unique challenges law and policy have created for rural communities of color – the "minority of the minority," whose very existence is often obscured.

Land dispossession facilitated en masse by state and federal laws in particular has helped catalyze the whitening of rural America, driving Indigenous and Black populations into rural ghettoes or out altogether. But many rural communities of color maintain or seek out ties to rural regions, often bearing disproportionate burdens of chronic poverty – as illustrated by rural America's fast-growing Latino population. While one can vilify the white populations that benefit from inequality and discrimination within these localities – just as one might do for racial inequality in cities and suburbs – this chapter proposes that the failure to protect rural populations of color is also a collective failure of law and government.

Chapter 7 addresses the myth that rural regions are populated with right-wing radicals who irrationally hate all government. The chapter takes a deep dive specifically into the rural relationship with the federal regulatory state. A granular look at rural populations' disaffection with the federal regulatory state does not reveal themes of radicalism. Rather, such an analysis reveals rational reactions to perceptions of procedural exclusion, disappointment with substantive outcomes, and a sense that federal agencies serve the interests of someone other than rural populations. Agencies are perceived instead to owe fealty to corporations, the urban affluent, or, from the perspective of rural racial minorities, to white people.

Although the radicalizing effects of social media do take hold and contribute to broader patterns of polarization, the chapter compares and contrasts subjective rural accounts in sociological literature with objective structural features of the regulatory state. The apparent consistency of rural feelings with some of these objective structural features lends credence to rural feelings as a logical and predictable response to the regulatory state's failure to accommodate rural conditions. The common perception among rural populations – that the regulatory state binds them while failing to protect them – finds footing in real conditions, particularly trends of regulatory retreat from rural life in certain spheres alongside regulatory encroachment into rural life in other spheres over the past several decades.

Finally, Chapter 8 argues that rural America needs to be reconceptualized as a commons. Chapters 2 through 7 establish how the extractive rural economy and laws driven by market supremacy have undermined rural regions' resilience, to society's collective detriment. Chapter 8 argues that the urban majority does, in fact, have some level of entitlement to the resources in rural communities, and that rural America as a whole should be understood as a common resource. However, what has been missing from the exercise of that entitlement to date is a concomitant ethos of stewardship. In other words, if the urban majority is entitled to take from the rural, the urban majority is necessarily obligated to take care of the rural.

Critically, the urban majority's impetus to steward rural America does not stop at natural resource conservation. That impetus extends to the workers, residents, places, and infrastructure that are also critical to collective and regional resilience. The chapter contemplates policies that embrace an ethos of stewardship with a view to regional and collective resilience, with a focus on agricultural land, energy production, and infrastructure. Drawing on examples from federal legislative initiatives, the chapter proposes that interventions into rural regions to radically restructure urban–rural dynamics – for reasons of fairness, pragmatism, and collective survival – are already within reach. The chapter concludes with five overarching principles that should be considered in rural governance interventions to help better share and steward the rural commons.

2

The Foundational Myths

The Myths of Rural Hyper-Simplicity, Rural Hyper-Complexity, and Rural Immateriality

Rural America has received quite a bit of attention over the past several years.[1] High-profile memoirs,[2] sociological investigations,[3] historical accounts,[4] legal analyses,[5] and political analyses[6] have proliferated since 2015. Works going back further in time, such as Thomas Frank's *What's the Matter with Kansas*,[7] Robert Ellickson's *Order without Law*,[8] and even the writing of W.E.B. Du Bois,[9] show that the modern preoccupation with urban–rural difference has, in fact, been around in one form or another for decades, since urbanization picked up steam in the nineteenth century.

This book draws on each of the above genres in order to incorporate firsthand observations with the many dimensions of a broader socio-legal context. In deciding where to start, I did contemplate whether I hail from a rural place or not. The U.S.

---

[1] Portions of this chapter were excerpted from Ann M. Eisenberg, *Distributive Justice and Rural America*, 61 B.C. L. Rev. 189 (2020) and Ann M. Eisenberg, *Rural Blight*, 13 Harv. L. & Pol'y Rev. 187 (2018) [hereinafter Eisenberg, *Rural Blight*].

[2] J. D. Vance, Hillbilly Elegy: A Memoir of a Family and Culture in Crisis (2016); Sara Smarsh, Heartland: A Memoir of Working Hard and Being Broke in the Richest Country on Earth (2018); Tara Westover, Educated: A Memoir (2018).

[3] Arlie Russell Hochschild, Strangers in Their Own Land: Anger and Mourning on the American Right (2016); Katherine J. Cramer, The Politics of Resentment: Rural Consciousness in Wisconsin and the Rise of Scott Walker (2016); Robert Wuthnow, The Left Behind: Decline and Rage in Rural America (2018); Loka Ashwood, For-Profit Democracy: Why the Government Is Losing the Trust of Rural America (2018); Jennifer Sherman, Dividing Paradise: Rural Inequality and the Diminishing American Dream (2021).

[4] Elizabeth Catte, What You Are Getting Wrong about Appalachia (2018); Steven Stoll, Ramp Hollow: The Ordeal of Appalachia (2017); Nancy Isenberg, White Trash: The 400-Year Untold History of Class in America (2017).

[5] Joan C. Williams, White Working Class: Overcoming Class Cluelessness in America (2017); Michelle Wilde Anderson, The Fight to Save the Town: Reimagining Discarded America (2022).

[6] Jane Kleeb, Harvest the Vote: How Democrats Can Win Again in Rural America (2020); Chloe Maxmin & Canyon Woodward, Dirt Road Revival: How to Rebuild Rural Politics and Why Our Future Depends on It (2022).

[7] Thomas Frank, What's the Matter with Kansas?: How Conservatives Won the Heart of America (2004).

[8] Robert C. Ellickson, Order without Law: How Neighbors Settle Disputes (1991).

[9] See W. E. B. Du Bois, The Souls of Black Folk: Essays and Sketches (1903).

FIGURE 2.1 Street view in downtown Ithaca, New York, Carol M. Highsmith, Library of Congress (2018)

Census Bureau has designated Ithaca, New York, population 30,000 (plus 30,000 seasonal students), as an urbanized or urban area of 50,000 or more people, reflecting Ithaca's relatively high population density, which also meets a certain threshold of population volume.[10] However, I've occasionally surveyed people over the years as to their views on this question. Opinions are mixed about whether Ithaca, whose downtown is shown in Figure 2.1, counts as rural and why or why not. At dinner with a law professor based in New York City who had spent time in Ithaca, I asked if he had thought Ithaca was rural. His response was swift and serious: "Uh, *yeah*," he said, his eyes bugging out slightly as he recalled navigating winding roads through a bleak, snowy landscape overlooking empty gorges like the one shown in Figure 2.2. But when I've asked my family whether I could conceivably brand myself as rural having grown up in Ithaca, their unanimous response has been, "Absolutely not."

[10] *Urban and Rural*, U.S. CENSUS BUREAU, www.census.gov/programs-surveys/geography/guidance/geo-areas/urban-rural.html [https://perma.cc/8V3C-2ASB]; *2010 Census–Urbanized Area Reference Map: Ithaca, NY*, U.S. CENSUS BUREAU, www2.census.gov/geo/maps/dc10map/UAUC_RefMap/ua/ua41914_ithaca_ny/DC10UA41914.pdf [https://perma.cc/KM9X-DWWQ].

FIGURE 2.2 Ithaca Falls on Fall Creek, one of two prominent cascades that support a local slogan, "Ithaca Is Gorges" (a play on the word "gorgeous") in Ithaca, New York, Carol M. Highsmith, Library of Congress (2018)

Ithaca does not count as rural, I'm told, because there are a lot of wealthy and educated people there and because university towns are just different. Isn't that kind of a slight to rural, I ask? So rural has to mean people are mostly poor or uneducated? Doesn't it mean something that Ithacans go to Rochester (almost two hours away) or Manhattan (at least four hours away) when they need "serious" healthcare? Or to Syracuse (an hour away) for the "good mall" or the more reliable, affordable airport? Or, Ithaca *does* count as rural, people say, because it's relatively small, geographically isolated, winter weather predominates life for half the year, and it doesn't have everything New York City does. But then, it's being measured against the most urban of urban metropolises, which doesn't seem fair either. Isn't everything rural compared to New York City?

The real story here, of course, is that rural is a contested concept and means different things to different people.[11] Academic and popular conceptions of rural remain highly varied. This can sometimes mean that different disciplines or viewpoints are talking past one another when it comes to understanding the challenges facing rural places.

---

[11] *See generally* Daniel T. Lichter & David L. Brown, *Rural America in an Urban Society: Changing Spatial and Social Boundaries*, 37 ANN. REV. SOCIO. 565 (2011).

The question of what defines and characterizes rural is ever present in conversations on rural America and the urban–rural divide.[12] And those definitions may make a difference in characterizing the object of conversation. For example, according to the Census Bureau's definition of rural as anything that is not classified as urban, as of 2018, approximately 63 million U.S. residents lived in rural areas, reflecting roughly 19 percent of the population.[13] By contrast, if one refers instead to *counties* designated as rural by the Centers for Disease Control and Prevention, populations within those counties are altogether lower in number, constituting 14 percent of the national population as of 2017, or roughly 46 million people.[14]

Like many works of law and rurality contemplating the rural at a higher level of abstraction, the discussion that follows "does not depend on granular distinction between urban and rural."[15] Yet, whatever definition one might adopt, some common misconceptions seem to miss the mark altogether. This chapter introduces and critiques what I think of as the foundational myths about how rural is characterized – meaning the perceptions of rural that lead people to believe rural answers are obvious, impossible, or just not that interesting or relevant. Addressing these myths first is a helpful starting point for providing some additional illustrations, beyond basic definitions relating to population size or distances across landscapes, about what and who this book is talking about when I say "rural," and why this inquiry about rurality and law is warranted. I will describe these three basic myths first – the myths of rural hyper-simplicity, rural hyper-complexity, and rural immateriality – and then provide a fuller truth for characterizing and understanding rural America today.

(1) The Myth of Rural Hyper-Simplicity

"Why don't they move?"
  "Why don't they access doctors and hospitals online?"
  "Why can't coal miners manufacture solar panels?"[16]

These common questions are infused with the myth of rural hyper-simplicity. This conception of the rural assumes uniform conditions across rural places and that a single, silver-bullet measure will address rural America's challenges. A common manifestation

[12] *Cf.* Lisa R. Pruitt & Bradley E. Showman, *Law Stretched Thin: Access to Justice in Rural America*, 59 S.D. L. Rev. 466, 488 (2014); Maybell Romero, *Rural Spaces, Communities of Color, and the Progressive Prosecutor*, 110 J. Crim. L. & Criminology 803, 810 (2020); Lisa R. Pruitt, *Rural Rhetoric*, 39 Conn. L. Rev. 159, 177–84 (2006).

[13] *Understanding and Using American Community Survey Data*, U.S. Census Bureau (2020) www.census.gov/content/dam/Census/library/publications/2020/acs/acs_rural_handbook_2020_ch01.pdf].

[14] Kim Parker et al., *What Unites and Divides Urban, Suburban and Rural Communities*, Pew Research Center (2018) [permalink: www.pewresearch.org/social-trends/2018/05/22/demographic-and-economic-trends-in-urban-suburban-and-rural-communities/].

[15] Jessica A. Shoemaker, *Fee Simple Failures: Rural Landscapes and Race*, 119 Mich. L. Rev. 1695, 1703 n.46 (2021).

[16] *Cf.* Sarah Jones, *Please Stop Telling Miners to Learn to Code*, Intelligencer: N.Y. Mag. (Dec. 31, 2019), https://nymag.com/intelligencer/2019/12/coding-jobs-wont-save-coal-country.html?regwall-newsletter-signup=true [permalink: https://perma.cc/2GZU-FDU7].

of the myth of rural hyper-simplicity is the perception that the majority of rural residents are still involved in agriculture, when in fact only a small minority are.[17]

(2) The Myth of Rural Hyper-Complexity

"It's not possible to generalize about rural America because it's so diverse."
   "West Virginia coal miners have nothing in common with Navajo coal miners."
   "Manufacturing and timber have nothing to do with each other."
   "Oregon and South Carolina are too different to compare."

Swinging to the opposite side of the spectrum of rural conceptualizations, many also believe that telling a cohesive story about commonalities across rural regions is not possible in light of variations among rural demographics, economics, histories, and the legal frameworks shaping different aspects of rural life. According to this myth, there is no way to generalize meaningfully about rural regions, which means there is no purpose in contemplating large-scale solutions to inherently variable rural problems.

(3) The Myth of Rural Immateriality

"The issues are not about place, they're about class."
   "It's not about place, it's about race."
   "Urban communities face challenges, too, so it doesn't make sense to focus on rural."

The third foundational myth is either that place is not all that relevant a lens through which to view societal issues, or that rural, in particular, is not a compelling focus because it is not unique or because other factors are more important.

RURAL AS A COMMON EXPERIENCE AND AN INTERSECTIONAL CONCEPT

My response to these foundational myths, which tend to motivate a dismissive attitude toward investigations of rural, is that they all have a bit of truth to them. Rural America is absolutely a complex and varied set of landscapes, populations, economics, laws, and politics. It is not a monolith. Yet, there are common themes that affect that world based on its rurality – meaning the challenges posed by sparser populations, distance from population centers, and a changing socioeconomic landscape.

So what *does* rural mean? Formal definitions characterize rurality by population scarcity, low overall population volumes, and distance from substantial population centers. After the 2010 census, the U.S. Census Bureau defined "rural" as anything

---

[17] According to a 2002 survey by the W.K. Kellogg Foundation, "Respondents perceive[d] rural America as being based on an almost completely agricultural economy. In reality, farm employment is 7 percent of all rural employment." W.K. KELLOGG FOUND., PERCEPTIONS OF RURAL AMERICA (2002), https://wkkf.issuelab.org/resource/perceptions-of-rural-america.html [https://perma.cc/S5VL-V3W5].

FIGURE 2.3 Urbanized areas and urban clusters, 2010
Source: U.S. Census Bureau, 2010 Census Urban Area Delineation Program

other than (1) an urbanized area of 50,000 or more people, or (2) urban clusters of between 2,500 and 50,000 people.[18] These designations are illustrated in Figure 2.3. After the 2020 census, the agency redefined rural by raising the minimum population threshold to 5,000, adding housing unit density, and eliminating the distinction between different types of urban areas.[19] Lichter and Ziliak explain, however, that "few scholars" embrace the Census Bureau's "narrow definition."[20] Most scholars agree that a spectrum best characterizes differing types of populations and landscapes, with extreme urbanity on the one end and extreme rurality on the other.

More scholars opt to use the Census Bureau's definition of "nonmetropolitan" to refer to rural localities.[21] The Census Bureau defines "nonmetropolitan" (or "nonmetro") as anything outside a metro area. It defines a "metropolitan area" according to the United States Office of Management and Budget delineation of a

---

[18] *Urban and Rural*, U.S. Census Bureau, www.census.gov/programs-surveys/geography/guidance/geo-areas/urban-rural.html [https://perma.cc/8V3C-2ASB].

[19] Michael Ratcliffe, *Redefining Urban Areas following the 2020 Census*, U.S. Census Bureau (Dec. 22, 2022), www.census.gov/newsroom/blogs/random-samplings/2022/12/redefining-urban-areas-following-2020-census.html [https://perma.cc/P4CK-LCNV].

[20] Daniel T. Lichter & James P. Ziliak, *The Rural-Urban Interface: New Patterns of Spatial Interdependence and Inequality in America*, 672 Annals Am. Acad. Pol. & Soc. Sci. 6, 10 (2017).

[21] *Id.*

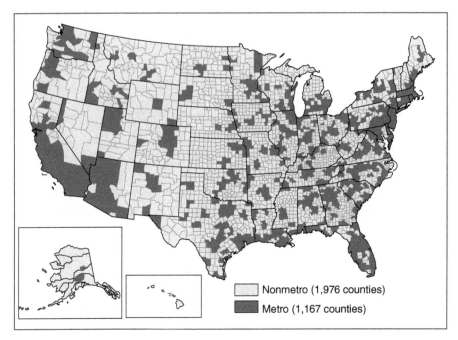

Nonmetro (1,976 counties)
Metro (1,167 counties)

FIGURE 2.4 Metro and nonmetro counties, 2013
Source: USDA, Economic Research Service using data from the U.S. Census Bureau

place considered "a core area containing a substantial population nucleus, together with adjacent communities having a high degree of economic and social integration with that core."[22] Note, though, that the Census Bureau disagrees that nonmetro and rural can be used interchangeably. It proposes that only 54.4 percent of rural residents live in formally designated nonmetro areas.[23] Figure 2.4 shows the breakdown of metropolitan and nonmetropolitan counties as of 2013.

As these competing definitions illustrate, formal legal or regulatory definitions, of which there are many (with many variations), are not necessarily the best metrics by which to understand rural America holistically today. This discussion takes a somewhat broader view. An isolated town of 2,501 people is likely to face similar challenges as one that has a population of 2,499. The trends that affect remote regions and smaller localities within the United States are also relevant to other places on different points along the urban–rural continuum. Life in a city of 51,000, even if

---

[22] *About*, U.S. Census Bureau, www.census.gov/programs-surveys/metro-micro/about.html [https://perma.cc/CBD8-KMP6].

[23] *Rural America*, U.S. Census Bureau, https://mtgis-portal.geo.census.gov/arcgis/apps/MapSeries/index.html?appid=49cd4bc9c8eb444ab51218c1d5001ef6 [https://perma.cc/8TYD-ZDHJ] (scroll down text box to section "Dispelling the Nonmetro Myth"). *See also* Lisa R. Pruitt, *Gender, Geography & Rural Justice*, 23 Berkeley J. Gender L. & Just. 338, 345 (2008) (noting that Census Bureau definition is broader than nonmetro).

technically considered "urban" or "metro," is still going to be different from life in Manhattan or Los Angeles and will share some of the challenges of the country's smaller towns and remote counties.[24] As of 2021, the USDA's Economic Research Service formally recognized 14 percent of the U.S. population as rural, accounting for 46 million people.[25] But many more than this already substantial figure are affected by the issues discussed throughout this book.

Rural America's many complexities – the complexities that would exist within any group of 46 million (or more) people spread throughout the country – do make telling a cohesive narrative about rural America challenging. Rural variations in topography, population, history, and industrial activity make generalizations difficult. As explained in a key treatise on rural poverty:

> Rural America includes not only some of the world's best farmland (in the Great Plains and the Corn Belt, for instance), high-producing dairy regions (such as in Upstate New York, Wisconsin, and New England), but also sprawling exurban areas on the outer edges of the nation's largest metropolitan areas; the vast arid range and desert lands in the Southwest; the deep, mountainous forests of the Pacific Northwest; the flat and humid coastal plain of the Southeast; the hardscrabble towns and hollows of the Appalachians; the rocky shorelines and working forests of New England, where rural villages look much as they did a hundred years ago; and the glaciers and fjords of Alaska.[26]

Inequality *within* rural America adds yet another wrinkle to the complexity of telling a singular story of a rural experience. For these reasons, Kimberlé Crenshaw's theory of intersectionality has taken root of late in law and rurality literature.[27] Intersectionality – the idea that individuals' and populations' lives are shaped by multiple, interacting axes of identity, privilege, and disadvantage – helps account for variations within the rural experience, while also allowing for a commonness to it. Rurality may indeed not always be the most important factor in an individual's or a population's experiences. Nevertheless, rurality warrants attention for several reasons.

---

[24] Ganesh Sitaraman et al., *Regulation and the Geography of Inequality*, 70 Duke L.J. 1763, 1765 (2021) (distinguishing between "superstar" cities and others that are being left behind in fashion similar to rural areas).

[25] ELIZABETH A. DOBIS ET AL., USDA ECON. RSCH. SERV., ECON. INFO. BULL. NO. 230, RURAL AMERICA AT A GLANCE (2021), www.ers.usda.gov/webdocs/publications/102576/eib-230.pdf?v=281 [https://perma.cc/N7KN-NBZ8].

[26] Kenneth M. Johnson, *Where Is Rural America and Who Lives There?*, *in* RURAL POVERTY IN THE UNITED STATES, 3–4 (Ann R. Tickamyer et al. eds., 2017).

[27] Michele Statz & Kaylie Evers, *Spatial Barriers as Moral Failings: What Rural Distance Can Teach Us about Women's Health and Medical Mistrust*, 64 HEALTH & PLACE 1 (2020); Michele Statz & Lisa R. Pruitt, *To Recognize the Tyranny of Distance: A Spatial Reading of* Whole Woman's Health v. Hellerstedt, 51 ECON. & SPACE 1043 (2019); Lisa R. Pruitt, *The Women Feminism Forgot: Rural and Working-Class White Women in the Era of Trump*, 49 U. TOL. L. REV. 537, 538 (2018); Hannah Haksgaard, *Rural Women and Developments in the Undue Burden Analysis: The Effect of* Whole Woman's Health v. Hellerstedt, 65 DRAKE L. REV. 663, 686 (2017). Crenshaw first articulated her theory in *Demarginalizing the Intersection of Race and Sex: A Black Feminist Critique of Antidiscrimination Doctrine, Feminist Theory and Antiracist Politics*, 1989 U. CHI. LEGAL F. 139, 140.

One reason is the nature of rurality itself. Rural residents, according to virtually all definitions, live outside large population centers. This fact alone carries with it a host of realities. Land is a more dominant part of life, and as such, land uses may have more direct and potent relationships with people's lives, livelihoods, and welfare.[28] The scarcer population renders local governments weaker, and people enjoy fewer protections by way of land use planning, zoning ordinances, and infrastructure.[29] The lack of development makes economic opportunities scarcer, driving more people to engage in hazardous or undesirable economic activity to survive.[30] The distance from population centers brings with it invisibility, a veil between rural residents and a mainstream population that may be either ignorant or indifferent to abuses that take place outside of cities.[31] Remote localities may seem unimportant to that mainstream population, an irrelevancy not worth taking on.

In addition to consistent qualitative themes concerning land, scarcity, invisibility, and law's more limited reach into daily life, some trends affect rural communities nationwide, even as those communities may be defined according to different frameworks. These trends often involve economic struggle, other quality-of-life issues, and challenges to regional prosperity. Nonmetro counties account for 85.3 percent of U.S. counties designated as "persistently poor" and 92 percent of counties with a child poverty rate of 40 percent or higher.[32] Rural workers experience higher rates of "working poverty" than urban workers.[33] From 2010 to 2020, the rural population declined consistently, reflecting "the first decade-long rural population loss in history."[34] Rural areas struggled more than cities to recover from the economic recession of 2007.[35]

---

[28] *See, e.g.,* THOMAS G. SAFFORD ET AL., UNIV. OF N.H.: CARSEY INST., JOBS, NATURAL RESOURCES, AND COMMUNITY RESILIENCE: A SURVEY OF SOUTHEAST ALASKANS ABOUT SOCIAL AND ENVIRONMENTAL CHANGE 14 (2011).

[29] *See* Michelle Wilde Anderson, *Sprawl's Shepard: The Rural County*, 100 CALIF. L. REV. 365, 369–70 (2012).

[30] *See generally* Benjamin E. Apple, *Mapping Fracking: An Analysis of Law, Power, and Regional Distribution in the United States*, 38 HARV. ENV'T L. REV. 217 (2014) (discussing rural municipalities' vulnerability to coercive, uncontrolled development scenarios due to scarcity of opportunities); Ann M. Eisenberg, *Beyond Science and Hysteria: Reality and Perceptions of Environmental Justice Concerns Surrounding Marcellus and Utica Shale Gas Development*, 77 U. Pitt. L. Rev. 183 (2015).

[31] Pruitt & Showman, *supra* note 12, at 482.

[32] *Rural Poverty & Well-Being*, ECON. RSCH. SERV.: USDA (Nov. 29, 2022), www.ers.usda.gov/topics/rural-economy-population/rural-poverty-well-being/ [https://perma.cc/RVP7-3D2P]; Bruce Weber & Kathleen Miller, *Poverty in Rural America Then and Now, in* RURAL POVERTY IN THE UNITED STATES 40–42 (Ann R. Tickamyer et al. eds., 2017).

[33] J. Tom Mueller et al., *Impacts of the COVID-19 Pandemic on Rural America*, 118 PNAS 1, 3 (2021), www.pnas.org/doi/10.1073/pnas.2019378118#core-r34 [https://perma.cc/5Q9M-NSLW].

[34] KENNETH M. JOHNSON, UNIV. OF N.H.: CARSEY RSCH., NAT'L ISSUE BRIEF #160, RURAL AMERICA LOST POPULATION OVER THE PAST DECADE FOR THE FIRST TIME IN HISTORY (2022), https://scholars.unh.edu/cgi/viewcontent.cgi?article=1446&context=carsey [https://perma.cc/C4HX-HQFT].

[35] Kevin. J. Bennett et al., *Geographic Differences in Recovery after the Great Recession*, 59 J. RURAL STUD. 111 (2018).

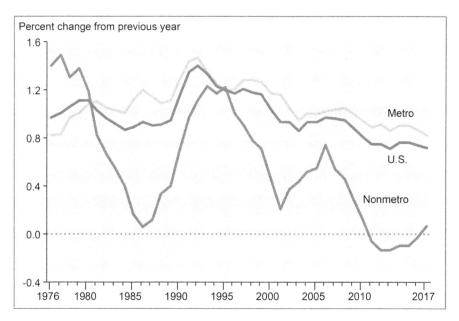

FIGURE 2.5 Population change by metro/nonmetro status, 1976–2017
Note: Metro status changed for some countries in 1980, 1990, 2000, and 2010.
Source: USDA, Economic Research Service using data from the U.S. Census Bureau

Scholars are still assessing the geographic variations of effects of the COVID-19 pandemic. Early studies suggested that rural communities' limited advantages (such as easier social distancing in places less reliant on mass transit) were offset by certain disadvantages (such as more limited access to remote work).[36] Although the pandemic did drive "a sharp turnaround in migration flows" for a time,[37] rural communities experienced higher mortality rates than urban populations and the rural workforce continues to lose working-age people.[38] Figure 2.5 shows trends in population change by metro/nonmetro status from 1976 to 2017.

Public health literature, in particular, recognizes the uniqueness of rurality and how it warrants special attention. Elizabeth Weeks describes "rural health care exceptionalism" in which "U.S. health policy has long recognized that rural health care is different, as demonstrated by a host of special designations, reimbursement

---

[36] Matthew M. Brooks et al., *Rural-Urban Differences in the Labor-Force Impacts of COVID-19 in the United States*, 7 Socius (2021), https://journals.sagepub.com/doi/full/10.1177/23780231211022094 [https://perma.cc/E7QD-XT4E].

[37] James C. Davis et al., *Rural America at a Glance*, USDA Economic Research Service (2022), www.ers.usda.gov/webdocs/publications/105155/eib-246.pdf?v=8695.5.

[38] Liz Carey, *Study: Rural Covid Mortality Influenced by Isolation, Demographics*, The Daily Yonder (Feb. 16, 2023), https://dailyyonder.com/study-rural-covid-mortality-influenced-by-isolation-demographics/2023/02/16/ [https://perma.cc/CE7V-6ZEX].

models, and subsidies that sustain rural healthcare providers, ensuring access to essential services for residents in those areas" in light of "the unique challenges facing rural healthcare delivery."[39] Studies in health and other fields that control for various factors, including place, race, and age, have demonstrated that "rural" can indeed be a significant factor in people's quality of life, meaning that rural residents share common structural experiences notwithstanding their diversity.[40]

As with other characteristics, place interacts with factors such as race, class, and gender to shape a person or community's experiences. Ultimately, a central premise of this book is that place matters in addition to the other factors that are considered relevant to marginalization in relation to law. And, in particular, "rural" should be recognized as a unique kind of place that brings unique experiences, challenges, and opportunities. These assumptions may not be controversial for geographers or rural sociologists. But in legal academia, which is so often concerned with law detached from place, I don't take acceptance of this premise for granted.[41]

RURAL AS A CONCEPT WITH LEGAL SALIENCE

The law's relationship with the rural has been a specific topic of investigation for scholars of law and rurality and related fields over the past two decades. A rural-legal analytical lens can involve a technical orientation or a theoretical one. The discussion earlier, for instance, reveals that formal designations of places as non-metropolitan or rural or something else – those designations themselves informed by shifting standards and subjective priorities – can affect law and policy outcomes such as access to healthcare resources.[42] Lisa Pruitt notes the variability and arbitrariness of such designations, pointing out that federal and state statutes and regulations vary in defining "rural" as having "a population less than 20,000, less than 8,300, no more than 1,500," or other metrics.[43] But those definitions can have serious consequences, as the designation of rural could affect outcomes as varied as "the duty owed under tort law, the scope of utility easements, and whether a warrantless search was justified."[44]

---

[39] Elizabeth Weeks, *One Child Town: The Health Care Exceptionalism Case against Agglomeration Economies*, 2021 UTAH L. REV. 319, 327.

[40] *See, e.g.*, Mark P. Doescher & J. Elizabeth Jackson, *Trends in Cervical and Breast Cancer Screening Practices among Women in Rural and Urban Areas in the United States* 11 (Rural Health Rsch. Ctr.: Univ. of Wash., Working Paper, 2008), http://depts.washington.edu/uwrhrc/uploads/RHRC_FR121_Doescher.pdf [https://perma.cc/93UY-5E84]; Mueller et al., *supra* note 33; Michele Statz and Paula Termuhlen, *Rural Legal Deserts Are a Critical Health Determinant*, 110 AM. J. PUBLIC HEALTH 1519 (2020).

[41] *See* Ann M. Eisenberg, *Navigating Legal Geographies*, 50 FORDHAM URB. L.J. 243 (2023).

[42] Pruitt & Showman, *supra* note 12, at 177–84 (discussing many legislative definitions of rural, the factors that shape those definitions, and the salience of rural designations to legal outcomes).

[43] *Id.* at 179.

[44] *Id.* at 235.

Like me, many scholars and advocates enter this field based on the suspicion, or the conviction, that rural is neglected both culturally and in our society's distributions of material benefits and burdens. Yet, investigating these hunches involves some complexity because, as explored in Chapter 3, much of our society understands rural residents to be among society's most powerful. Whether studies engage with rural in a narrower or broader sense, these investigations often reveal meaningful lessons for law's relationship with geography and vice versa. Thus, law and rurality scholarship can probably best be understood as a critical methodology falling under the same umbrella as law and political economy, in which analysis aims to critique law and legal institutions through lenses of power, politics, and attunement to real-world conditions as opposed to more traditional or mainstream analysis focused on legal doctrine.[45]

Rural legal scholarship frequently converges on two main issues in the law's relationship with the rural: (1) the omission concern[46] and (2) the stereotype or misinformation concern.[47] The omission concern centers on the fact that rural needs are often forgotten by legal decision-makers. Centers of legislative and judicial power tend to be based in cities.[48] Despite urbanites' common complaint that rural representatives dominate state and federal legislatures, the vast majority of the national population is urban and suburban. Thus, law has a tendency to advance urban perspectives, which may neglect even the existence of rural populations and conditions.

Yet, even when decision-makers address rural issues, their misinformed sense of rural life – the stereotype concern – may cause them to do so poorly.[49] These disconnects, scholars have argued, result in "urbanormative" law, or law that fails to appropriately contemplate the needs of populations not living in urban centers.[50]

---

[45] Acknowledging its weak points, including occasional internal contradictions, Richard Thompson Ford describes "Critical Theory" as including "an ever-expanding list of identity-based movements that are critical of some aspect of the status quo (only?) insofar as it affects a specific community." It "also denotes a *method* of theoretical orientation with some historical relationship to Marxian, postmodern, or post-liberal philosophy." Richard Thompson Ford, *Critique, Ideology, and Aesthetics*, 92 U. COLO. L. REV. 1013, 1014 (2021).

[46] *See, e.g.*, Katherine Porter, *Going Broke the Hard Way: The Economics of Rural Failure*, 2005 WIS. L. REV. 969, 970 ("When scholars collect empirical data, they frequently fail to sample rural residents. When reform proposals for legislation are debated, the impact of such laws on rural residents is often ignored .... [R]ural Americans are ghosts in the legal system."); Debra Lyn Bassett, *Distancing Rural Poverty*, 13 GEO. J. ON POVERTY L. & POL'Y 3, 4 (2006) (criticizing inattention to rural struggles after Hurricane Katrina).

[47] *See, e.g.*, Debra Lyn Bassett, *Ruralism*, 88 IOWA L. REV. 273, 279 (2003) ("[R]uralism entails the projection of stereotyped attributes by a more powerful majority group onto a less powerful minority group."); Bud W. Jerke, *Queer Ruralism*, 34 HARV. J. L. & GENDER 259, 260 (2010); Debra Lyn Bassett, *The Rural Venue*, 57 ALA. L. REV. 941, 941 (2006).

[48] *See* Ann M. Eisenberg, *Navigating Legal Geographies*, 50 FORDHAM URB. L.J. 243, 247 (2023).

[49] *See* STUDIES IN URBANORMATIVITY: RURAL COMMUNITY IN URBAN SOCIETY 3 (Gregory M. Fulkerson & Alexander R. Thomas eds., 2014).

[50] *See* Lisa R. Pruitt & Marta R. Vanegas, *Urbanormativity, Spatial Privilege, and Judicial Blind Spots in Abortion Law*, 30 BERKELEY J. GENDER L. & JUST. 76, 77 (2015).

Rural areas likely need to be treated differently; they often do have unique needs. However, *how* they should be treated differently is often imperfectly understood, given the lack of study and knowledge about rural life and the shrinking portion of the population that has firsthand experience with it. Pruitt has critiqued definitions of rural like the Census Bureau's – which defines rural as "everything else" – as treating rural simply "as the 'other,' in contrast or opposition to an implicit urban norm," ultimately treating rural as deviant or strange.[51]

As an example of how conceptions of rural can shape legal outcomes beyond formal legal definitions, scholars have argued that courts treat rural property differently because of stereotypes about rural, and that this differential treatment may contribute to widespread patterns of rural properties falling into disrepair.[52] In *Rural Rhetoric*, Pruitt observes that courts treat the laws of nuisance, ownership, and easements differently in a rural versus an urban context. "In many instances," she argues, "the law respects the private property rights of rural landowners more than those of urban ones, based on assumptions about how the lives of their respective inhabitants differ."[53]

In *Rural Property Law*, Alan Romero similarly argues that courts apply property law differently in urban and rural areas, especially in nuisance, adverse possession, landlord-tenant, prescriptive easement, and surface water cases.[54] He also suggests that this divergent treatment may stem from misguided beliefs about the nature of rural life, positing that judges may believe that "rural tenants need less assurance of habitability or less protection from landlords" and "rural development isn't as important as urban development."[55] The underlying stereotype evokes the image of a self-sufficient individual or family with a strong reliance on land-based activity. This image may be the reality for some rural property owners and may, in fact, reveal the courts' reflection of rural political priorities. However, presuming these conditions as the default may also neglect other concerns, such as safety and infrastructure development.

Pruitt and Romero highlight in their respective reviews of court decisions: (1) a higher tolerance for nuisances on rural private property, including nuisances related to poor property maintenance; (2) a lower tolerance for public intrusion onto rural land, such as for infrastructure development, including higher compensation for such intrusions; (3) stronger protections for rural landlords and weaker ones for rural tenants; (4) liberal rural homestead protections; and (5) a higher burden for establishing adverse possession claims on rural private property. Taken altogether, these protections may serve to keep property in the hands of negligent or absentee property owners, protect hazardous conduct, and limit the potential for transfers of interests into more productive private or public stewards.

---

[51] Pruitt & Showman, supra note 12, at 168.

[52] *See generally* Ann M. Eisenberg, *Rural Blight*, 13 Harv. L. & Pol'y Rev. 187 (2018).

[53] Pruitt & Showman, supra note 12, at 191.

[54] Alan Romero, *Rural Property Law*, 112 W. Va. L. Rev. 765, 765–66 (2010).

[55] *Id.* at 797.

It can be difficult to differentiate among what an appropriate intuition is about urban–rural differences, what constitutes a stereotype, and what conclusions logically stem from anecdotal evidence. For instance, it may seem natural that rural areas would have a higher tolerance for certain nuisances, such as agricultural activity, in light of traditional economic activities and relative population sparseness.[56] Clearly, though, meaningful study and understanding are preferable to knee-jerk instincts about "what rural places are like." This literature suggests that a half-informed sense of rural conditions can serve to ossify laws and policies with concerning unintended consequences.

RURAL AS A CATEGORY WITH SUBTYPES

How is it possible to characterize rural America in a concise way, despite all its complexity? I have found particularly helpful writing by researchers at the Carsey Institute at the University of New Hampshire, who categorize rural America into "four rural Americas." Rural diversity notwithstanding, common trends across these landscapes and populations can be identified. The four rural Americas are each shaped by a handful of key factors that reflect how economic activity does or does not sustain them. The four rural Americas include: (1) amenity-rich rural America; (2) chronically poor rural America; (3) declining resource-dependent rural America; and (4) amenity-decline rural America, an "in-between" category.[57]

This book, as has perhaps become evident, is mostly concerned with types two through four. Although amenity-rich rural places do have challenges, their concerns more closely resemble those seen in urban places. Being rural is not as much of a concern for relatively affluent places like Aspen and Vail, Colorado, for instance – although inequality within those places undoubtedly exists and likely has inflections of rural challenges, such as a lack of employment choices and housing shortages for locals working at ski resorts.[58] Ithaca, with its heavily publicly subsidized university that regularly brings affluent urbanites to the area, probably counts as "amenity-rich," which helps explain why it might be considered distinct from other places with similar geographies, due to those places' more acute economic hardships.

According to the Carsey Institute report, chronically poor rural America shares some similarities with declining rural America.[59] Both communities are concerned

---

[56] *But see* Pruitt & Showman, *supra* note 12, at 160 ("The assumptions judges make about rural places and people are often incapable of being empirically proven.").

[57] LAWRENCE C. HAMILTON ET AL., UNIV. OF N.H.: CARSEY INST., PLACE MATTERS: CHALLENGES AND OPPORTUNITIES IN FOUR RURAL AMERICAS 26–28 (2008).

[58] *See* Nicholas Riccardi, *Aspen Split between Wealthy Visitors and the Working Poor that Serve Them*, ASSOCIATED PRESS (Jan. 12, 2015), https://skift.com/2015/01/12/aspen-split-between-wealthyvisitors-and-the-working-poor-that-serve-them/ [https://perma.cc/5LC2-7C8F].

[59] HAMILTON ET AL., *supra* note 57, at 27.

about employment opportunities, crime, and drug use. Two main differences are that chronically poor rural America has lost less population and is constituted of more non-white populations.[60] This category describes substantial parts of the rural South, including central Appalachia, many Native American reservations, and other pockets of concentrated poverty across Western states.

The declining resource-dependent communities referenced by category 3 are predominantly white, comprised mostly of at least second-generation residents who grew up in the area and remained there in the long term. The decline is largely driven by young adults leaving. In addition to population loss, job opportunities and drug manufacturing and sales are prominent regional problems.[61] This category describes parts of Appalachia, the deindustrializing Midwest, and timber communities in the Pacific Northwest.

RURAL AS A PLACE BURDENED WITH CHRONIC POVERTY

Chronic rural poverty, the issue that most directly affects category 2 communities, has a long and difficult history. Although it is usually measured as an economic phenomenon by departments such as the U.S. Census Bureau, poverty may be defined as "a multidimensional concept that involves insufficient income relative to need and limited access to resources such as education, health care, and social and political power."[62]

The persistence of rural poverty is one feature that may set it apart from urban poverty. Rural poverty emerged as a national policy issue in the 1930s, when the Great Depression drew attention to dire living conditions for certain populations outside cities.[63] In 1968, a report from the President's National Advisory Commission on Rural Poverty stated, "Rural poverty is so widespread, and so acute, as to be a national disgrace[.]"[64] The Johnson administration's 1964 War on Poverty created a legislative framework largely still in effect today and made notable strides to address rural challenges.[65] The American Rescue Plan Act, an aid package passed in 2020 in response to the COVID-19 pandemic, involved a historic injection of resources into rural communities on the level of the War on Poverty, the nascent effects of which are explored in more depth in Chapter 8.[66]

---

[60] *Id.*

[61] *Id.* at 26.

[62] Weber & Miller, *supra* note 32, at 28, 38.

[63] *Id.* at 35.

[64] *Id.* at 31.

[65] *See id.* at 39–41 (discussing War on Poverty and stating that rural poverty declined during the 1960s under the Johnson administration); *see also* Donald E. Voth, *A Brief History and Assessment of Federal Rural Development Programs and Policies*, 25 U. MEM. L. REV. 1265, 1272–75 (1995).

[66] Dylan Matthews, *Joe Biden Just Launched the Second War on Poverty*, VOX (Mar. 10, 2021) www .vox.com/policy-and-politics/22319572/joe-biden-american-rescue-plan-war-on-poverty [https://perma .cc/7JGE-S8QL]

Despite these large-scale efforts, rural poverty has proven more tenacious than urban poverty.[67] Since 1959, poverty rates in rural America have outpaced their urban counterparts.[68] As of 2009–2013, approximately one-third of rural counties were considered high poverty, compared to one-sixth of metro counties.[69] Since 2020, the COVID-19 pandemic has exacerbated many preexisting rural economic challenges.[70]

Thus, concentrated, chronic rural poverty remains a substantial problem today. Chronic rural poverty is exacerbated by rural socioeconomic decline. In turn, communities in decline are susceptible to the spread of poverty.[71] Communities in decline have been in the national spotlight since many white rural voters embraced President Trump's populist, isolationist rhetoric in the 2016 presidential election, with promises to bring back jobs lost in struggling regions.

However, the inattention to longstanding chronic poverty is a critical problem. Communities in decline tend to be majority white, while rural communities of color have been disproportionately burdened by chronic poverty since well before the onset of modern rural decline. As of 2013, rural African Americans had the highest incidence of poverty at 37.3 percent; rural Native Americans had the second highest rate at 34.4 percent; and rural Hispanics had the third highest rate at 28.2 percent. Rural whites, by contrast, experienced a poverty rate of 15.9 percent, which is similar to rates of urban poverty,[72] although rates for white populations may be higher depending on the region. While communities in decline certainly warrant attention – and are vulnerable to poverty – a discussion of rural decline should also include a discussion of persistent rural poverty.

RURAL AS A PLACE WITH CHANGING ECONOMICS

Despite concerns about rural poverty in the 1960s, rural communities were collectively more prosperous in the mid and late twentieth centuries than they are now,[73] although the 2020s may be seeing a change in course due to pandemic-driven

---

[67] Weber & Miller, *supra* note 32, at 33.

[68] *Id.* at 40.

[69] *Id.* at 51. These 828 counties were "concentrated primarily in Appalachia, the southern Black Belt and Mississippi Delta, along the Mexican border, and on Native American tribal reservations." *Id.* at 50.

[70] Mueller et al., *supra* note 33.

[71] *Id.* at 32 (explaining that most rural poverty is in the Southeast, but deindustrialization since the 1980s has led to the spread of poverty in the Midwest and Northeast, as did the Great Recession).

[72] Mark H. Harvey & Rosalind P. Harris, *Racial Inequalities and Poverty in Rural America, in* RURAL POVERTY IN THE UNITED STATES 146 (Ann R. Tickamyer et al. eds., 2017).

[73] *See* Eduardo Porter, *The Hard Truths of Trying to "Save" the Rural Economy*, N.Y. TIMES (Dec. 14, 2018), www.nytimes.com/interactive/2018/12/14/opinion/rural-america-trump-decline .html [https://perma.cc/c86P-CJXC] (explaining that "[r]ural communities once captured a greater share of the nation's prosperity" and detailing the sustained job creation in rural America during the 1990s).

population migrations.[74] The changing rural landscape stems in large part from changes in rural economic activity. Rural livelihoods have ebbed and flowed in and out of various sectors over the past hundred years, as the nation shifted away from a majority agrarian society to an industrialized one.[75] The overall effect, though – when viewed through the lens of human history, throughout which most people have lived subsistence lifestyles – has been a relatively abrupt transition.[76] And contrary to common misconceptions, rural livelihoods have never been synonymous with agriculture in the modern era. A century ago in the 1920s, approximately 60 percent of U.S. residents lived in rural areas, and 40 percent of the population as a whole worked on farms.[77] Today, as mentioned earlier, roughly 14 percent of U.S. residents live in rural areas, but a mere 1 to 2 percent of the population as a whole works on farms.[78] Those involved in agricultural work also tend to have at least one additional source of income.[79]

More recent decades have also seen dramatic transformations. As of 1970, in "high-density" rural areas, agriculture, forestry, fishing, manufacturing, and mining accounted for approximately 38 percent of employment altogether. In "low-density" rural areas, these sectors accounted for 36 percent of employment.[80]

The substantial proportions of those employment numbers do not paint the full picture of the significance of these traditional rural livelihoods to communities

---

74 JAMES C. DAVIS ET AL., USDA: ECON. RSCH. SERV., ECON. INFO. BULL. NO. 246, RURAL AMERICA AT A GLANCE (2022), www.ers.usda.gov/webdocs/publications/105155/eib-246.pdf?v=1425.7 [https://perma.cc/52LL-VB6D]; Kenneth M. Johnson, *Recent Data Suggest Rural America Is Growing Again after a Decade of Population Loss*, UNIV. OF N.H.: CARSEY SCH. OF PUB. POL'Y (Dec. 6, 2022), https://scholars.unh.edu/cgi/viewcontent.cgi?article=1453&context=carsey [https://perma.cc/T27T-PYBU].

75 CAROLYN DIMITRI ET AL., USDA: ECON. RSCH. SERV., ECON. INFO. BULL. NO. 3, THE 20TH CENTURY TRANSFORMATION OF U.S. AGRICULTURE AND FARM POLICY 2–5 (2005), https://naldc.nal.usda.gov/download/22832/PDF [https://perma.cc/DC2L-JF7Y].

76 *Cf.* STOLL, *supra* note 4, at 28–30 (observing that until only very recently in human history, the vast majority of people were subsistence agrarians).

77 Weber & Miller, *supra* note 32, at 34, 36.

78 *Id.* at 36.

79 *The Importance of Off-Farm Income to the Agricultural Economy*, UNIVERSITY OF MISSOURI EXTENSION (2022), www.cobank.com/documents/7714906/7715332/The-Importance-of-Off-Farm-Income-to-the-Agricultural-Economy.pdf/119d4727-ba95-3f4b-519e-5c2d915a2032?t=1663350230900 [https://perma.cc/LN5M-YUB7].

80 THE WHITE HOUSE, PRESIDENT BARACK OBAMA: COUNCIL OF ECON. ADVISERS, STRENGTHENING THE RURAL ECONOMY – THE CURRENT STATE OF RURAL AMERICA (2010) [hereinafter CURRENT STATE OF RURAL AMERICA], https://obamawhitehouse.archives.gov/administration/eop/cea/factsheets-reports/strengthening-the-rural-economy/the-current-state-of-rural-america [https://perma.cc/P623-6JXH]. The exact breakdown of rural livelihoods is as follows: agriculture, forestry, and fishing accounted for 13 percent of jobs in high-density rural areas and 23 percent of jobs in low-density rural areas; manufacturing accounted for 23 percent of jobs in high-density rural areas and 10 percent of jobs in low-density rural areas; and mining accounted for 2 percent of jobs in high-density rural areas and 3 percent of jobs in low-density rural areas. Other major sectors included government, the service sector, wholesale and retail trade, finance, insurance, real estate, and "other." *Id.*

dependent upon them. These livelihoods often center on large-scale productive activity with a substantial land use or environmental footprint. These industries have been distinct from other significant employers, such as the service or retail sectors, in the magnitude of their presence and their relationships with local governments. Industries such as coal and timber may account for millions of dollars in tax revenue through measures such as severance taxes, which are then distributed to rural municipalities, counties, and reservations.[81] Thus, although these industries employed just over one-third of residents in the 70s, their role in a regional way of life often loomed even larger than the statistics suggest.

By 2007, these industries had declined dramatically.[82] Between 1970 and 2007, agriculture, forestry, fishing, manufacturing, and mining went from accounting for more than one-third of rural employment to less than one-fifth.[83] The localized effects have been more dramatic for many communities, however.

In rural Southeast Alaska, for instance, forestry was once the region's economic driver, providing a peak of 3,400 jobs in 1990. This figure dropped to just 214 in 2009.[84] As of 2011, 75 percent of that region's residents believed that the loss of forestry

---

[81] *See* RORY MCILMOIL & EVAN HANSEN, DOWNSTREAM STRATEGIES, THE DECLINE OF CENTRAL APPALACHIAN COAL AND THE NEED FOR ECONOMIC DIVERSIFICATION 1 (2010), www.downstreamstrategies.com/documents/reportsj5ublication/DownstreamStrategies-DeclineOfCentralAppalachianCoal-FINAL-1-19-10.pdf [https://perma.cc/55PX-6JTJ] (discussing the coal industry's role in filling the tax coffers of local governments in Appalachia); *see also* Michelle W. Anderson, *The Western, Rural Rustbelt: Learning from Local Fiscal Crisis in Oregon*, 50 WILLAMETTE L. REV. 465, 481 (2014) (discussing the relationship between federal timber funds paid in lieu of taxes and regional reliance on the industry in the northwest); Alan Ramo & Deborah Behles, *Transitioning a Community away from Fossil-Fuel Generation to a Green Economy: An Approach Using State Utility Commission Authority*, 15 MINN. J. L. SCI. & TECH. 505, 515 (2014) (discussing the tax revenue Hopi and Navajo tribes derived from their coal mines); Julie Turkewitz, *Tribes that Live off Coal Hold Tight to Trump's Promises*, N.Y. TIMES (Apr. 1, 2017), www.nytimes.com/2017/04/01/us/trump-coal-promises.html [https://perma.cc/ZJ8M-LHLS] (explaining how half of the Crow Tribe's non-federal budget comes from royalties and taxes on coal extracted from a mine located on the reservation; the mine also supports 170 jobs).

[82] CURRENT STATE OF RURAL AMERICA, *supra* note 80. The exact breakdown of these sectors is as follows: agriculture, forestry, and fishing accounted for 6 percent of jobs in high-density areas and 12 percent in low-density areas; manufacturing accounted for 13 percent of jobs in high-density rural areas and 7 percent in low-density rural areas; and mining accounted for 1 percent in high-density rural areas and 3 percent in low-density rural areas. *Id.*

[83] *See id.* (detailing how traditional rural livelihoods once made up roughly 36 percent to 38 percent of rural employment; that number has decreased to roughly 20 percent). Since some of these livelihoods – such as forestry and mining – are rural by nature, changes in those livelihoods had less of an effect on urban communities. The numbers may look similar for manufacturing in urban places: in 1970, 25 percent of the workforce as a whole worked in manufacturing, compared to 8.5 percent today. Sara Bauerle Danzman & Jeff D. Colgan, *Robots Aren't Killing the American Dream. Neither Is Trade. This Is the Problem.*, WASH. POST (Mar. 10, 2017), www.washingtonpost.com/news/monkey-cage/wp/2017/03/10/robots-arent-killing-the-american-dream-neither-is-trade-thisis-the-real-problem/ [https://perma.cc/5JV4-UZ6M]. These losses in manufacturing, however, have had a more substantial impact on rural communities. *See* Anderson, *supra* note 81, at 467–68.

[84] SAFFORD ET AL., *supra* note 28, at 14.

jobs was negatively affecting their communities.[85] In North Carolina, manufacturing jobs dropped from 761,000 in 2000 to 429,000 in 2010, a reduction of 44 percent that disproportionately affected rural communities.[86] Former timber communities of the Pacific Northwest are still in crisis following reductions in timbering on public lands.[87] Coal communities in central Appalachia struggle with a regional economy on the brink of collapse.[88] Iowa has lost 30 percent of its farms since 1977.[89] The story may differ depending upon the region in question, but common themes are losses in livelihoods, population, and ways of life.

These data show that the makeup of rural livelihoods has shifted substantially in modern U.S. history. Over the course of the same period from the 1970s to the late 2000s, economic growth disproportionately benefited large urban centers.[90] With the economic recession of 2008, rural communities as a whole fell below zero population growth for the first time in the country's history.

The consequences of this economic decline have been severe. Mass migration to cities due to the changing economic landscape has affected both the physical and the social rural landscape. Shrunken populations have a ripple effect on communities' already precarious economic health. As populations shrink, local governments receive less tax revenue and are, in turn, less able to provide basic services, such as police protection. Homes and businesses stand empty, and as they fall into disrepair, they impose a new burden on cash-strapped local governments. Rural hospitals and libraries have closed throughout the country, leaving remaining residents underserved.[91] As the built and infrastructural environment decays, new potential

---

[85] *Id.* at 5.

[86] David L. Carlton & Peter A. Coclanis, *The Roots of Southern Deindustrialization*, 61 CHALLENGE 418, 418 (2018).

[87] Anderson, *supra* note 81, at 471 (describing the "crisis" in Oregon timber industry).

[88] *See* CALVIN A. KENT, NAT'L ASS'N OF CTYS., THE CRUEL COAL FACTS: THE IMPACT ON WEST VIRGINIA COUNTIES FROM THE COLLAPSE OF THE COAL ECONOMY 1 (2016), www.cbermu.org/wp-content/uploads/2017/08/2016-09-Cruel_Coal.pdf [https://perma.cc/4X7C-LN6G] (stating that the "38 percent decline in West Virginia coal production plus the 71 percent fall in coal prices since 2008 have led to a collapse of the State's coal economy").

[89] Matthew Patane, *How We Got Here: Iowa Farms Grow in Size, but There Are Fewer of Them*, CEDAR RAPIDS GAZETTE (June 17, 2019), www.thegazette.com/IowaIdeas/stories/agriculture/how-we-got-here-iowa-farms-grow-in-size-but-there-are-fewer-of-them-family-farms-consolidationiowa-state-research-20180623 [https://perma.cc/6ZNP-4XK6].

[90] *See Rural Employment and Unemployment*, USDA: ECON. RSCH. SERV. (May 10, 2022), www.ers.usda.gov/topics/rural-economy-population/employment-education/rural-employment-and-unemployment/ [https://perma.cc/92RE-X6FS] (explaining that while urban communities have recovered from the Great Recession, rural employment rates remain low compared to pre-recession levels); Carlton & Coclanis, *supra* note 86, at 419 (asserting that a loss of rural jobs "has disproportionately hit the small-town and rural South, particularly its heavily white populations, and has opened up enormous disparities between these areas and the larger cities of the region"); Evert Meijers & Dick van der Wouw, *Struggles and Strategies of Rural Regions in the Age of the 'Urban Triumph,'* 66 J. RURAL STUD. 21, 21–22 (2019).

[91] Sheldon Weisgrau, *Issues in Rural Health: Access, Hospitals, and Reform*, 17 HEALTH CARE FIN. REV. 1, 1–7 (1995); *see* Jon Marcus & Matt Krupnick, *The Rural Higher-Education Crisis*, ATLANTIC (Sept.

residents and investors are drawn to more livable places. Young people continue to move away because of a lack of opportunity.[92] Meanwhile, disproportionate rural "deaths of despair" by opioids or suicide persist.[93]

Yet, the nature of the industries that left these communities did not necessarily allow for a clean break. Traditional rural livelihoods meant that longstanding industrial activities left legacies beyond lost jobs and socioeconomic despair. The quality of water and air in mining communities remains precarious, for example; many of the mountaintops of the Appalachian mountain range have been permanently felled to retrieve coal.[94] Power plants like the Navajo Generating Station have "fouled the air and scarred the land that the tribe holds sacred."[95] Mill towns struggle to remediate the manufacturing centers that now sit as hazardous brownfields.[96] And the pollutants emitted by large agribusiness operations that displaced residents and transformed communities often go unchecked.[97]

The past several decades are also significant because of three transitional moments. First, during the 1970s, the already declining rural population seemed to have balanced out. In a period known as the "rural renaissance," rural areas, in fact, grew at a faster rate than cities.[98] Yet, certain legal and economic developments – notably including the 1980s farm crisis and deregulatory initiatives by the federal government, discussed later in this book – helped steer rural prosperity downward just after that era. More recently, the 2008 Great Recession proved another decisive event. Widespread housing and business foreclosures and abandonments seemed

---

27, 2017), www.theatlantic.com/education/archive/2017/09/the-rural-higher-education-crisis/541188/ [https://perma.cc/XHW4-ZJTS] (explaining that rural areas must "contend with drug and mental-health issues, poverty, and a lack of high-speed access to the internet"); *see also* Darrell M. West & Jack Karsten, *Rural and Urban America Divided by Broadband Access*, BROOKINGS BLOG (July 18, 2016), www.brookings.edu/blog/techtank/2016/07/18/rural-ajid-urban-america-divided-by-broadband-access/ [https://perma.cc/22MM-ZQXM] (detailing how rural areas have slower broadband than urban areas).

92 Alana Semuels, *The Graying of Rural America*, ATLANTIC (June 2, 2016), www.theatlantic.com/business/archive/2016/06/the-graying-of-rural-america/485159/ [https://perma.cc/8GX6-Y79F].

93 *2017 Drug Overdose Death Rates*, CTRS. FOR DISEASE CONTROL & PREVENTION (last reviewed Mar. 22, 2021), www.cdc.gov/drugoverdose/deaths/2017.html [https://perma.cc/22E8-KE3K] (describing the disproportionately harsh effects of the opioid crisis on rural communities).

94 Patrick McGinley, *Collateral Damage: Turning a Blind Eye to Environmental and Social Injustice in the Coalfields*, 19 J. ENV'T. & SUSTAINABILITY L. 304, 373 (2013).

95 James Rainey, *Lighting the West, Dividing a Tribe*, NBC NEWS (Dec. 18, 2017), www.nbcnews.com/specials/navajo-coal [https://perma.cc/DSW6-V8PT].

96 U.S. ENV'T. PROT. AGENCY, REVITALIZING AMERICA'S MILLS: A REPORT ON BROWNFIELDS MILL PROJECTS 2, 24 (2015), www.epa.gov/sites/production/files/2015-09/documents/mill_report_110306.pdf [https://perma.cc/K3AV-AE83].

97 *See, e.g.*, Margaret Carrel et al., *Pigs in Space: Determining the Environmental Justice Landscape of Swine Concentrated Animal Feeding Operations (CAFOs) in Iowa*, 13 INT'L J. ENV'T. RSCH. & PUB. HEALTH 849 (2016) (detailing harmful level of pollution produced by the swine industry).

98 *See* J. Paul Newell, *Rural Healthcare: The Challenges of a Changing Environment*, 47 MERCER L. REV. 979, 981 (1996) ("The 1970s were labeled a 'rural renaissance,' with the rate of rural population growth outpacing urban growth for the first time in the twentieth century. However, this trend was reversed in the 1980s, primarily because of the depressed rural economy.").

to smother a spark that was otherwise fueling a path toward revitalization.[99] And of course, the COVID-19 pandemic reshaped economic sectors, plunged many into unemployment, and contributed to widespread illness and death, again, the full breadth of which still remains to be seen.

Today, the rural economy is characterized by an aging population and an ethnically diversifying workforce. Rural economic activity was dominated by four industries as of 2022: government, manufacturing, retail, and healthcare/social assistance.[100] But legacy industries continue to loom even as they fade, while many regions and local governments search for a path forward. This book is therefore not concerned solely with poverty and economic struggle – already pressing problems – but also with what appears to be the large-scale, systematic unraveling of many rural local governments and related social and economic systems throughout the country.

RURAL AS CONCEPTUALIZED IN THE RURAL ELECTRIFICATION ACT OF 1936

Commentary often frames the challenges facing the modern countryside as novel and flummoxing. Headlines repeatedly bemoan: *How can we possibly address these major changes at such a large scale?* Although modern rural challenges do have some novel features, this commentary is also often quick to dismiss the many interventions that have pursued geographic equity during the past century. These interventions have seen mixed successes, but nonetheless offer a rich foundation for contemplating potential avenues to address current conditions in distressed rural regions.

In early 1936, Congress took up a draft of the Rural Electrification Act (REA). The Rural Electrification Administration had been created a year prior as a temporary entity mandated to bring electricity to the countryside. In discussion in the Senate on February 25, 1936, senators were tasked with assessing whether to pass legislation that would appropriate millions of dollars to make the Administration permanent and extend its activities, and what form that legislation should take. The senators' discussion of the draft REA helps contextualize today's conversation on rural marginalization. Of particular interest is what was different at that time and what remains the same today.

Funnily enough, even in the drafting of an act for rural electrification, senators were not entirely certain what "rural" was. Senator George Norris of Nebraska, the bill's main sponsor in the Senate, explained to his colleagues that the bill "attempted" a definition of rural.[101] That definition provided that rural "[s]hall be

---

[99] Annie Lowrey, *The Great Recession Is Still with Us*, ATLANTIC (Dec. 1, 2017), www.theatlantic.com/business/archive/2017/12/great-recession-still-with-us/547268/ [https://perma.cc/LD4U-4ZLM]; Gillian B. White, *Rural America's Silent Housing Crisis*, ATLANTIC (Jan. 28, 2015), www.theatlantic.com/business/archive/2015/01/rural-americas-silent-housing-crisis/384885/ [https://perma.cc/2GVN-9B74].

[100] DAVIS ET AL., *supra* note 74.

[101] 80 CONG. REC. 2759 (1936).

deemed to mean any area of the United States not included within the boundaries of any city, village, or borough having a population in excess of 1,500 inhabitants."[102] However, Senator Norris explained, "The limit of 1,500 is an arbitrary selection. I do not know whether it is right or not. It strikes me as being fair, but it may be that the number should be smaller, or that it ought to be larger."[103] He clarified, "We cannot lay down a hard and fast rule as to just how much density of population there shall be or in how much of a compact territory it will be" because of varying levels of density of farm populations.[104]

Senators during those discussions more often than not treated "rural" as synonymous with "farmer." "Rural electrification" was interchangeably referred to as "farm electrification" and "getting electricity to the farmers." Indeed, as of the 1930s, just under half the national population was still rural, and a slight majority of that rural population was employed in agriculture.[105]

Farmers' contributions to the country were treated as part of the rationale behind the intervention to electrify the countryside. Senator Norris explained:

> The farmer thinks just as much of [electricity] as does the man who dwells in the city. In the end the farmer is the best customer, because he needs it for all the purposes for which the city dweller needs it, and in addition to that he needs it and utilizes it for many other purposes for which the city dweller has no use whatsoever.
>
> The farmer saws his wood, separates his cream, fills his silo, pumps his water, and in many instances milks his cows by electricity. That means that the farmer, when he once has electricity installed and uses it, thinks more of it than anything else he has on his farm. Would not any of us? Are we going to say to the farmer, "You cannot have this modern element of civilization that everyone else insists on having. You must go without it. Yet you toil and produce the food that keeps us all. You are the foundation of the pyramid, but to you we will deny this luxury, if it may be called as such, this modern necessity of human existence."[106]

Despite their emphasis on farmers, Senator Norris and his co-drafters wanted electrification of rural areas "to include both the farm and the nonfarm population thereof" because some regions might "not have sufficient density of farm population to warrant the installation of an electric distribution system."[107] Senator Norris explained that private power companies had already found the "cream" of areas for service provision – meaning the places of highest density and, therefore, the highest return on their investments. The "idea" of the Rural Electrification Administration, he proposed, was "to include just as much of the lean territory as can be included."[108]

[102] *Id.*
[103] *Id.*
[104] *Id.*
[105] DIMITRI ET AL., *supra* note 75.
[106] 80 CONG. REC. 2757 (1936).
[107] *Id.*
[108] *Id.*

Legislators' treatment of "rural" and "farmer" as synonymous in 1936 offers an important lesson about modern society's confusion as to what to make of rural marginalization. As mentioned earlier, modern rural America is *not* synonymous with farming or with the other extractive industries it has historically been known for. This change over the past century has left broader U.S. society and its increasingly urban majority uncertain about what rural contributions to society *are*, if not the vision of the traditional family farm or the coal mine or an equivalent. In other words, the shift away from larger-scale rural extraction today has created confusion as to whether rural regions are earning their keep – and thus, whether they deserve the basic necessities of infrastructure. Chapter 8 explores common oversights about rural regions' ongoing and potential contributions to society. But the discussion also ought to ask whether any locality should have to be a site of extraction to be considered a worthy part of the national ecosystem.

In addition to their pragmatic concerns, the senators' discussion of rural electrification also treated the task as an ethical issue. Earlier in the debate, Senator Norris observed, "Electricity under our civilization is no longer a luxury. It is a necessity."[109] Embedded in this statement was the assumption that government has certain obligations to furnish a particular quality of life to its constituents, regardless of where they live or what they do.

The conceptualizations of rural in the REA debates might not mirror modern conditions, but they mirror modern questions. What are the *practical and ethical* drivers for how and why our laws and institutions distribute resources across populations and landscapes?

---

[109] *Id.*

3

The Myth of Rural Empowerment

This chapter turns to the myth that rural communities hold all the power.[1] But for its substantive complexity, this myth could have been included among Chapter 2's foundational myths. Like those myths, the myth of rural empowerment inspires the sense that rural disadvantage is not a sympathetic or relevant lens of analysis. This myth prompts urbanites to ask, "Why should I care about them?" Especially after the 2016 presidential election, urban voters saw themselves as hostage to rural voters. Although Trump could not have been elected without the votes of millions of suburbanites and city dwellers, the narrative of angry rural voters in Trump country spread quickly. Cities and their residents are the underdogs, this myth proposes. Rural populations hold the cards.

Some commentators point to the fact that electoral structures do weight rural votes and representation disproportionately, in a fashion that is troubling for representative democracy. Yet, Klein and Pruitt have argued that the idea of outsized rural political representation is itself "grossly overstated," and have labeled this idea as a myth.[2] And the myth is a dangerous one: the inflated idea of rural empowerment obscures rural disadvantage, in turn exacerbating that disadvantage by making it seem unworthy of exploration.

Klein and Pruitt compellingly complicate the assumptions behind the premise of outsized rural political representation. My own view is that although rural populations do sometimes benefit from outsized political power, this power does not somehow neutralize the many forms of rural disadvantage. And that disadvantage became particularly apparent to me when I learned about the challenges rural local governments are dealing with in the face of depopulation and the empty, crumbling buildings an urbanizing country has left behind.

---

[1] Excerpts from this chapter were taken from Ann M. Eisenberg, *Addressing Rural Blight: Lessons from West Virginia and WV LEAP*, 24 J. AFFORDABLE HOUS. & CMTY. DEV. L. 513 (2016) [hereinafter Eisenberg, *Addressing Rural Blight*] and Ann M. Eisenberg, *Rural Blight*, 13 HARV. L. & POL'Y REV. 187 (2018) [hereinafter Eisenberg, *Rural Blight*].

[2] Kaceylee Klein & Lisa R. Pruitt, *Rural Bashing*, 57 U. RICH. L. REV. 965, 971 (2023).

DEPOPULATION AND THE BUILT ENVIRONMENT

Shortly after I arrived in West Virginia in 2014, Jesse, the Clinic's lead land use attorney, came by my desk and asked whether I wanted to work on dilapidated buildings. I smiled and shrugged as if to say, "Sure! Why not?" But I did not know how a lawyer would "work on dilapidated buildings." Would I be getting a hammer?

I quickly came to appreciate the why and the what of vacant and dilapidated buildings as the inevitable successor to depopulation. As of 2014, the Clinic had been operational for a few years. The program's faculty, staff, and students had made inroads with communities all around the state, developing relationships with local government employees, activists, and other organizations. The Clinic was in high demand for its services, providing counseling and assistance on drafting comprehensive plans and ordinances. West Virginia communities recognized these processes as a way to pursue economic diversification and infrastructure development, to think about strategies to attract new residents and service providers, or to maximize the potential of amenities that were already there.

But the Clinic kept hearing one concern that did not fall squarely under the umbrella of traditional land use planning: vacant and dilapidated properties. As coal jobs were lost, and as young people moved away and the state's population dropped, the area's volume of residents no longer matched the communities' built environments. From 2010 to 2020, West Virginia lost 3.2 percent of its population, making it one of only three states to lose population during that period.[3] For the past two decades, deaths have outpaced births in West Virginia.[4] But the physical structures for a larger population remain.

Echoing the cycles that hit cities like St. Louis, Detroit, and Baltimore after mid century white flight to the suburbs,[5] West Virginia's downtowns and main streets emptied out and began to crumble. Historic theaters with boarded-up windows, half-burnt mansions, crumbling houses, and empty gas stations or big box stores were not an unusual sight throughout the state. Morgantown was not immune to these trends either. I regularly passed the historic Warner Theater on Morgantown's Main Street, built in 1924 as an art deco beauty, now sitting empty, derelict, and sad (Figure 3.1).

These buildings are not just eyesores. They are often dangerous, ready to catch fire, collapse on someone, attract vermin, or otherwise pose risks to the

---

3   Am. Counts Staff, *West Virginia Population Declined 3.2% From 2010 to 2020,* U.S. Census Bureau (Aug. 25, 2021), www.census.gov/library/stories/state-by-state/west-virginia-population-change-between-census-decade.html [https://perma.cc/7W8C-BGSQ].

4   John Raby, *Leaving Home: West Virginia Population Drop Is Largest in US,* AP News (May 22, 2021), https://apnews.com/article/al-state-wire-west-virginia-lifestyle-census-2020-business-9b94594a74d6b7ab1bee153a425981d9 [https://perma.cc/B47X-FLR8].

5   Christopher J. Tyson, *Municipal Identity as Property,* 118 Penn St. L. Rev. 647, 664 (2014); James R. Cohen, *Abandoned Housing: Exploring Lessons from Baltimore,* 12 Hous. Pol'y Debate 415, 415–16 (2001); Elizabeth M. Tisher, *Re-Stitching the Urban Fabric: Municipal-Driven Rehabilitation of Vacant and Abandoned Buildings in Ohio's Rust Belt,* 15 Vt. J. Env't. L. 173, 174 (2013).

FIGURE 3.1 The Warner Theatre marquee in Morgantown, WV, 2015. West Virginia Collection, Carol M. Highsmith Archive, Library of Congress

neighboring area.[6] But the buildings' aesthetic effects matter, too. People and businesses want to move away from these properties, not toward them. Properties emptying and falling into dereliction are both symptom and cause of a downward cycle of socioeconomic decline.

These problem properties are also quite complicated to deal with legally, which explained why people sought help from a law clinic. Depending on the issue, different statutes may be implicated, such as the laws on tax foreclosure, the building code, or the fire code. Landowners have rights to notice and process when a local government seeks to enforce a regulation or do something on their property, some of which have a timeline that can take years. Landowners' status may be complicated by cotenancy, bankruptcy, corporate designation, residence out of state, or simply by being unknown. Most of the local governments approaching the Clinic were struggling with their problem properties due to the complexity and expense of dealing with them.

HOW LOCAL GOVERNMENTS DEAL WITH PROBLEM PROPERTIES IN THEORY

It is theoretically possible for a local government to address one or more of these properties in a smooth, straightforward fashion. Ideally, when a problem property warrants action, the municipality should have already laid a foundation for

---

[6] *Cf.* 35 PA. STAT. AND CONS. STAT. ANN. § 1712.1 (West 2002) (defining "blighted property" to include premises declared a public nuisance, posing an attractive nuisance to children, any dwelling that is "dilapidated, unsanitary, unsafe, vermin-infested," or lacking facilities required by housing code, properties that pose fire hazards or other dangers, properties with accumulations of trash and debris or "haven[s] for rodents or other vermin," properties that were delinquent on taxes for two years or more, and properties considered vacant or abandoned).

addressing these properties in law and policy.[7] To lay such a foundation, it should have adopted a comprehensive plan, a zoning ordinance, and a building code, complying as needed with provisions of state law.[8]

With this foundation in place, when a property violates the zoning ordinance or the building code, a local government actor, such as a code enforcement officer, issues a citation.[9] For example, if the property owner allows trash and vermin to collect on the front lawn, the code enforcement officer would direct the owner to correct the violations or face fines and, eventually, proceedings in court.[10] Ideally, property owners respond to such citations with corrective action, and the cycle either ceases or begins again.

The cases in which landowners never correct deficiencies are the ones that contribute to dereliction and vacancy, conditions sometimes collectively referred to as "blight." Some properties fall into disrepair because of landowners who simply refuse to maintain them, but this seems relatively rare.[11] Much of the property neglect in rural areas actually comes from cases of vacant properties with absentee owners or ownership that is unclear.[12] These may include speculators who purchased a property at a tax sale without intending to use it; heirs who live out of state or are unaware they inherited a property; neglectful landlords; foreign or out-of-state investors; people who died or moved to retirement facilities without making plans for the property; or mortgage lenders who did not foreclose on abandoned homes during the

---

[7] *See, e.g.*, W. Va. Univ. Law: Land Use & Sustainable Dev. L. Clinic, From Liability to Viability: A Legal Toolkit to Address Neglected Properties in West Virginia 4 (2015) [hereinafter Liability to Viability], https://wvleap.wvu.edu/files/d/cf7aade6-10ca-4df7-b154-6956dbad3b85/from-liability-to-viability.pdf [https://perma.cc/22DA-44DL] ("Addressing dilapidated properties is a long-term project that requires capitalizing on community partnerships and community planning .... [M]aintaining properties typically requires the use of an effective code enforcement program and a registration system to keep track of vacant and uninhabitable properties."); *see also id.* at 7 ("[C]omprehensive plans are an essential tool for guiding a community's goals and resources, particularly for dilapidated properties.").

[8] *See* Patricia E. Salkin, American Law of Zoning § 6:6 (5th ed. 2017).

[9] *See* Nicole Stelle Garnett, *Ordering (and Order in) the City*, 57 Stan. L. Rev. 1, 4 (2004); *see, e.g.*, Code Enforcement, City of Va. Beach, www.vbgov.com/government/departments/housing-neighborhood-preservation/code-enforcement/Pages/default.aspx [https://perma.cc/G43C-AH8U].

[10] *See, e.g.*, Code Enforcement, Burlington, N.C., www.ci.burlington.nc.us/1542/Code-Enforcement [https://perma.cc/97FU-4T9U]; *Code Enforcement*, Ferndale, www.ferndalemi.gov/services/code-enforcement [https://perma.cc/9HJB-YM4E]. These processes vary by state, locality, and strategy, however. For instance, a municipality may also opt to sue to have a property declared a nuisance. *See* Steven E. Barlow et al., *Ten Years of Fighting Blighted Property in Memphis: How Innovative Litigation Inspired Systems Change and a Local Culture of Collaboration to Resolve Vacant and Abandoned Properties*, 25 J. Affordable Hous. & Cmty. Dev. L. 347, 356 (2017); Creola Johnson, *Fight Blight: Cities Sue to Hold Lenders Responsible for the Rise in Foreclosures and Abandoned Properties*, 2008 Utah L. Rev. 1169, 1190.

[11] *See, e.g.*, On-site Citations, W.V. Univ. Coll. of Law: WV LEAP, https://wvleap.wvu.edu/fundamental-tools/on-site-citations [https://perma.cc/ XWW7-2675] (discussing noncompliance and responses in the city of Charleston).

[12] *See* Eisenberg, *Addressing Rural Blight*, *supra* note 1, at 533.

housing and foreclosure crisis of 2008.[13] Owners of abandoned malls, former industrial sites, and other defunct businesses may be corporations that no longer exist or maintain local contacts, and owners of abandoned schools may be the cash-strapped local governments themselves.[14]

Properties such as these decay rather rapidly, as no one is tending to them and the owners are difficult to hold accountable. In turn, empty, dilapidated structures attract vermin and crime, create fire and structural hazards, reduce neighboring properties' values, and hurt local government tax revenues and overall community socioeconomic health.[15]

When a high volume of these properties crops up, a local government ideally takes action in response. Condemnation and eminent domain are perhaps the most common legal tools local governments can use for properties that reach such a dramatic state of disrepair and danger. A well-functioning local government acting in good faith would first look to its blight ordinance or another statute.[16] The statute would define blighted properties as having one or a set of the problems discussed here, including hazardous physical defects and the absence of a property owner willing to make repairs.[17] The local government would then officially designate a property as "blighted."[18] The landowner would be entitled to due process protections, requiring the local government to provide notice of the designation to the extent possible.[19]

Eventually, absent action from the landowner, the local government or related entity would take over ownership of the property.[20] The local government would then raze or rehabilitate the building and sell it to a new owner who would put it to productive use. If a community had a large number of problem properties, the local

---

[13] *See id.* at 546 n.152; Allen Best, *Unfinished Zombie Housing Developments Haunt the Rural West,* HIGH COUNTRY NEWS (Colorado) (Mar. 12, 2012), www.hcn.org/issues/44.4/unfinished-zombie-housing-developments-haunt-the-rural-west [https://perma.cc/7R6Y-6T5A].

[14] *See, e.g.,* Betsy H. Sochar, *Shining the Light on Greyfields: A Wal-Mart Case Study on Preventing Abandonment of BigBox Stores through Land Use Regulations,* 71 ALB. L. REV. 697, 703 (2008) ("Currently, thousands of abandoned big box[ ] [stores] litter municipalities across the United States.").

[15] *See* Eisenberg, *Addressing Rural Blight, supra* note 1, at 518, 546 n.3.

[16] *See, e.g.,* City of Shelton v. Fuge, No. CV010074857S, 2002 WL 1009845, at *1 (Conn. Super. Ct. Apr. 23, 2002) (analyzing City of Sheldon's Anti Blight Ordinance enacted pursuant to Connecticut Code § 7-148 "to ensure that proper procedures exist for the rehabilitation, reconstruction, or reuse of vacant and blighted buildings in order to protect the health and safety of the people").

[17] *See, e.g.,* 35 PA. STAT. AND CONS. STAT. ANN. § 1712.1 (West 2002) (defining, among other options, blighted property to include premises that are nuisances because of physical conditions, properties that are "dilapidated, unsanitary, unsafe, vermin infested or lacking in the facilities and equipment required by the housing code of the municipality," and properties that have been declared abandoned by the owner).

[18] *See, e.g.,* Redevelopment Auth. of City of York v. Bratic, 45 A.3d 1168, 1170 (Pa. Commw. Ct. 2012) (City Planning Commission certified property as blighted under state statute).

[19] *See id.* (discussing series of letters sent to landowner, opportunities for appeal, and opportunities to correct deficiencies).

[20] *See id.*; Charleston Urb. Renewal Auth. v. Courtland Co., 509 S.E.2d 569, 571 (W. Va. 1998) (property was subject to acquisition by eminent domain).

government could use one of several common large-scale approaches, including creating a land bank or designating some form of community development zone.[21] A land bank creates an avenue for a local government or a quasi-public entity to acquire, hold, and flip problem properties using eminent domain.[22] Local governments may also use nuisance abatement lawsuits to pursue the same goal of essentially acquiring and redistributing a property to get it into the hands of a responsible owner, or at least, to mitigate the property's negative effects.[23]

Officials and practitioners throughout West Virginia brought their towns' problem properties to the Clinic in large part because these properties are legally complex and resource-intensive to deal with. In addition to the many challenges associated with absentee owners and navigating various applicable areas of law, there was also the dilemma of what to do if people were actually living in these properties. Poverty and limited rural housing stocks often meant people had no place else to go or could not afford to make repairs.

THE WV LEAP PROGRAM AND THE BARRIER OF URBANORMATIVITY

The Clinic wanted to help, so Kat – the Clinic's director, who took a chance on hiring me despite my lack of a background in land use law – worked some grant-writing magic and secured funding for a project to do so. The grant funded a year-long initiative called the West Virginia Legal Education to Address Abandoned and Neglected Properties program (WV LEAP).[24] The first part of the program involved a listening tour around the state.[25] Kat or another Clinic representative, often with me in tow to take notes on my laptop, would travel to a West Virginia town, meet with local government representatives, and hear the challenges they faced in dealing with their problem properties, as well as success stories. After a certain number of those interviews had been conducted, phase two involved using that information to develop and publish a legal toolkit that would be distributed throughout the state for local governments to use.[26]

During the listening phase, I got used to hopping in on Clinic rides of two to three hours without much forethought, often huddling in the Morgantown Sheetz parking lot with my coffee to be picked up before the sun rose. Working around the whole state meant sometimes that was just the necessary commute for the day. We spent a lot of time in the car on route 79.

---

[21] *See* Anne E. Kline, *A Case for Connecticut Land Banks*, 88 Conn. Bar J. 210, 214 (2015).

[22] *Id.*

[23] S. Adeline McKinney, *The North Carolina Banking Institute Symposium on the Foreclosure Crisis: Municipalities Fight Effects of Foreclosure with Litigation and Neighborhood Stabilization Program Grants*, 14 N.C. Banking Inst. 257, 259 (2010).

[24] Eisenberg, *Addressing Rural Blight*, *supra* note 1, at 513, 532.

[25] *Id.*

[26] Liability to Viability, *supra* note 7.

Sitting in on the listening sessions was eye-opening for me in terms of seeing just how little some small, remote municipalities had to work with. I went along with Kat for one interview to a smaller town a couple hours south of Morgantown on a gray day that did not lend itself to optimism. We met that day with the town's code enforcement officer in a setup that was beginning to feel familiar: a small municipal office with fluorescent lighting and a few chairs and a table, not much activity to speak of, and an atmosphere that reminded me of the dentist's office I visited as a child in the 80s.

The code enforcement officer, a sturdy white man in his thirties or so, did not speak about the town's problem properties with an air of professional detachment. He was depressed about his work, his voice inflected with a hint of despair. He explained that, for a lot of the properties falling into dereliction, he did know who the owners were. But he couldn't get them to cooperate. He would issue a citation under the building code for a violation. Then he would follow up with threats of more formal and serious legal action.

But, he explained, the property owners would call his bluff. He did not, in fact, have the budget to take uncooperative property owners to court. The municipality did not have the resources to take building code enforcement to its full extension, which is the threat of municipal acquisition of the property's title through condemnation. The municipality couldn't do that if it wanted to, but it also didn't want to. What was the town supposed to do with a bunch of crappy, derelict properties? It didn't have the money to knock the buildings down or rebuild them, and it didn't want to take on the liability of owning a problem property. Even if it could repair or rebuild them, who would buy them anyway?

So the code enforcement officer would threaten, he explained. But then he would "back off" when the time for consequences came. "You can't get blood from a stone," he sighed. I didn't know if he was talking about the property owners or the municipality.

Kat advised people to share their thoughts about problems beyond just the need for money and funding. Everyone needed more money, she would explain. That's a given. We were trying to help by looking at legal tools and strategies.

But it did seem like more money would help. The question Kat and I mulled over on the ride back: How are people in these communities supposed to do something with nothing? We wondered whether "How to Do Something with Nothing" should be the title of the legal toolkit.

At one point, my task for WV LEAP was to consolidate information on federal funding programs available to address vacant, abandoned, and dilapidated properties. A prominent one was the U.S. Department of Housing and Urban Development's Community Development Block Grant program, through which local governments could secure grants to tackle local infrastructure and land use issues.[27]

---

[27] *Community Development Block Grant Program*, U.S. Dep't Hous. Urb. Dev. (Dec. 22, 2022), www.hud.gov/program_offices/comm_planning/cdbg [https://perma.cc/LSG2-TVMD].

Other programs were geared toward historic preservation, affordable housing, or environmental issues.[28] A savvy locality could potentially piece together quite a bit of support through these programs.

But I struggled to find information or resources specific to dealing with problem properties in small or remote localities. Many of the resources in academic literature or publications for practitioners seemed to assume an urban setting. Resources discussing challenges and success stories in Baltimore, Detroit, St. Louis, Syracuse, and similar cities tended to refer to high-volume efforts and large-scale tools. These cities, which remained sizable despite their own challenges with depopulation, were using approaches like the land banks I mentioned earlier, in which the city or a quasi-public entity would acquire and flip problem properties using eminent domain. For West Virginia's small towns and their modest budgets, it was not clear how helpful these approaches were. I complained to Jesse one day about the lack of information on how small towns or counties can deal with problem properties. He sighed, and grumbled, "Everyone only cares about cities!"

Investigating the lack of resources on rural challenges led me to discover academic literature on the concept of urbanormativity. Urbanormativity explained much of why we couldn't find much writing or discussion to help inform our project. Pruitt and Vanegas explain critical rural studies' concept of urbanormativity:

> Thomas et al. define urbanormativity as "an assumption that the conditions of urbanism found in metropolitan areas are normative; a corollary is that a departure from an urban lifestyle is deviant." Seale and Fulkerson paraphrase this: "This is another case where the dominant group enjoys visibility and social perceptions of normalcy while less powerful groups are either ignored or understood through a stigmatized or prejudiced lens." Seale and Fulkerson also note that an "urbanormative lens would presuppose easy access to most of life's basic needs and wants."[29]

Perhaps more simplistically, I came to understand urbanormativity to mean that urbanites often assume everyone else is an urbanite, and often fail to realize that things they take for granted are not available to everyone, such as a high-speed internet connection. It is a form of classism with a spatially oriented twist. It is also a form of ignorance – a failure to "check one's spatial privilege."[30] Urbanormativity, in turn, interacts with the stereotype of rural as backward or primitive because it presupposes that rural ways of life are necessarily lesser or inconceivable.

Trying to articulate instances of urbanormativity has itself been eye-opening, as the response I sometimes receive is, "Well, rural people are different because they

---

[28] *See, e.g., Historic Preservation Fund*, U.S. NAT'L PARK SERV., www.nps.gov/subjects/historicpreser vationfund/project-grants.htm [https://perma.cc/Z9Q4-FX4N].

[29] Lisa Pruitt & Marta R. Vanegas, *Urbanormativity, Spatial Privilege, and Judicial Blind Spots in Abortion Law*, 30 BERKELEY J. GENDER L. & JUST. 76 (2015) (internal citations omitted).

[30] *See id.*

actually *are* backward." A good rural person, I'm told, is one who wants to move to a city, stop being such a burden, get a useful, modern job, and vote for Democrats.

Urbanormativity can be borne of ignorance or of bias. If you're in a city, it is easy, perhaps understandable, to forget the countryside. And I'm not suggesting that a neighborhood activist in Baltimore needs to be inclusive of rural Maryland. But when policymakers, funders, and the creators of necessary resources forget that a lot of people live outside cities, that oversight is neither inclusive nor helpful for rural communities' integration, dignity, and welfare within mainstream society – or even just for figuring out what a good small-town ordinance on vacant properties should look like.

UNDERSTANDING RURAL DIFFERENCE

This was not the first time I had been attuned to rural difference in law. As a law student in 2011, I used a modest grant to return to the site of my Peace Corps service in Morocco to investigate a hunch. My hunch was that Morocco's new, much-lauded, progressive women's rights law, known as the Moudawana, was not actually reaching the countryside. The women I spoke to in the remote, predominantly Indigenous Azilal Province largely confirmed that suspicion. Underage marriage for girls had been outlawed, yet underage girls in rural communities were being married off in droves. One woman told me in an interview, "What Moudawana is there? There is no Moudawana. There's a Moudawana for people with money .... If I had money, I'd do whatever I like with the law too."[31]

Rural difference in law also emerged as a theme during a summer in law school, when I interned at a human rights nongovernmental organization (NGO) in New Delhi. I worked in the organization's reproductive rights department, which fought to ensure equal access to maternal healthcare, abortion, and related services. The maternal mortality statistics for rural India were staggering.[32] Through collaboration with the NGO's international team and events like a national convening of activists at a rain-battered monastery in Goa, I heard stories of pregnant and laboring women dying in taxis because the hospitals were hours away. India's Supreme Court had actually made many of these barriers to accessing care illegal. The court had recognized, for instance, that the Indian Constitution's "right to life" meant the "right to health."[33] But if the other arms of the government did not provide adequate funding and support for resources like rural hospitals, what did those rights really mean?

---

[31] Ann M. Eisenberg, *Law on the Books vs. Law in Action: Under-Enforcement of Morocco's Reformed 2004 Family Law, the Moudawana*, 44 CORNELL INT'L L.J. 693, 710 (2011).

[32] *See* C. Meh et al., *Trends in Maternal Mortality in India over Two Decades in Nationally Representative Surveys*, 129 BJOG 550 (2022).

[33] Consumer Educ. & Rsch. Ctr. v. Union of India, (1995) 3 SCC 42 (India).

I did not expect to see parallels across Morocco, India, and West Virginia. But a common theme was there: Rural difference mattered. And it mattered in unique ways for law. Law had a harder time traveling over mountains and through valleys to reach people who were spread out and remote from centers of concentrated amenities and power. Poverty and limited resources could be hidden in far-off places, away from protest squares, journalists, and well-intentioned reformers. Rural neglect and exploitation seemed self-justifying for those who opted to neglect and exploit rural regions.

Views expressed by West Virginia local government officials during the listening tour mirrored many of these themes, and often echoed the sentiments of the depressed code enforcement officer. Findings that emerged through WV LEAP listening sessions included the following:

- Criminal activities, drug activity, methamphetamine labs, and other threats to public safety were perceived as serious problems with neglected properties.
- Limited resources and a lack of funding were universally perceived as obstacles to addressing blight.
- Communities' systems for addressing neglected properties often took an ad hoc, complaint-based approach, which was perceived as not achieving a systematic impact on blight.
- Absentee landowners were reported to be a significant obstacle. They were perceived as being less knowledgeable of buildings falling into disrepair and less accountable in the local community. Respondents believed that substantial time and resources were devoted to figuring out who the landowners were and finding them – with no guarantee of results due to local governments' lack of enforcement tools for out-of-state owners.
- A lack of legal authority or relevant ordinances, the time-consuming nature of legal processes (such as due process requirements in code enforcement), and the futility of using the court system were perceived as obstacles to taking effective action.
- Some landlords were seen as "slumlords," taking advantage of lax enforcement of code standards or putting multiple families in single-family housing. In turn, officials did not want to condemn those properties because the renters would then have no place to live due to housing shortages.
- Tax delinquency was perceived as fueling a vicious cycle. Neglected properties had delinquent taxes and lowered neighboring property values, and the impacts on local government budgets made local governments less able to address the properties. The three-year tax lien foreclosure process was reported to result in neglect.
- Mortgage delinquency and out-of-state banks were problematic. Sometimes ownership between the bank and the borrower was unclear, and some banks either would not repossess properties or not maintain them once they did.

- Complex property titles and determinations of ownership were complicated further by "property that has passed down automatically from one generation to the next without a will (or through wills that give the property to 'all of the children equally')," giving ownership interests to multiple – sometimes hundreds – of heirs.[34]
- Where local governments were able to acquire neglected properties, there was concern about returning the property to productive use economically. For instance, a municipality that demolished an abandoned structure could spend tens of thousands of dollars on the process and end up burdened with an empty lot of minimal value. Respondents were similarly concerned about limited incentives for developers to rehabilitate properties due to limitations on returns on investments and limited local economies. Liens were perceived as an ineffective way to recoup costs due to competition with other liens.
- Communities were interested in preserving historic properties, but preservation processes and coordination with specialized committees added complications to legal processes. Old housing stock that was built prior to the adoption of any applicable codes or ordinances was considered a problem.
- Properties with fire damage and asbestos were perceived as more expensive and legally complex to address. Respondents were generally concerned about a lack of clarity in the law or a lack of informational resources.
- Although it was not a main priority, some respondents were concerned about uncooperative landowners and landowners' lack of pride or personal investment in their properties.
- Respondents were concerned about elderly residents with fixed incomes or who resided in nursing homes and had unknown caretakers for their properties, and related complications with property titles.
- Property owners' emotional ties to structures, limited financial resources, and local officials' concerns about community relations were also issues. Some code enforcement officials were hesitant to impose citations on those in difficult circumstances because properties were often in disrepair due to landowners' limited incomes in the first place, and landowners would not be able to pay fines anyway. Some code officials did not approach nuisance abatement in a standardized way, but rather worked with individual property owners (if cooperative) based on their needs. Some considered this to be successful, while others were concerned about selective enforcement.

As reflected in these findings, addressing vacant and dilapidated properties in rural communities involves unique challenges related to rural conditions, which warrant tailored attention in law, policy, and discourse. Rural communities differ

---

[34] *Heirs Property*, W. VA. UNIV. COLL. OF LAW: LEAP (2015), https://wvleap.wvu.edu/additional-tools/highlight-heirs-property [https://perma.cc/BV3S-4HMZ].

from urban ones in many important ways, ranging from geographical layouts to local economies and cultural values.[35] Disparities in resources may be the most salient difference. A small, rural town is less likely to have the institutions and services necessary to engage in effective planning, conduct effective code enforcement, and if needed, acquire the title to a neglected property and dispose of it in an economically sustainable way.[36] Although urban governments also struggle with these issues, rural communities may lack basic legal tools urbanites take for granted, such as a building code.[37]

Meanwhile, urbanormative discussions and literature on this topic tend to presuppose well-structured governments, established legal frameworks, and diverse resources to draw upon.[38] Urbanormative assumptions do not just mean a lack of resources for rural practitioners. This disconnect, in this context and others, can "lead to policies and funding mechanisms that are formulated for metropolitan problems but are applied with a broad brush."[39] It can also lead to laws "being dictated by an urban majority" to "govern the rural culture," despite that majority being "ignorant of the ways of the people whose lives they are controlling."[40]

As I've mentioned, a common refrain of rural law and policy scholarship is that rural circumstances tend to be ignored, or when acknowledged, poorly understood. Discourse on rural blight is no exception. Little research establishes the prevalence of vacant, abandoned, and dilapidated properties in rural areas. Existing data – including a one-third rate of residential building vacancy in some rural counties, or up to a 100 percent vacancy rate in some places if fully abandoned "ghost towns" are counted – indicate that blight is just as much a problem in rural communities as it is in urban ones.[41] Yet, a search of popular research databases suggests that

---

[35] Lisa R. Pruitt & Bradley E. Showman, *Law Stretched Thin: Access to Justice in Rural America*, 59 S.D. L. REV. 466, 485 (2014).

[36] *Cf. id.* at 486–88 ("It is ... a hallmark of rural living that residents must travel greater distances, at greater cost to access all sorts of services and institutions ... includ[ing] courts, and ... services provided by lawyers, as well as others that are often ancillary to legal issues[.]").

[37] Ezra Rosser, *Rural Housing and Code Enforcement: Navigating between Values and Housing Types*, 13 GEO. J. ON POVERTY L. & POL'Y 33, 38 (2006).

[38] *Cf.* George Homsy & Mildred Warner, Nat'l Ass'n of Dev. Orgs.: ICMA Ctr. for Sustainable Cmtys., Defying the Odds: Sustainability in Small and Rural Places 1 (2013) ("While the likes of New York, Boston, Chicago, and Seattle have the money, expertise, and regional power base to implement large-scale sustainability programs, thousands of small cities and rural towns struggle to protect the environment.").

[39] Shannon Van Zandt et al., *Small-Town Housing Needs: Resource Inefficiencies and Urban Bias*, 39 CMTY. DEV. 75 (2008), https://doi.org/10.1080/15575330809489670.

[40] Debra Lyn Bassett, *Ruralism*, 88 IOWA L. REV. 273, 292 (2003).

[41] *See* Dawn Jourdan et al., *Meeting Their Fair Share: A Proposal for the Creation of Regional Land Banks to Meet the Affordable Housing Needs in the Rural Areas of Texas*, 19 J. AFFORDABLE HOUSING & CMTY. DEV. L. 147, 155 (2010) (discussing rural counties in Texas with 28 percent vacancy); Michelle Wilde Anderson, *Dissolving Cities*, 121 YALE L.J. 1364, 1364 (2012) (describing ghost town phenomenon); Bill Estep, *Historic Coal Towns Are Fighting to Survive. Could Three of Them Merge into One?*, LEXINGTON HERALD LEADER (Oct. 26, 2017, 1:09 PM),

rural blight is addressed in only a small fraction of articles discussing blight.[42] This seems disproportionately low, given that just under one-fifth of Americans reside in rural areas and 72 percent of the country's land is rural.[43]

THE CHALLENGE OF RURAL BLIGHT

Because of conditions relating to rurality, the process I described earlier for dealing with problem properties is not necessarily accessible to smaller localities. And these challenges are not unique to West Virginia. The small town of Cairo, Illinois, illustrates how blight arises and perpetuates a vicious downward cycle for a rural community.[44] With a population of around 15,000, Cairo thrived into the early twentieth century because of its commerce-friendly location at the intersection of the Ohio and Mississippi Rivers.[45] Its population gradually decreased to under 3,000 as of 2014, in part because of competition from railway and interstate traffic, and because of the closure of Cairo's largest employer, the Burkart Foam Company.[46] During

---

www.kentucky.com/news/state/article181032761.html [https://perma.cc/H4GK-P5C7] (discussing one-third vacancy rate in Lynch, Kentucky); *but see* Kate Abbey-Lambertz, *These Are the American Cities with the Most Abandoned Houses*, HUFFINGTON POST (Feb. 13, 2016, 9:30 AM), www.huffingtonpost.com/entry/cities-with-most-abandoned-houses-flint_us_56be4e9ae4b0c3c5505171e7 [https://perma.cc/ZB8R-FPB8] (discussing one-sixth vacancy rate in Flint, Michigan, and one-fifth rate in Detroit).

[42] A brief, nonscientific perusal of online resources illuminates the attention rural blight receives in the overall discourse on blight. As of this writing, a search for "urban blight" yields 1,330 results on Westlaw and 288,000 results on Google. Meanwhile, a search for "rural blight" yields 10 Westlaw results and 2,330 Google results, respectively – roughly suggesting that rural blight is addressed in less than 1 percent of discussions of blight (0.6 percent on Westlaw and 0.8 percent on Google). A search for "blight" in the same paragraph as "rural," with "rural" mentioned at least twice – accounting for the fact that "rural blight" is not necessarily a commonly used term, but blight may be discussed in a rural context – expands the Westlaw results to 62 articles, or 4 percent of articles addressing blight. As 16 percent of Americans reside in rural areas, one might expect a proportionate balance to yield a 16 percent rate of discussion of rural blight – which would result in 254 results for rural blight on Westlaw (rather than fewer than 100) and 56,000 on Google (rather than 2,260).

[43] *See* John Cromartie, *Rural Areas Show Overall Population Decline and Shifting Regional Patterns of Population Change*, USDA ECON. RSCH. SERV. (Sept. 5, 2017), www.ers.usda.gov/amber-waves/2017/september/rural-areas-show-overall-population-decline-and-shifting-regional-patterns-of-population-change/ [https://perma.cc/4F7B-AQYL].

[44] For another case study, see Michelle Wilde Anderson, *Who Needs Local Government Anyway? Dissolution in Pennsylvania's Distressed Cities*, 24 WIDENER L.J. 149, 151 (2015) (discussing decline of Rust Belt town of Braddock, Pennsylvania, with a 24 percent vacancy rate).

[45] *See* James Wilkinson, *The Town that Time Forgot: Incredible Photos Show How Nature Is Reclaiming the Eerie, Near-Abandoned City of Cairo, Illinois*, DAILY MAIL (Aug. 25, 2016, 20:22 EDT), www.dailymail.co.uk/news/article-3759263/Eerie-photos-Cairo-Illinois-abandoned-cityMississippi-Ohio-rivers.html [http://perma.cc/P7N6-T9YD].

[46] *See id.; see also* Kirk Siegler, *Tired of Promises, A Struggling Small Town Wants Problems Solved*, NPR (Mar. 28, 2017, 5:01 AM), www.npr.org/2017/03/28/521118179/tired-of-promises-a-struggling-small-town-wantsproblems-solved [https://perma.cc/F6QW-H7RB]; *Burkart Foam Plant to Close*, SE. MISSOURIAN (Sept. 15, 2001), www.semissourian.com/story/42693.html [https://perma.cc/7MGQ-SVCW].

that time, the town also transitioned from majority white to majority Black.[47] As of 2019, Alexander County, where Cairo is located, was one of the poorest and most quickly depopulating counties in the country.[48]

Cairo's properties have followed in step with its economic and population decline. Entire blocks have been condemned, and "partly burned mansions with roofs caving in" characterize the landscape.[49] The town's only grocery store and gas station closed in 2015, in addition to the bowling alley, a furniture store, and other private businesses.[50] While there have been efforts to demolish some properties and otherwise revitalize Cairo, state grant funding "dried up long ago" and the county housing authority went bankrupt.[51]

In 2014, a small group of residents began documenting the problem properties, and community members also began the process of creating a comprehensive plan.[52] Comprehensive plans are typically nonbinding land use and development visions for communities.[53] They lay a foundation for more powerful local land use governance, including zoning ordinances, and are required to receive grant support from the U.S. Department of Housing and Urban Development (HUD) and other funders.[54] Cairo's earlier comprehensive plan developed in 1973 had never been implemented.[55]

The comprehensive plan effort came to fruition in November 2014, with the document specifically identifying blight and the city's 26 percent vacancy rate as needs to be addressed.[56] However, a discouraging sign as to Cairo's progress occurred in 2017, when HUD authorities deemed two of the town's public housing complexes uninhabitable and beyond repair.[57] The condemnation of the buildings – plagued with water damage, mold, roaches, bed bugs, insufficient insulation, and poor plumbing, heating, and electrical systems – at first seemed like vindication for the

---

[47] *See* Monica Davey, *Their Public Housing at the End of Its Life, Residents Ask: What Now?*, N.Y. Times (May 17, 2017), www.nytimes.com/2017/05/17/us/cairo-public-housing-hud-poverty.html [https://perma.cc/L6SU-QH76].

[48] *See* Siegler, *supra* note 46.

[49] *Id.*

[50] *Id.*; Wilkinson, *supra* note 45.

[51] *See* Siegler, *supra* note 46; *Burkart Foam Plant to Close*, *supra* note 46.

[52] *See* Steve Matzker, *Residents Mobilize to Help Cairo*, S. Illinoisan (June 15, 2014), https://thesouthern .com/news/local/residents-mobilize-to-help-cairo/article_4dd63244-1539-53ab-80f1-3391022deb19 .html [https://perma.cc/CK9E-2Q8K]; *Burkart Foam Plant to Close*, *supra* note 46.

[53] *See* Forestview Homeowners Ass'n v. Cook, 309 N.E.2d 763, 771 (Ill. App. Ct. 1974) (explaining that "[a] comprehensive zoning plan is a scheme or formula of zoning that reasonably relates the regulation and restriction of land uses, including establishment of districts therefor, to the health, safety and welfare of the public, and thus to the police power" and helps to guide zoning decisions).

[54] *See* Matzker, *supra* note 52; *Burkart Foam Plant to Close*, *supra* note 46; *see also* 1350 Lake Shore Assocs. v. Casalino, 816 N.E.2d 675, 685 (Ill. App. Ct. 2004) (noting that absence of comprehensive plan weakens presumption of valid zoning ordinance).

[55] *Burkart Foam Plant to Close*, *supra* note 46.

[56] CITY OF CAIRO, COMPREHENSIVE PLAN (2014).

[57] Davey, *supra* note 47.

many residents who had complained.[58] But when approximately 400 residents were told to vacate their homes in April 2017, many had to leave Cairo altogether to find adequate housing because "places like Cairo have no excess supply of safe, available low-income housing."[59] As one resident articulated, "[w]e all know there's nowhere to use a [public housing] voucher in Cairo."[60] According to HUD, rebuilding was not an option because of the lack of a willing private partner.[61] In 2022, HUD closed another housing complex.[62]

Commentary from 2021 expressed hope that a state-supported river port might foretell a "comeback" for Cairo.[63] Yet, Cairo's struggle illustrates several problems rural communities encounter with the processes described earlier as the standard for blight remediation. First, many rural local governments lack the capacity to take on ownership and repairs of a problem property.[64] To do so requires substantial resources and may expose the local government to liability associated with property hazards.[65] For instance, it seems unlikely that Cairo could acquire or remediate its public housing complexes given its prior inability to address smaller properties.

Meanwhile, a large-scale initiative would seem difficult for Cairo without external support. Land banks, redevelopment authorities, and receivership are among the popular tools used in urban blight remediation, but these approaches usually involve a local government creating a public or quasi-public entity that operates as a sort of real estate business. Land banks, for example, "are typically sophisticated entities that are independent of local governments with their own budgets and staff."[66] Yet, all of these initiatives "require resources and coordination that may be beyond many rural communities … [which] may not have the human or fiscal resources necessary to accomplish the relatively sophisticated land acquisition and distribution activities involved in land banking" and similar approaches.[67]

As rural local governments have a more limited capacity overall, a lower volume of vacant properties, and a smaller market for redeemed properties, land banks and similar large-scale approaches might not be realistic blight remediation mechanisms for them to implement.[68] Although Cairo's comprehensive plan calls for a land

---

[58] *Id.*

[59] *Id.*

[60] *Id.*

[61] *Id.*

[62] Molly Parker, *"I Don't Know Where I'm Going to Go": HUD Displaces Even More Residents in This Small City*, PROPUBLICA (Nov. 23, 2022, 1:00 PM), www.propublica.org/article/hud-demolishes-public-housing-displaces-residents-cairo [https://perma.cc/ZUM5-R97D].

[63] Peter Hancock, *A Comeback for Cairo?*, NEWS-GAZETTE (Champaign) (Sept. 27, 2021), www.news-gazette.com/business/economy/a-comeback-for-cairo/article_9dfbc242-8498-5235-8b07-9de220e3d30d.html [https://perma.cc/9LGS-9HFC].

[64] Jourdan et al., *supra* note 41.

[65] *See* Eisenberg, *Addressing Rural Blight*, *supra* note 1, at 513, 530.

[66] Jourdan et al., *supra* note 41, at 149.

[67] *Id.* at 157.

[68] *See* Eisenberg, *Addressing Rural Blight*, *supra* note 1, at 530.

bank to address a portion of its downtown,[69] the city does not seem to have created a land bank in the years since the plan's drafting. Even at the level of the individual parcel, if a local government could reach the step of redeveloping the property, the parcel will likely have a relatively low economic value and the rural area may well lack interested buyers.[70]

HUD's statement about the lack of a willing partner to redevelop Cairo's public housing similarly illustrates this issue. Cairo's struggle to survive involves a full spectrum of problem properties. Its blight ranges from crumbling, vacant mansions to uninhabitable, yet occupied, housing. These conditions resemble blight-related problems that arise in cities. Yet, Cairo exhibits many of the traits of rurality that shape rural blight and impede its remediation. Few people were available to document properties. Because of a lack of a comprehensive plan until 2014, Cairo has had more limited land use guidance to direct remediation and development and has had to start its land use policy from scratch. No private developers were willing to work on the public housing problems, according to HUD; and limited housing options were driving people out of town.

ADDRESSING RURAL BLIGHT

With Kat's permission, I wrote an academic paper about the lessons we were learning through WV LEAP, given that it reflected "a rare instance of systematic study of rural blight by attorneys and planners."[71] According to a synthesis of the feedback we heard, in addition to my own research, four common rural conditions seemed to hamper rural blight remediation in West Virginia and elsewhere. First, these rural places were characterized by limited resources and economic activity, including higher rates of poverty, lower household incomes, more limited local government fiscal and human resources, and more limited infrastructure. This meant fewer resources to tackle the problem properties, and more limited markets to return them to once rehabilitated.

Second, rural cultural tendencies meant a greater likelihood to rely on informal services and dispute resolution mechanisms, an "ethos of independence and self-reliance," an attachment to private property rights, and more limited political accountability, alongside heightened social and interpersonal accountability.[72] This meant communities were not necessarily primed to look to local government, or any government, as the solution to their problems.

Third, rural communities often have more limited planning and legal frameworks, such as a community being unincorporated (and therefore lacking governance

[69] CITY OF CAIRO COMPREHENSIVE PLAN, *supra* note 56.
[70] Eisenberg, *Addressing Rural Blight, supra* note 1, at 530 (citing Jourdan et al., *supra* note 41, at 157).
[71] *See* Eisenberg, *Rural Blight, supra* note 1, at 203; Eisenberg, *Addressing Rural Blight, supra* note 1.
[72] Eisenberg, *Addressing Rural Blight, supra* note 1, at 523.

authority) or the absence of building codes, comprehensive plans, and zoning ordinances. This meant these communities had fewer tools to work with to tackle one or more problem properties. The learning curve and effort it would take to create such a framework were disproportionately high.

Finally, the variability of rural issues meant a standardized approach to tackling problem properties in rural areas was not necessarily obvious. While one town might be stymied by an abandoned theater, another might be dealing with an old school, and yet another might be dealing with fifteen houses, or a long-vacant brownfield. Given the different ownership types, legal frameworks, and environmental considerations associated with each, it would take some investigation to come up with an overarching formula for success – if one even existed.

While the challenges faced by West Virginia local governments seemed daunting, many local government officials did have success stories to share. The Clinic's legal toolkit, developed based on this input, helped move the needle.[73] The toolkit was tailored to West Virginia and its rural context, making it a unique resource for West Virginia localities. Unlike resources created for bigger cities, the toolkit starts at a point for communities that may need to lay a foundation from scratch, such as by adopting a building code for the first time. It then progresses from relatively simple, low-cost tools to address problem properties, such as creating local registration systems for inventorying the properties, and advances to more sophisticated, complex tools, such as land banks and the exercise of eminent domain.

As I continued to research problem properties in rural communities in subsequent years, I came to appreciate rural blight as emblematic of much more than an instance of urbanormativity in resources and policymaking on this discrete issue. The stakes of addressing the crumbling rural built environment extend beyond a few problem properties, both in terms of scale and in terms of what blight's widespread presence signifies. Rural blight is an apt symbol for overall rural decline, as it symptomatizes a variety of legal, social, and economic systems that are not functioning well. Whatever the optimal roadmap for rural America may be, the ubiquity of rural depopulation and an emptying built environment implicate society as it leaves rural communities to "the slow ravages of abandonment and disintegration."[74]

THE MYTH OF RURAL EMPOWERMENT

This brings me back to the myth featured in this chapter's title. During the time when I was doing a deep dive into rural local governments' struggles to provide even the most basic services, I kept hearing about how powerful rural communities were. I was thinking about rotting foundations, meth labs, the formatting of foreclosure

---

[73] LIABILITY TO VIABILITY, *supra* note 7.

[74] Michelle W. Anderson, *The Western, Rural Rustbelt: Learning from Local Fiscal Crisis in Oregon*, 50 WILLAMETTE L. REV. 465, 500 (2014).

notices, depressed code enforcement officers, dwindling municipal and county budgets, and asbestos mitigation. I was thinking about how Morgantown's Target store – ironically dubbed "Target Mountain" by locals, as if it were part of the natural landscape – and Ithaca's depressing mall managed to siphon away all the business from historic downtowns. This meant Morgantown did not have a single locally owned ice cream shop and Ithaca's downtown pedestrian area couldn't even keep a McDonald's. I was thinking about trailer parks, catastrophic flooding, and fracking.

But the United States had been traumatized by Trump's election (well, half of it had been). And someone had to be blamed. And it is true that voters in more population-sparse states have an outsized influence on presidential elections and the composition of the Senate. The initial compromise made by the drafters of the Constitution sought to entice new states to join the Union through the creation of a bicameral legislature that did not match up to each state's population proportionately. Because congressional representation determines representation in the Electoral College, the outsized rural vote extends to presidential elections.[75] Similar structures sometimes mean state voting and politics have similar patterns, with disproportionately rural and conservative state legislatures dominating progressive cities, as with Austin, Texas, and Charlotte, North Carolina.

These conditions are manifestly bad for democracy, dangerous for a free society, and otherwise undesirable. Reform of these institutions' structures is clearly necessary. However, it is rarely acknowledged that outsized rural representation has become more outsized in part *because of* rural depopulation, and that rural depopulation has resulted from decades of policies, explored in subsequent chapters, that have aggressively fueled that depopulation without regard to the consequences. These choices have made the rural population less dense and all the more disproportionately weighted in elections than it was prior to depopulation. Why don't we ever blame, at least in part, the relentless march toward mostly coastal, urban agglomeration economies, whether people want them or not, for an increase in outsized rural voting power? Also, what does this outsized representation mean for rural populations if it does not seem to result in a better quality of life for them? That is rural voters' fault because they "vote against their interests," I am told, a concerning proposition explored in Chapter 6.

In 2021, I was invited by the *Harvard Law Review Forum* to publish a response to the journal's lead article by Professor Sarah Swan, "Constitutional Offloading at the City Limits." The article explores how courts seem to afford rural municipalities greater constitutional authority to shape their own fates as compared to larger cities. I conclude this chapter with the full text of my response here as a study on the notion of rural empowerment versus my observations about relative rural powerlessness.

---

[75] Maria Liasson, *A Growing Number of Critics Raise Alarms about the Electoral College*, NPR (June 10, 2021), www.npr.org/2021/06/10/1002594108/a-growing-number-of-critics-raise-alarms-about-the-electoral-college [https://perma.cc/NNQ7-AMUA].

Power and Powerlessness in Local Government: A Response
to Professor Swan

Are rural communities powerful or powerless? This question arises regularly in today's national public and scholarly discourses.[76] The collective interest in the issue of rural power stems in large part from hotly contested national and state elections in which strong, polarized political preferences play out along geographic lines.[77] Election maps show us how consistently sparsely populated regions, in which people live in small towns or remote counties, emerge an indignant-conservative red.[78] Big cities, by contrast, predictably materialize with the forbearing-liberal blue. Especially with ever-polarized public health measures implicated by the ongoing pandemic – which has affected matters as intimate as whether face masks are required or not and where[79] – we are all acutely cognizant of whether we live in a red state or a blue state, or a red county or a blue municipality.

These enduring, polarized political patterns have drawn attention to an "urban–rural divide" in politics, prompting inquiries into how the nation arrived at this point and what the implications are.[80] One central implication is the inordinate power that residents of sparsely populated regions wield in various political bodies, including the Electoral College and legislatures at the federal and state level.[81] For instance, because of the distribution of electoral votes per population in the Electoral College, "one Wyoming voter has roughly the same vote power as four New York voters [in presidential elections]."[82] In this sense, more sparsely populated communities are powerful to a degree that threatens representative democracy itself in a disturbing system of rule by a predominantly older, whiter, more conservative minority.[83] Commentary focused on this aspect of the

---

[76] Ann M. Eisenberg, *Power and Powerlessness in Local Government: A Response to Professor Swan*, 135 HARV. L. REV. F. 173 (2022).

[77] *See, e.g.*, Kirk Siegler, *Biden's Win Shows Rural-Urban Divide Has Grown since 2016*, NPR (Nov. 18, 2020, 5:00 AM), www.npr.org/2020/11/18/934631994/bidens-win-shows-rural-urban-divide-has-grown-since-2016 [https://perma.cc/A7UE-GL2A].

[78] *See* Alice Park et al., *An Extremely Detailed Map of the 2020 Election*, N.Y. TIMES (Mar. 30, 2021), www.nytimes.com/interactive/2021/upshot/2020-election-map.html [https://perma.cc/NX62-SVUB].

[79] *See* Mike Olson, *Columbia Mayor Steve Benjamin Responds to AG's Letter Regarding Mask Mandate in Schools*, ABC COLUMBIA (Aug. 10, 2021, 6:12 PM), www.abccolumbia.com/2021/08/10/columbia-mayor-steve-benjamin-responds-to-ags-letter-regarding-mask-mandate-in-schools [https://perma.cc/52TF-9QJT].

[80] *See* Josh Kron, *Red State, Blue City: How the Urban-Rural Divide Is Splitting America*, ATLANTIC (Nov. 30, 2012), www.theatlantic.com/politics/archive/2012/11/red-state-blue-city-how-the-urban-rural-divide-is-splitting-america/265686 [https://perma.cc/Z9AZ-HJCN].

[81] *See* Eric W. Orts, *Senate Democracy: Our Lockean Paradox*, 68 AM. U. L. REV. 1981, 1981 (2019).

[82] Chris Kirk, *How Powerful Is Your Vote?*, SLATE (Nov. 2, 2012, 6:04 PM), www.slate.com/articles/news_and_politics/map_of_the_week/2012/11/presidential_election_a_map_showing_the_vote_power_of_all_50_states.html [https://perma.cc/TY6M-TA5W].

[83] *See* Kenneth Owen, *Minority Rule Cannot Last in America*, ATLANTIC (Dec. 2, 2020), www.theatlantic.com/ideas/archive/2020/12/minority-rule-cannot-last-america/617272 [https://perma.cc/45FG-PQ8E].

question of rural power tends to conclude that rural communities are indeed powerful – and dangerously so.

Yet, while the political urban–rural divide reveals the rural as dangerously powerful, the economic urban–rural divide reveals the rural as the underdog. Larger cities dominate the economy.[84] This dominance is sometimes attributed to cities attracting talent or being innately more appealing. However, national and global economic restructuring through deregulation, liberalized trade, consolidated agriculture, developments in the energy and environmental sectors, the weakening of unions, and automation have all contributed to depopulating and deteriorating rural landscapes.[85] Cities are also not necessarily easy to move to, with the widespread skyrocketing of housing costs and local resistance to inclusionary zoning.[86]

Meanwhile, poverty rates are higher and more entrenched outside dense urban centers.[87] Rural residents still struggle to access high-speed broadband internet, public transportation, and affordable doctors and lawyers. Health outcomes are consistently worse in rural communities than in urban ones.[88] The 2008 recession and the ongoing pandemic have exacerbated all of these trends, shuttering more rural businesses and challenging regional economic vitality.[89] In this sense, then, many rural communities are relatively disempowered in the daunting economic losses they have borne and challenges they still face.

Both of these geographically themed divides have broad relevance for the role of local government in the United States, given local government's centrality to both political representation and community economic development. In her article "Constitutional Off-Loading at the City Limits," Professor Swan very usefully tackles a question of law, geography, and political and economic power.[90] Namely, she assesses how courts treat municipalities attempting to engage in "constitutional off-loading," by which municipalities infringe upon a constitutional right based on the rationale that the right can be exercised extraterritorially, typically in a nearby jurisdiction.[91] Swan analyzes courts' uniformly divergent constitutional treatment

---

[84] *See* Richard C. Schragger, *Federalism, Metropolitanism, and the Problem of States*, 105 Va. L. Rev. 1537, 1603 (2019).

[85] *See generally* Jennifer Sherman, Dividing Paradise (2021) (documenting a variety of factors driving a decline in traditional rural ways of life).

[86] *See, e.g.*, J. K. Dineen, *"No Slums in the Sunset": Backlash over Affordable Housing Development Intensifies in Western S.F. Neighborhood*, S.F. Chron. (Jan. 20, 2021, 3:14 PM), www.sfchronicle.com/bayarea/article/Slum-charges-fly-in-fracas-over-affordable-15880321.php [https://perma.cc/US3L-5PHG].

[87] *See* Janet L. Wallace & Lisa R. Pruitt, *Judging Parents, Judging Place: Poverty, Rurality, and Termination of Parental Rights*, 77 Mo. L. Rev. 95, 117 (2012).

[88] *Rural Health Disparities*, Rural Health Info. Hub (Apr. 22, 2019), www.ruralhealthinfo.org/topics/rural-health-disparities [https://perma.cc/UR87-ARAJ].

[89] *See* Hanna Love & Mike Powe, *Rural Small Businesses Need Local Solutions to Survive*, Brookings (Dec. 1, 2020), www.brookings.edu/research/rural-small-businesses-need-local-solutions-to-survive [https://perma.cc/C2UD-CH8W].

[90] *See* Sarah L. Swan, *Constitutional Off-Loading at the City Limits*, 135 Harv. L. Rev. 831 (2022).

[91] *Id.* at 848.

of local governments depending on their size, in which a more restrictive rule is applied to large municipalities and a more lenient rule is applied to small ones. What results from this divergent treatment is one set of constitutional expectations and rules for large cities and another set for the small towns that make up many rural communities and suburbs. This "horizontal tailoring" – defined as "when the same legal principle is applied differently within the same level of government"[92] – introduces new implications for the many tensions in politics, economics, and culture that track along U.S. landscapes.

This response first provides a brief summary of Swan's article. It then offers a normative critique of Swan's primary conclusion that the problems and benefits associated with the phenomenon she observes will "ultimately push toward a more balanced localism for all" and may help defuse urban–rural polarization.[93] Specifically, the response argues that having divergent constitutional standards for different types of local government is more concerning than Swan's analysis proposes, although the discussion also suggests that horizontal tailoring may not actually be as surprising or novel as the article implies. Courts' questionable reliance on place-based stereotypes, the democratic deficits associated with local governance, and varying standards for localism and constitutional protections all deserve more scrutiny as possible contributors to the urgent societal rifts described earlier, and as likely not yet reflecting optimal distributions of political and economic power.

Constitutional off-loading begins with municipalities' efforts to exclude undesirable land uses. As a common example, a municipality may try to argue that an ordinance that would prevent a proposed strip club from opening within its borders is not an unconstitutional violation of First Amendment rights because there are strip clubs available in a nearby urban center or elsewhere within its county.[94] Swan observes a pattern in courts' treatment of this argument: Small municipalities are frequently able to advance the argument of extraterritorial availability successfully, while large municipalities are uniformly not allowed to do so.[95]

Thus, in cases concerning small municipalities, courts accede that towns could "entirely ban commercial live entertainment"[96] and "zone out such uses completely" despite First Amendment protections.[97] Courts rely on ideas such as "reasonable alternatives," "nearby access," and "artificial" and "arbitrary" local government boundaries to justify allowing exclusion.[98] Courts tell cities, on the other

---

[92] *Id.* at 861 (emphasis omitted).
[93] *Id.* at 888.
[94] *See id.* at 841–43.
[95] *Id.* at 843, 853–54.
[96] *Id.* at 846 (quoting Jules B. Gerard & Scott D. Bergthold, Local Regulation of Adult Business § 4:4 (2020)).
[97] *Id.* (quoting Gerard & Bergthold, *supra* note 96, §4:6).
[98] *Id.* at 850.

hand, that it is "hard to imagine" someone suggesting a city like Chicago could prohibit free speech or religious liberty "on the rationale that those rights may be freely enjoyed in the suburbs."[99]

At first glance, Swan explains, one might conclude that courts are giving small municipalities special treatment and that this horizontal tailoring gives them greater power to pursue self-determination through more robust opportunities to off-load constitutional obligations on neighboring localities.[100] Big cities are forced to bear more diverse land uses despite their potential undesirability, whereas small municipalities have greater control over keeping the perceived undesirables out. In this sense, small towns – including the thousands of small towns that comprise much of rural America[101] and the many suburbs outside urban centers whose conservative political leanings often resemble rural ones[102] – are relatively powerful. The implication for the urban–rural divides described earlier is that "small conservative 'red' towns can maintain and even deepen their conservative community character through exclusions, while large 'blue' cities are prohibited from crafting their progressive community character through similar exclusionary methods."[103]

But, Swan argues, the story is more complex than that. Courts' respect and enforcement of jurisdictional borders are what make those borders meaningful – what make them exist at all, in fact. Thus, there is a catch to small towns' apparently greater discretion to off-load constitutional obligations on neighboring jurisdictions. Courts' acquiescence to this practice reflects not their respect for small-town autonomy, but their disregard for small-town borders.[104] The treatment of small municipalities' borders as permeable reveals the limits of local municipal sovereignty on a small scale. By contrast, in being told by courts that they must be constitutionally inclusive, large cities are empowered as locally sovereign – more than as mere political subdivisions of the state, and instead as equivalents of the state.[105] Thus, Swan concludes, the joke is on the small towns: They can have their cake (constitutional off-loading) but not eat it too (maintain the respect afforded to a strong, meaningful political subdivision or standalone jurisdictional entity).[106] In this sense, then, many rural communities and suburbs are once again revealed as relatively powerless in the form of their reduced constitutional significance.[107]

---

[99] *Id.* at 856.

[100] *See id.* at 869.

[101] *See* ROBERT WUTHNOW, THE LEFT BEHIND 5 (2018).

[102] *See* KATHERINE J. CRAMER, THE POLITICS OF RESENTMENT 13 (2016).

[103] Swan, *supra* note 90, at 836.

[104] *See id.* at 877.

[105] *See id.* at 883–84.

[106] *See id.* at 877–79.

[107] *Cf.* Alan Romero, *Extraterritorial Land Use Regulation and Bridging the Urban-Rural Divide*, 87 UMKC L. REV. 867, 867–68 (2019) (noting that many rural residents are governed by counties rather than municipalities, and that cities that do not represent rural residents may be allowed to regulate them, exacerbating urban–rural tensions).

Swan concludes that the benefits of courts horizontally tailoring constitutional off-loading likely outweigh whatever problems the practice poses.[108] Small municipalities' ability to exclude exacerbates the proliferation of homogeneous, exclusive, wealth-hoarding enclaves throughout the country, in turn contributing to today's geographically imbued political polarization.[109] But the alternative – top-down, paternalistic mandates for constitutional inclusivity – can contribute to backlash and political polarization in its own way.[110] Swan concludes that both options – "respect or force" – are problematic.[111] Too much deference to small towns "threaten[s] to increase political polarization" by "enabl[ing] these localities to adopt an increasingly extreme constitutional community character."[112] Yet paternalistic mandates risk "breed[ing] resentment."[113]

Since courts are damned if they do (allow unmitigated localism) and damned if they don't (mitigate localism with paternalistic mandates), Swan argues that they may as well engage in horizontal tailoring of constitutional off-loading, giving small localities the impression of power with the one hand – by letting them engage in constitutional off-loading – while minimizing it with the other – by treating their borders as less constitutionally significant than those of large cities, after which "claims to localism are weakened."[114]

Swan reasons that this approach represents an "evening [of] the localism playing field"[115] by laying a conceptual basis to counteract various evils that strong small-town borders have facilitated, including racial segregation, disregard for externalities imposed on neighboring communities, and other parochial or selfish interests.[116] Swan anticipates that courts could use this conceptual foundation to diminish small towns' localism – and, therefore, their capacity for harm[117] – by resisting small localities' efforts "to become more visible[,] … seeking acknowledgement as valid constitutional interpreters and actors."[118] This, in turn, may help the process of reducing urban–rural polarization by "'unbundl[ing]' the urban and rural packages offered" by the political parties associated respectively with each place.[119]

Swan's analysis also emphasizes the practical consequences that flow from horizontal tailoring for cities. Most significantly, the analysis offers large cities a

---

[108] Swan, *supra* note 90, at 853 (characterizing horizontal constitutional off-loading as having offsetting costs and benefits for small towns and large cities, respectively).

[109] *Id.* at 880, 885.

[110] *Id.* at 867–68.

[111] *Id.* at 868.

[112] *Id.*

[113] *Id.* at 869.

[114] *Id.* at 871; *see id.* at 870–71.

[115] *Id.* at 888.

[116] *Id.* at 872–76.

[117] *Cf. id.* at 868, 880.

[118] *Id.* at 880.

[119] *Id.* at 887.

conceptual tool to be used in preemption battles.[120] Conservative states have been aggressively trying to preempt large, progressive cities' efforts to pursue liberal legislation, such as antidiscrimination ordinances, plastic bag bans, and regulation of extractive industries. If courts' approach to constitutional off-loading can be understood as tacitly elevating large cities' constitutional status to an even footing with states, cities have stronger claims against preemption.

Other than highlighting the benefits of these consequences, Swan's analysis does not quite tackle the question of whether horizontal tailoring in constitutional off-loading is a sound doctrinal approach. The bait-and-switch that small communities reach for – special treatment that is ultimately condescension, which helps confuse powerlessness and power – brings to mind two related pieces of literature. The first is Professor Lisa Pruitt's "Rural Rhetoric," a longstanding pillar of the rural legal studies canon and an important empirical study on how state courts conceptualize and treat the rural.[121] The second is Professor Rick Su's "Democracy in Rural America," which examines the role of local government in furthering representative democracy outside large cities.[122]

"Rural Rhetoric" and Swan's analysis touch on similar themes involving place-based stereotypes, what courts in turn do with those stereotypes, and the implications of courts' reliance on stereotypes. Both Swan and Pruitt observe that, in our public and legal imagination, places outside of cities are often romanticized as safe, wholesome, clean, quiet, and interconnected – as opposed to the chaos and dangers supposedly lurking in the big city.[123] Yet both Swan and Pruitt observe that there is a cost to a widespread understanding of a romanticized version of place. Neighborliness and a sense of safety, for instance, are associated with homogeneity and exclusivity. When courts assume towns are "safe," they not only likely overlook actual dangers faced by vulnerable members of those communities, but they also make more nefarious assumptions about the nature of the community.

Both Swan and Pruitt conclude that, when courts apply law to localities based in stereotypes, courts reify and cement those stereotypes, reconstituting these places in the courts' own conceptualization of them.[124] Thus, a court that gives legal weight to a community's perceived homogeneity in turn reconstitutes the community as homogeneous. Swan concludes that treating small communities in this way may be a natural outgrowth of the different public and legal conceptualizations of small and large municipalities and, alongside the risks associated with paternalism, makes it seem almost unavoidable.[125] Pruitt concludes, by contrast, that courts' "frequent reliance on nostalgic stereotypes" results in inattention to real conditions in these

---

[120] *Id.* at 884–85.
[121] *See* Lisa R. Pruitt, *Rural Rhetoric*, 39 CONN. L. REV. 159 (2006).
[122] *See* Rick Su, *Democracy in Rural America*, 98 N.C. L. REV. 837 (2020).
[123] *See* Swan, *supra* note 90, at 865–71; Pruitt, *supra* note 121, at 169.
[124] *See* Swan, *supra* note 90, at 836; Pruitt, *supra* note 121, at 172.
[125] *See* Swan, *supra* note 90, at 836.

places and "is generally disappointing."[126] It seems worth asking, then, whether horizontal tailoring in constitutional off-loading is as advantageous as Swan suggests, or whether the practice is more reflective of the many problems she describes with the approach before she concludes that it holds promise.

"Democracy in Rural America" turns the lens on small local governments and their deficits as vehicles for democratic empowerment outside large urban centers. Su argues "that rural communities currently lack the power to address many of the challenges they face today and that this powerlessness is rooted in the manner in which rural local governments are defined in American law."[127] Rural local governments were not designed to be representative of local democratic interests in the first place, Su argues, because they were designated on maps as subdivisions for state control, with local government employees, such as sheriffs, often still today employed directly by the state and not expected to answer to the locality.[128] These historical roots combined with local disenfranchisement means a rural community "can sometimes bear little relationship to the local government that governs [it]" – meaning a decision passed at the local level is likely to be flawed in its representation of local will.[129] In terms of local autonomy and pathways to self-determination, states' widespread adoption of twentieth-century home rule often excluded towns, viewing them as fundamentally different legal creatures than large cities, with far fewer powers. In short, Su says, "home rule largely left rural America out."[130] The absence of local autonomy has been coupled in recent decades with the growing role in rural affairs of state and federal agencies, which "are not directly responsive to local constituents"[131] and further exacerbate a sense of rural powerlessness.[132] Ultimately, Su concludes, rural towns and counties are very limited in their ability to channel the interests of their residents.

Su's article offers some additional context for Swan's analysis. First, Su concludes that the popular conception of rural local governments as bastions of self-governance, a romanticized notion that Swan references, is simply not an accurate reflection of the modern reality.[133] Second, and more centrally, legislatures and courts have historically treated cities and towns as fundamentally legally different, with different structures and different rights and responsibilities. Viewed in this light, horizontal tailoring of constitutional off-loading becomes quite a bit less surprising because cities and towns have never truly been considered the same level and creature of

---

[126] Pruitt, *supra* note 90, at 234; *cf.* Richard C. Schragger, *The Limits of Localism*, 100 MICH. L. REV. 371, 376 (2001) (characterizing the choice between localism and paternalism as a false dichotomy).

[127] Su, *supra* note 122, at 839.

[128] *See id.* at 855–60.

[129] *Id.* at 855.

[130] *Id.* at 863.

[131] *Id.* at 867.

[132] *Id.* at 867–68.

[133] *See* Swan, *supra* note 90, at 836; Su, *supra* note 122, at 867–68.

local government. Perhaps horizontal tailoring as described here is not really horizontal tailoring of a different standard across two equivalent levels of government, but more like slightly diagonal tailoring of a different standard across a level of government with substantial internal variation linked to population size.

Putting all these pieces together – place-based stereotypes, democratic deficits, constitutional protections, and varying standards for localism – it is tempting to conclude that small towns are indulged with localism when they do not need it and denied localism when they do. In other words, courts give small municipalities leeway to shape their own destinies when a strip club wants to come to town – after all, the sensitive, traditional locals would simply be unable to bear such an affront to their moral values. But then, small municipalities are denied the opportunity to shape their own destinies when they need it to influence regional livelihoods and opportunities in a way that can actually keep their communities afloat.

Some small-town residents are, of course, perfectly happy with homogenization and exclusion, and they can make those interests known through their local governments. But, when courts elevate those interests over others – such as the rights of sexual, political, and religious minorities – they are perhaps not actually doing communities qua communities any favors, but merely ceding small localities to the local fiefdoms that antimajoritarian safeguards are designed to protect against.[134] Meanwhile, failing to enable meaningful local input on other land uses, such as major federal energy projects, helps further undermine struggling regional economies. This may work out just fine for the wealthier small-town suburbs that siphon off the benefits of metropolitan centers without bearing any of the costs, as Swan points out.[135] But, for the rural populations that do not have that luxury, the limits of small-town government have been very costly.

These tensions call into question Swan's conclusion that the benefits and burdens associated with divergent responsibilities between small towns and cities ultimately weigh in favor of horizontal tailoring of constitutional off-loading. Courts' divergent treatment of local governments based on size is probably appropriate in many circumstances. I have argued in prior work that a small, remote municipality is a fundamentally different creature than the City of Chicago.[136] But the juxtaposition Swan highlights seems more concerning than her conclusion that it "evens the localism playing field" because small towns are punished for their exclusionary tactics with reduced constitutional significance.

---

[134] *See* Swan, *supra* note 90, at 868 (suggesting that constitutional off-loading risks undermining "uniform protection of rights everywhere in the country" (quoting Mark D. Rosen, *The Surprisingly Strong Case for Tailoring Constitutional Principles*, 153 U. PA. L. REV. 1513, 1632 (2005))); *cf.* Schragger, *supra* note 126, at 372–74 (characterizing much of the localism debate as a conflict between individual rights and community norms, and arguing that the definition of "community" – as a product of contested political norms – is central to whether a particular community's norms are entitled to respect).

[135] *See* Swan, *supra* note 90, at 875; Su, *supra* note 122, at 859.

[136] *See generally* Eisenberg, *Rural Blight*, *supra* note 1 (arguing that small, remote local governments need specialized support to take on community development initiatives effectively).

It seems as if instances of rural and suburban empowerment – whether relating to politics, land use, or even rhetorical imagery – are outdated, based on outdated notions of national population distribution and outdated notions of what communities outside cities are and can be. If courts condescend to treat small towns as closed-minded and intolerant, courts help make rural communities and suburbs as much, in turn helping to drive the young, the progressive, and those of minority backgrounds to more population-dense locales where their interests stand to receive greater protection.[137] Small towns' weak borders do not offer much consolation for this deleterious population sorting.

Meanwhile, small towns' ability to engage in constitutional off-loading in some contexts has not borne fruit for small towns by way of affording them meaningful avenues to self-determination. For those who have always seen at least some small towns as underdogs, modest municipalities having weak constitutional significance is neither a revelation nor an adequate consolation prize for their occasional wins. When a small municipality tries to pass a controversial ordinance – such as by aiming to exclude or regulate hydraulic fracturing or monopolistic, industrial agricultural activity – a state can and often will preempt them. That horizontal tailoring of constitutional off-loading affords states more ammunition to disregard small towns' constitutional significance does not seem neutral or positive in this context, but in fact rings in subjugation.

As Su points out, small towns' power deficits might help explain in part why political appeals to a sense of voicelessness have proven disproportionately impactful outside cities.[138] Despite their seemingly robust land use decision-making power, small towns and sparsely populated counties have failed to take control over whether plants can close and effectuate mass layoffs;[139] over how to refill tax coffers drained of former timber and coal revenues;[140] over keeping the local nuclear plant from

---

[137] *Cf.* Schragger, *supra* note 126, at 376 (arguing that law institutes one particular version of the local to the exclusion of multiple possible alternative localisms).

[138] *See* Su, *supra* note 122, at 840; Ian Scoones et al., *Emancipatory Rural Politics: Confronting Authoritarian Populism*, 45 J. PEASANT STUD. 1, 7–9 (2018).

[139] *See generally* Fran Ansley, *Standing Rusty and Rolling Empty: Law, Poverty, and America's Eroding Industrial Base*, 81 GEO. L.J. 1757, 1758 (1993) (describing grassroots efforts to keep employers in the face of deindustrialization); Brady Dennis & Steven Mufson, *In Small Towns across the Nation, the Death of a Coal Plant Leaves an Unmistakable Void*, WASH. POST (Mar. 28, 2019), www.washingtonpost .com/national/health-science/thats-what-happens-when-a-big-plant-shuts-down-in-a-small-town/2019/03/28/57d62700-4a57-11e9-9663-00ac73f49662_story.html [https://perma.cc/DD6F-S9GU] (describing economic challenges in small towns that lose coal plants); John Seewer, *Ripples from U.S. Nuclear Plant Closings Overwhelm Small Towns*, AP NEWS (Mar. 26, 2017), https://apnews.com/article/ nv-state-wire-us-news-ap-top-news-mi-state-wire-oh-state-wire-612d238dffbe47c0a6da47d2b6541439 [https://perma.cc/3PND-TRUF] (describing economic challenges in towns that lose nuclear plants).

[140] *See generally* Anderson, *supra* note 74, at 469 (detailing fiscal struggles among local governments that have lost economic activity in the timber industry); Adele Morris et al., *The Risk of Fiscal Collapse in Coal-Reliant Communities*, BROOKINGS (July 15, 2019), www.brookings.edu/research/the-risk-of-fiscal-collapse-in-coal-reliant-communities [https://perma.cc/5HBF-MA2L] (detailing the risk of local government fiscal collapse in coal-reliant communities).

giving residents cancer;[141] over whether to keep natural gas drilling and pipelines out;[142] over whether the local hospital will close;[143] over whether local doctors' offices will be flooded with opioids;[144] over keeping consolidated agribusiness in check;[145] over access to national transportation and telecommunications infrastructure;[146] over keeping small businesses afloat against unfettered corporate competition;[147] and over preventing school consolidation.[148] But maybe, at the very least, they can keep the strip club at bay.

---

[141] *See generally* LOKA ASHWOOD, FOR-PROFIT DEMOCRACY: WHY THE GOVERNMENT IS LOSING THE TRUST OF RURAL AMERICA 161 (2018) (detailing environmental and health struggles of rural residents engaged with local nuclear plants).

[142] *See* Heidi Gorovitz Robertson, *Cities and Citizens Seethe: A Case Study of Local Efforts to Influence Natural Gas Pipeline Routing Decisions*, 122 W. VA. L. REV. 881, 883 (2020); Heidi Gorovitz Robertson, *When States' Legislation and Constitutions Collide with Angry Locals: Shale Oil and Gas Development and Its Many Masters*, 41 WM. & MARY ENV'T L. & POL'Y REV. 55, 58–61 (2016).

[143] *See generally* U.S. GOV'T ACCOUNTABILITY OFF., GAO 21-93, RURAL HOSPITAL CLOSURES: AFFECTED RESIDENTS HAD REDUCED ACCESS TO HEALTH CARE SERVICES 20–22 (2020), www .gao.gov/assets/gao-21-93.pdf [https://perma.cc/6F8M-W32U]; Taylor Sisk, *As Appalachian Hospitals Disappear, Rural Americans Grapple with Limited Care*, NAT'L GEOGRAPHIC (July 14, 2021), www .nationalgeographic.com/history/article/appalachian-hospitals-are-disappearing [https://perma.cc/ J2VH-U79V].

[144] *See* Effler v. Purdue Pharma L.P., 614 S.W.3d 681, 684 (Tenn. 2020) (holding that plaintiffs' allegation that drug manufacturers "knowingly participated in the illegal drug market" was sufficient to state a claim); City of Charleston v. Joint Comm'n on Accreditation of Health Care Orgs., 473 F. Supp. 3d 596 (S.D. W. Va. 2020) (finding that municipalities stated a claim adequate for standing in a negligence lawsuit against an organization that collaborated with opioid manufacturers to issue pain-management standards); Scott Higham et al., *76 Billion Opioid Pills: Newly Released Federal Data Unmasks the Epidemic*, WASH. POST (July 16, 2019), www.washingtonpost.com/investigations/76-billion-opioid-pills-newly-released-federal-data-unmasks-the-epidemic/2019/07/16/5f29fd62-a73e-11e9-86dd-d7f0e60391e9_story.html [https://perma.cc/NCH7-ZD4U] (noting that rural communities were hit particularly hard by the opioid crisis).

[145] *See* Alexander A. Reinert, *The Right to Farm: Hog-Tied and Nuisance-Bound*, 73 N.Y.U. L. REV. 1694, 1695 (1998) (describing state right-to-farm laws, which restrict local governments' ability to pass ordinances restricting agricultural activity).

[146] *See* Aditi Shrikant, *Why Air Service Is so Crucial for Small Cities*, VOX (Nov. 12, 2018, 7:01 AM), www .vox.com/the-goods/2018/11/12/18080806/air-service-small-cities-crucial [https://perma.cc/24C7-SGMJ] ("For smaller towns and cities, the availability of air travel is always on the chopping block as airlines cut small-plane service and consolidate in major cities."); Ganesh Sitaraman et al., *Regulation and the Geography of Inequality*, 70 DUKE L.J. 1763, 1785–98 (2021).

[147] *See* Love & Powe, *supra* note 89.

[148] *See* Robert M. Bastress, *The Impact of Litigation on Rural Students: From Free Textbooks to School Consolidation*, 82 NEB. L. REV. 9, 30–31 (2003).

4

The Myth of Rural Unsustainability

When I tell urban audiences that I think distressed rural regions warrant more robust interventions to turn their fates around, I encounter a fair amount of skepticism.[1] One version of that skepticism conceptualizes any rural localities that would benefit from such interventions, or that might need such interventions to survive, as artificial creations, like Disney World. Aghast, an urbanite might ask me, "Why should *we* [in our dynamic, organic, self-sustaining urban locality] have to *subsidize them* [in their frivolous, obsolete, unnatural, unwieldy way of life?]" It's as if a public measure to more aggressively deploy rural broadband or to reopen a rural hospital is a form of unjust urban alimony payment to a rural ex-spouse who will fritter away hard-earned urban money on trucks and guns.

The myth of rural unsustainability turns on ideas about costs, efficiency, and dynamism. According to this myth, because rural populations, by definition, are more spread out, they are more costly to sustain than their more densely packed urban counterparts. Urban life is more sustainable because it offers a more efficient means of service provision. That is, urban life is conducive to economies of scale, whereas rural life is not. Therefore, urban life is the more efficient, less wasteful societal model, poised not only to make the best use of scarce resources but also to keep carbon emissions per capita lower through that efficient use of resources.[2]

Rural life, by contrast, is assumed to be inefficient, wasteful, and requiring heavy subsidization. It is therefore only sustainable as a form of parasitism on organic urban prosperity.[3] Commentators question, for instance, the fairness of policy approaches

---

[1] Portions of this chapter were excerpted from Ann M. Eisenberg, *Economic Regulation and Rural America*, 98 WASH. U. L. REV. 737 (2021).

[2] Richard Florida, *Why Bigger Cities Are Greener*, BLOOMBERG (Apr. 19, 2012), www.bloomberg.com/news/articles/2012-04-19/why-bigger-cities-are-greener [https://perma.cc/T64M-VKRA].

[3] Matthew Yglesias, *The Inefficiency of Rural Living*, SLATE (June 6, 2012), https://slate.com/business/2012/06/the-inefficiency-of-rural-living.html [https://perma.cc/7BVV-WWWF] ("[I]t's completely impossible to provide modern health care services to a rural population."); *see also id.* (critiquing how "we disproportionately subsidize inefficient rural telecommunication and transportation infrastructure" alongside rural healthcare); Nathan Arnosti & Amy Liu, *Why Rural America*

such as "over-charg[ing] metropolitan America for mail delivery in order to create a cross-subsidy to provide discount mail to rural America."[4]

This chapter argues that rural communities are sustainable, meaning capable and worthy of being maintained. The myth of rural unsustainability becomes far weaker when one questions the market-supremacist assumptions that underlie it. In that same vein, cities are less dynamic and more dependent than many believe, while rural communities still offer important, unique contributions to society, which are explored in more depth in Chapter 8. Central to the discussion that follows, we also know rural communities are sustainable because robust legal traditions have helped intentionally sustain them for decades – and the modern unraveling of those frameworks is often a missing piece of today's conversations on rural decline.

First, let's start with the concept of economies of scale. The narrative of rural unsustainability often refers to an assumed, universal aspiration to achieve economies of scale in infrastructure and service provision. However, this commentary rarely provides an explicit definition for the concept. This is because, I posit, in a market-supremacist world, it is assumed that achieving economies of scale is an objective need rather than a subjective priority informed by value judgments. But a simple example of the economy of scale might be the labor and expenses a baker would put into making a single cookie – still having to buy and measure all of the ingredients in bulk, mix them, shape the cookie, and bake the cookie – versus making an entire batch of cookies with only the slightly heightened proportionate amount of labor, mostly directed to shaping additional cookies. A "diseconomy of scale" exists when the average cost of production increases with increased output.[5]

It is true that rural population sparseness builds additional costs into the provision of virtually any product, service, or development because of the costs associated with distance, such as needing to traverse the distance and increased uncertainty associated with that distance.[6] On the other side of that coin, because rural populations are more limited, there are fewer consumers to offset those higher costs, meaning rural diseconomies of scale will be more likely in most types of economic activity.[7] Drawing upon the cookie example, it would be as if the baker had thirty customers for dozens of cookies within one mile, but then had to drive a small amount of

---

Needs Cities, BROOKINGS (Nov. 30, 2018), www.brookings.edu/research/why-rural-america-needs-cities/ [https://perma.cc/7ZT9-BJR3] ("Prosperity in cities and metropolitan areas effectively subsidizes public investments in rural areas.").

4   Yglesias, *supra* note 3.
5   Bradley T. Borden, *Taxing Shared Economies of Scale*, 61 BAYLOR L. REV. 721, 724 (2009) (describing the "cost-reducing potential of economies of scale" as "the decline in average cost per-unit as output rises").
6   ORG. FOR ECON. COOP. & DEV., OECD RURAL POLICY REVIEWS: STRATEGIES TO IMPROVE RURAL SERVICE DELIVERY 25–26 (2010) [hereinafter OECD].
7   *See id.* at 3 (noting "delivering any particular service" is "more expensive in a rural location than in urban centres" because of lower population density, larger distances to travel, and smaller numbers of people that preclude economies of scale).

cookies ten miles away for two customers; those latter customers do not necessarily seem worth the additional costs due to their diseconomies of scale.

In the private sector, most companies would prefer to direct their services to urban centers because they can offer their products at a higher volume with lower relative costs.[8] Urban communities, simply by having more people, also offer more demand for products. So, for example, a private internet service provider, much like the electric companies of the 1920s and 30s, would avoid the "lean territory," seeking instead to establish itself to serve an urban community, not just because the urban community would offer more consumers, but also because the provider would make a more efficient use of its own resources by yielding higher returns per capita.[9] Once a provider achieves a level of production and consumption that can be sustained, that threshold is considered to be "at scale." When it comes to developments or services with high fixed costs, such as the installation of permanent infrastructure fixtures, the prospect of rural investments seems all the less appealing.[10]

The aspiration to achieve economies of scale also arises in the context of public and quasi-public amenities, such as schools and hospitals.[11] Although schools and hospitals do not produce the goods initially contemplated by this theory about business yields, they do have outputs and operating costs.[12] The idea here, too, is that more output will tend to make for more efficient use of costs. Thus, a rural school or hospital that serves three people would likely be considered not "at scale."[13] The principle of the economy of scale favors consolidation, at least to an extent.[14]

---

[8] *Cf.* Borden, *supra* note 5, at 722–23 (noting businesses' motivations to create economies of scale due to their cost-reducing potential from decline in average cost per-unit as output rises).

[9] *Cf.* Sharon Strover, *Reaching Rural America with Broadband Internet Service*, CONVERSATION (Jan. 16, 2018, 10:08 PM), https://theconversation.com/reaching-rural-america-with-broadband-internet-service-82488 [https://perma.cc/6P4D-FU79] (noting role of population sparseness and fewer customers from whom to recoup costs as reasons rural residents have limited access to quality internet service); OECD, *supra* note 6, at 3 (noting higher costs of service provision in rural areas).

[10] OECD, *supra* note 6, at 33 (describing increase in minimum efficient scale in service provision due to technological change, as well as high fixed costs associated with technologies, both of which conflict with shrinking rural demand and minimal cost savings in rural communities); Borden, *supra* note 5, at 750 (describing small-scale output as a "typical barrier to entry" in a new market).

[11] *See* Robert J. Tholkes & Charles H. Sederberg, *Economies of Scale and Rural Schools*, 7 RSCH. RURAL EDUC. 9 (1990); Monica Giancotti et al., *Efficiency and Optimal Size of Hospitals: Results of a Systematic Search* PLoS ONE 1 (Mar. 29, 2017) www.ncbi.nlm.nih.gov/pmc/articles/PMC5371367/ [https://perma.cc/6TVM-73N7]; *see also* OECD, *supra* note 6, at 16, 20–21 (suggesting that services can be grouped into three types: private, public (e.g., police protection, firefighting services, building inspection, or waste disposal), and collective/joint).

[12] *See* Tholkes & Sederberg, *supra* note 11, at 9, 10–13 (providing review of literature on economies of scale from the 1950s through 1990); *see also* George J. Stigler, *The Economies of Scale*, 1 J. L. & ECON. 54 (1958).

[13] *See, e.g.*, H.R. 1109, 84th Gen. Assemb., 2d Extraordinary Sess. (Ark. 2004) (Arkansas law mandating school district consolidation or annexation when attendance drops below 350 students).

[14] *See* Borden, *supra* note 5, at 723–24.

When the economies-of-scale standard is applied to rural communities as a whole, their very existence – and the dilemma of whether the broader community should support them – is called into question.[15] Those who emphasize the primacy of economies of scale tend to suggest that declining rural communities are not self-sustaining enough to justify the public expenditures that they need to function.[16] A particular municipality's entire economic activity – local wages earned, property taxes collected, and developers attracted, for example – may still be lower than the local and external public inputs, so-called subsidies, that would be needed to meet residents' needs. Those inputs would also need to be disproportionately higher on a per-resident basis than they would be for residents in urban communities.

Proposals to pursue revitalization policies for rural communities are always called to account for the ever-present question of supposed rural inefficiency when measured on the basis of costs per capita, and increasingly, on the measure of greenhouse gas emissions per capita. But what the myth of rural unsustainability inevitably fails to recognize is that the above line of thinking focuses on relatively narrow questions. Indeed, the principle that populations warrant public investment and support only if they are the most efficient use of the resources in question bears troubling logical conclusions, even for urban populations.

In any case, the discussion that follows illustrates how the comparison of urban–rural efficiency is not that simple. It also shows how a community's worth and contributions to society cannot necessarily be summed up on an accounting sheet, a perspective that past regulatory policy seemed to embrace more readily.

ONGOING RURAL NECESSITY ALONGSIDE EXAGGERATED URBAN SUPERIORITY (AND THE INTERDEPENDENCE OF BOTH)

A key question that the earlier narrative raises is: Are cities really that much more efficient and less wasteful than rural localities and regions? Is population density alone the paragon of development goals? Ample commentary recognizes or assumes that certain benefits do come with population density, and I do not dispute the obvious logic behind this idea.

However, modern American cities remain far from the idealized image of the dynamic, innovative urban utopia. In their book chapter entitled "The Myth of Urban Self Sufficiency," environmental scientists Day and Hall articulate how cities are emblematic of the unsustainability of modern life in the United States altogether. Manhattan, for instance, is often referenced as an icon of green living because of Manhattanites' relatively high use of public transportation, walking, and

---

[15] *See* David Schleicher, *Stuck: The Law and Economics of Residential Stagnation*, 127 YALE L.J. 78, 143–45 (2017).

[16] *See* Yglesias, *supra* note 3 (pointing out the inefficiency in providing services like broadband internet, brick-and-mortar mail, and medical services to rural communities).

biking. But Day and Hall challenge this depiction of overall urban greenness and the related conceptualization of cities in general as "the sustainable future."

First, "large urban megaregions" require constant, substantial imports of raw and processed materials to survive.[17] Those materials are often shipped from distant places, creating "large indirect energy and material demands that are not accounted for in calculations of urban energy use,"[18] meaning urban greenness is often overestimated. "[A]lmost everything from building materials to artificial lighting to clothing to food that is used in a city is produced elsewhere, often at high energy costs."[19] Those imports also frequently come from "energy-intensive and highly polluting industries such as aluminum- and steel-making," which have been "outsourced to regions and countries where labor is cheaper and environmental regulations are less stringent."[20] In turn, the production of those imported resources is increasingly invisible to urban consumers, meaning they may also fail to appreciate the unsustainability concerns associated with urban life. Day and Hall conclude, "In spite of their enormous requirements for materials and energy, and their enormous generation of wastes, many see urban living as the sustainable future for most of humankind in the twenty-first century. But there are serious issues for urban areas, especially very large ones ... given the interrelated problems of climate change, and energy and resource scarcity, and the importance of natural systems for society. These interrelated problems will pose constraints for all of society, but they will be much more challenging and difficult to solve for very large urban areas."[21]

Density alone also does not necessarily achieve low emissions and other measures of environmental sustainability. Day and Hall conclude that "[a]s a policy measure to reduce [greenhouse gas] emissions, increasing density appears to have severe limitations and unexpected tradeoffs."[22] A study by energy scholars Jones and Kammen, for instance, found "no evidence for net [greenhouse gas] benefits of population density in urban cores or suburbs when considering effects on entire metropolitan areas."[23] Rather than location or population density, they observe, "[i]ncome is the single most important contributing factor to household carbon footprint."[24]

Sociologists Fulkerson and Thomas have written extensively about urban dependency on nonurban places and resources. They explain that in sociological

---

[17] *Id.* at 32.

[18] *Id.* at 28.

[19] *Id.*

[20] *Id.*

[21] JOHN W. DAY & CHARLES HALL, AMERICA'S MOST SUSTAINABLE CITIES AND REGIONS: SURVIVING THE 21ST CENTURY MEGATRENDS 27 (2016).

[22] *Id.*

[23] DAY & HALL, *supra* note 21, at 29 (quoting Christopher Jones & Daniel M. Kammen, *Spatial Distribution of U.S. Household Carbon Footprints Reveals Suburbanization Undermines Greenhouse Gas Benefits of Urban Population Density*, 48 ENV'T SCI. & TECH. 895 (2013), https://doi.org/10.1021/es4034364).

[24] *Id.*

literature, "The dependency of cities upon rural communities that supply food and natural resources, and indeed any number of manufactured goods for trade, has at times been acknowledged, but all too often is not, or its importance overlooked."[25] They propose that in fact, urbanormativity – the idea that cities are normal and non-cities are deviant – "is the ideological justification for extracting resources from rural areas."[26] Human ecologist William Rees takes the point of urban dependency a step further. He argues "that modern industrial society and modern cities are inherently unsustainable," in part due to cities being "utterly dependent on access to abundant energy and material resources."[27] They also "generat[e] large quantities of wastes."[28]

If one understands cities as "concentrated areas of material and energy consumption and waste production that are dependent on large areas of productive ecosystems and waste sinks" located far away, and as "requir[ing] enormous inputs and outputs to continue to exist as they are,"[29] rural communities start to seem less unsustainable by comparison. One might, in fact, say that the extractive rural economy *subsidizes* cities.

Both urban and rural localities (and everything in between) face sustainability challenges in terms of their use of resources. But what this literature on urban dependency illustrates is that an understanding of "efficiency" should involve more than a narrow calculus of costs per capita in service provision, or a localized assessment of transportation use. The rural supply of labor and materials to support lifestyles along the urban–rural spectrum often remains invisible.

Yet, while scholars have argued that rural regions are an underappreciated necessity to society as a whole for what they already do, they are also essential for what we collectively need them to do, especially in light of climate change picking up momentum. Conservation law expert Laurie Ristino argues, "Rural America has a key role to play in our national resilience because it is the locus of our nation's ecosystem services, including food and fiber provisioning."[30] Calling rural "the foundation of our future sustainability," Ristino notes that rural residents act as stewards to the bulk of the nation's natural resources.[31] Yet, "[t]o our collective detriment, neither these rural landscapes nor the human communities that largely rely on

---

[25] Alexander R. Thomas & Gregory M. Fulkerson, City and Country: The Historical Evolution of Urban-Rural Systems (2021).

[26] *Id.*

[27] *Id.* (quoting William E. Rees, *Cities as Dissipative Structures: Global Change and the Vulnerability of Urban Civilization, in* Sustainability Science: The Emerging Paradigm and the Urban Environment 247–273 (Michael P. Weinstein & R. Eugene Turner eds., 2012).

[28] *Id.* at 33.

[29] Day & Hall, *supra* note 21, at 29 (quoting Christopher M. Jones & Daniel M. Kammen, *Quantifying Carbon Footprint Reduction Opportunities for U.S. Households and Communities*, 45 Env't Sci. & Tech. 4088 (2011), https://doi.org/10.1021/es102221h).

[30] Laurie Ristino, *Surviving Climate Change in America: Toward a Rural Resilience Framework*, 41 W. New Eng. L. Rev. 521, 522–23 (2019).

[31] *Id.* at 527.

them are, in general, resilient."[32] Ristino calls for us "to reimagine rural America as the engine of our collective resilience," proposing that Congress could pass "a resilience-based Farm Bill" that prioritizes "environmental health, food security, and economic well-being."[33]

In a similar vein, legal scholars Wiseman, Wiseman, and Wright observe that "[r]educing carbon emissions requires electrifying most energy uses and building large quantities of new zero-carbon electricity generation and transmission lines. This effort, in turn, will demand a national transformation of land use, particularly in rural, conservative areas."[34] The authors argue that there is potential for mutual benefit between farmers who want to preserve their way of life and states wanting to reduce carbon emissions. The massive amounts of federal subsidies currently directed to farmers to keep land fallow could be redirected to incentivize renewable energy development on that farmland instead.[35] "Marginal farmland can once again be put to productive use by hosting solar panels, supplying essential climate mitigation while preserving agricultural livelihoods, and using the land beneath the panels for ecological or other purposes."[36]

Like Ristino, they focus on the Farm Bill, and argue that Congress should revise the next Farm Bill to pursue these aims. These proposals and related ones to modernize rural contributions to society – to reconceptualize and transform rural America into the "engine of our collective resilience" – are explored in Chapter 8.

THE LEGAL FRAMEWORK THAT PRIORITIZED GEOGRAPHIC EQUITY AND RESILIENCE IN INFRASTRUCTURE ACCESS

This literature suggests that a fundamental rethinking of modern Western life itself is warranted in light of the looming threats of climate change and unsustainable patterns of consumption and development. But in a narrower sense, returning to the ongoing rhetorical referendum on rural relevance, we can at least ask whether economies of scale and related ideas about population density are the only measure by which we should assess the viability and desirability of public interventions that help keep different geographic regions thriving. In light of rural regions' essentiality to the rest of the world, it would behoove non-rural populations to think more deeply about rural sustainability in particular – meaning not just that rural regions earn their own keep according to some metric of efficiency, but that it is essential for our society to invest in sustaining rural regions.

In the century leading up to the 1970s, federal economic regulatory policy embraced the idea that rural communities needed unique forms of protection if

---

[32] *Id.* at 527.
[33] *Id.* at 538.
[34] Hannah J. Wiseman et al., *Farming Solar on the Margins*, 103 B.U. L. Rev. 525, 528–29 (2023).
[35] *Id.* at 530.
[36] *Id.* at 531.

they were going to be able to survive – and that their survival was worthwhile. Indeed, there was more recognition, generally, of public intervention as a necessary precursor to private growth.[37] As with the Rural Electrification Act (REA), both practical and ethical drivers motivated Congress to invest in and protect rural regions.

The 1887 Interstate Commerce Act (ICA), which introduced new regulations overseeing the railroad industry, reflected Congress's first significant intervention to control a major economic sector.[38] The ICA laid the groundwork for the next several decades of economic regulation of infrastructure industries by introducing the mandate for service providers not to discriminate among localities, to charge "reasonable and just rates," and to publish tariffs in the interest of transparency.[39]

The ICA's provisions "appl[ied] to any common carrier or carriers engaged in the transportation of passengers or property wholly by railroad, or partly by railroad and partly by water when both are used, under a common control, management, or arrangement," in interstate or international travel.[40] A common carrier was understood to be engaged in transportation of products or passengers for the benefit of the public, as opposed to those who typically engaged in ad hoc contractual arrangements.[41] The ICA also created the Interstate Commerce Commission (ICC) in order to implement and oversee the new regulatory regime.[42]

In the 1886 debates over the ICA, legislators consistently returned to the vulnerability of small and remote towns, as well as the "interior" of the country, to high rates and exploitation by unscrupulous railroad operators seeking to maximize their profits.[43] Common concerns included the risks of the countryside depopulating, businesses having to close, and allowing or facilitating the concentrated growth of a few commercial

---

[37] *See* Paul Stephen Dempsey, *The Dark Side of Deregulation: Its Impact on Small Communities*, 39 ADMIN. L. REV. 445, 447–49 (1987).

[38] Interstate Commerce Act of 1887, Pub. L. No. 49-104, 24 Stat. 379. The Supreme Court laid the foundation for Congress to pursue such a move a decade earlier with its decision in *Munn v. Illinois*, 94 U.S. 113 (1876), which established that state governments could regulate private businesses that affect public interests.

[39] Interstate Commerce Act §§ 1, 2, 6.

[40] *Id.* at § 1.

[41] *Munn*, 94 U.S. at 121–32 ("[C]ommon carriers ... are held to 'exercise a sort of public office,' and have public duties to perform .... [They stand] in the very 'gateway of commerce,' and take toll from all who pass."); Note, *National Transportation Policy and the Regulation of Motor Carriers*, 71 YALE L. J. 307, 307 (1961) [hereinafter *National Transportation Policy*] ("A common carrier may be defined as one who holds himself out as willing to carry any or specified commodities for all who may choose to employ him; upon making this offer he becomes legally obligated to serve all shippers at reasonable rates and without discrimination. A contract carrier, on the other hand, is one who does not hold himself out to serve the public; he incurs no special legal obligations.").

[42] Interstate Commerce Act § 11.

[43] Congress's attention was brought to this topic by "a pre-Populist agrarian political movement" of farmers who "object[ed] to the excessively high rates being charged them by the monopoly railroads for grain movements to eastern markets." Dempsey, *supra* note 37, at 448.

centers if the railroads' ability to discriminate among localities remained unchecked.[44] For instance, Senator Camden of West Virginia commented that manufacturers and shippers in parts of the country with disadvantaged access to transportation "may be either forced into bankruptcy or compelled to remove their business to the cities or competitive railroad centers."[45] He observed that this would have "the effect of driving population and business enterprise from the country and the towns to the cities and centers of railroad competition, and of creating for one section over another section commercial advantages which no power ought to be permitted to exercise."[46]

Senator Miller of New York expressed a similar concern about commercial disadvantages to remote places and problems associated with compelling residents and businesses to move to cities. He proposed that "diversified industries should be spread all over the country and not brought together in a few great centers."[47] Miller argued that inequitable rail rates, by coercing relocation to urban centers for access to cheap transportation, were "making a few great centers rich – rich not out of newly created wealth, but rich simply because you transfer wealth from other portions of our country to those great centers."[48] Miller condemned "[t]he abnormal growth of our great cities," attributing it "almost entirely to the discriminations

---

[44] *See* 17 CONG. REC. 3,872 (1886) (Senator Sherman of Ohio argued, "One of the great evils of our times in commercial transactions is the vast concentration of capital and labor in great commercial centers. What has built up Chicago? It is simply because Chicago has enormous advantages over every interior town."); 17 CONG. REC. 4,186–87 (1886) Senator Camden, criticizing draft language limiting the nondiscrimination principle, said,

> In my judgment there can be no reason given for it except the reason to legislate in favor of the cities and the large competitive shipping points, to build them up and to depopulate the towns and the distribution of manufactories throughout the country .... I want to see cities grow, but they ought not to grow at the expense of the country at large.

18 CONG. REC. 857 (1887) Congressman Henderson argued,

> Their coming builds up towns and enriches communities; so, too, their unjust management has often destroyed cities and towns and torn down hard-earned fortunes. Railroad owners must learn the new lesson that is coming to us all in this country, and that is to be content with a reasonable profit on investments, and that labor, small capital, and small shippers have their rights just as well as stock owners and powerful shippers.

17 CONG. REC. 7,281 (1886) Congressman Reagan argued that allowing service providers to discriminate

> enables the transportation companies to control the manufacturing interests of the country and to drive them from noncompetitive points and from the rural parts of the country, where living is cheaper and health better, to the great commercial centers .... This is a power which no government of a free people would dare to exercise, and which no wisely administered government would think of exercising, and yet the railroad companies demand and insist on the right to exercise this vast and dangerous power. And under it they are impoverishing some cities, towns, and communities, without any fault of theirs, and enriching others having no other merit to this favor than the arbitrary power of the transportation companies.

[45] 17 CONG. REC. 3,553(1886).
[46] 17 CONG. REC. 3,553(1886).
[47] *Id.* at 3,727.
[48] *Id.*

of railroad companies."[49] He argued that, but for this discrimination, "instead of a few great and overgrown centers where wealth is accumulated enormously … there would now be scattered all over this broad country in every little village and hamlet the great industries which collect around a few great competing points."[50]

Legislators were not merely concerned with fairness to small and remote places and their residents, but also with the public benefits of having widespread, equitable access to affordable transportation, at least for shipping purposes.[51] Senator Cullom of Illinois remarked upon the benefits to consumers, arguing, "[e]very portion of this country … is alike interested in having the products of different sections of the country moved long distances at cheap rates, which benefit the people who require these products as well as the people who raise them."[52] He emphasized further that it was in "the interest of the whole country" that domestic products find a market somewhere, making this "not simply a question of whether Tom Jones can get his corn to market in Springfield," but rather, "what the general policy shall be in order to encourage commerce all over this land."[53]

Like today, the prospect of protecting remote and sparsely populated places had detractors in the late nineteenth century. For instance, New York Senator Platt criticized the possibility of all localities along railroad branches receiving comparable rates. Platt raised concerns about efficiency, questioning the wisdom of charging the same rates for near and remote places "without reference to the cost of construction or the amount of business which is to be upon those branches" for branches that ran "through a sparsely populated country … and where there is very little business and over a road which it has cost no less to build."[54] Much commentary seemed to agree that an overly strict rule could cause harm, and exceptions were built into the legislation based upon potential hardships to railroad operators.[55] The bill passed

---

[49] *Id.*

[50] *Id.* In a perhaps less sympathetic line of reasoning, some legislators exhibited the view that urban communities generally were sites of moral decay and that rural communities should be sustained because the residents were more moral or industrious. *See, e.g.,* 17 CONG. REC. 4,404 (1886) (Senator Sherman arguing that railroad discrimination "destroys the smaller towns or communities, where vice does not prevail so largely as in great cities … where public opinion to a certain extent controls vice and controls all the habits of mankind. Corruption breeds in cities"); 17 CONG. REC. 3,877 (1886) ("There are a great many people in the cities. They sow not, neither do they spin.").

[51] Indeed, the entire reason railroads were able to expand involved "the economic incentives of generous federal and state land grants, loans, bonds, purchases of stock, and remission of taxes" based on the recognition "that the economic development of the interior of the North American continent required that a transportation infrastructure be built." Dempsey, *supra* note 37, at 448.

[52] 17 CONG. REC. 3,867 (1886).

[53] *Id.* at 3,867–68; *see also id.* at 3,876 (Senator Miller arguing that "[i]f the West can not find a market for its vast surplus, then New England, New York, and Pennsylvania will have no market for their manufactured products").

[54] 17 CONG. REC. 834 (1886).

[55] *See, e.g.,* 17 CONG. REC. 3,870 (1886) (Senator Gorman of Maryland stating,

> every railroad expert, I think, who appeared before the committee … admit [sic] that a rule which prohibits a railroad company from charging more for hauling a car-load 300 miles than is charged

the Senate with 47 votes in favor, 4 votes against, and 25 absences on May 12, 1886, and it passed the House with 219 votes in favor, 41 votes against, and 58 absences on January 21, 1887.

This discussion is not meant to suggest that the post-ICA railroad system was perfect. The evolution of the industry was always plagued by controversy, exploitative practices, and financial complexities.[56] The ICC was also not necessarily the most potent administrator, at least initially.[57] Nonetheless, the ICA's intervention was largely effective in enabling small, remote, and rural places to access rail lines. In 1917, the national core rail network for freight and passenger service had 254,000 miles, compared to 140,000 today.[58] A passenger during that era could travel from Maine to Florida without changing trains.[59] By 1929, "[a]lmost every town and village in the nation enjoyed rail passenger service."[60]

Rural access to the rail lines, in turn, yielded the positive, or at least insulating, effects for economic development in remote communities that the ICA's drafters anticipated. In the early twentieth century, "thanks to the railroads, corporations now saw the whole country as a unified market, encouraging businesses to expand beyond the borders of a particular state or region. America was now a national economy, rather than a series of regional ones[.]"[61] As an example, historian Richard Orsi argues that the Southern Pacific Railroad played an integral, even intentional role, in Western "regional economic development, small-farm settlement, agricultural change, and environmental policy."[62] These relationships make sense, ultimately. A functioning, affordable transportation sector is a necessary precursor to economic growth, just as the absence of transportation will necessarily stifle commerce.[63]

> for hauling a car-load 1,000 miles over the same road and in the same direction is just and proper; but they all contend that there are innumerable instances constantly occurring where exceptions must be made, or great injustice would result. Therefore, the rule should not be a rigid one.).

[56] *See* CHRISTIAN WOLMAR, THE GREAT RAILROAD REVOLUTION: THE HISTORY OF TRAINS IN AMERICA 5–26 (2012) (discussing Southern courts' role in convicting large groups of freed Black people through the early 1900s so that their cheap prison labor could be used for railroad construction); *id.* at 207 (discussing widespread rail company bankruptcies during 1890s due to economic downturn); RICHARD J. ORSI, SUNSET LIMITED: THE SOUTHERN PACIFIC RAILROAD AND THE DEVELOPMENT OF THE AMERICAN WEST, 1850–1930 298 (2005) (discussing controversy over rate regulation in early 1900s).

[57] *See* WOLMAR, *supra* note 56, at 308–19 (describing railway displacement of Native Americans, corruption among rail executives, and rampant railway company consolidation despite the advent of the ICC, as well as the ICC's ineffectuality until 1906).

[58] *See id.* at 308–09; AM. SOC'Y OF CIV. ENG'RS, 2017 INFRASTRUCTURE REPORT CARD: A COMPREHENSIVE ASSESSMENT OF AMERICA'S INFRASTRUCTURE 71 (2017), https://2017.infrastructurereportcard.org/wp-content/uploads/2019/02/Full-2017-Report-Card-FINAL.pdf [https://perma.cc/9ZY7-BBWU].

[59] WOLMAR, *supra* note 56, at 308–09.

[60] Dempsey, *supra* note 37, at 450

[61] WOLMAR, *supra* note 56, at 308–09.

[62] ORSI, *supra* note 56, at xvii.

[63] Dempsey, *supra* note 37, at 463 ("Trade routes are the arteries of the economic system, linking every city, town, and hamlet to the life blood of commerce. 'Transportation and economic development are

Congress amended the ICA with the Motor Carrier Act of 1935 (MCA) to bring trucks and buses under the ICC's purview alongside railroads, in significant part due to the railroads' insistence that it was unfair for them to be the sole transportation industry impeded by strict regulation.[64] Similar strains in public sentiment also drove the MCA's passage. Competition among truckers during the Great Depression had reached extreme levels, and "[s]ome feared that continuation of such unrestrained market forces might lead to a loss of service or higher prices for small shippers and communities, leaving the surviving carriers to concentrate on high-revenue traffic."[65]

Rural priorities seemed more mixed during debates over the MCA as compared to the ICA. During the 1934 debates over the bill in the House of Representatives, one congressman submitted telegrams from constituents pointing out that rural communities that still lacked rail access depended disproportionately on the trucking industry. Federal regulation of trucks, they argued, would increase the costs associated with trucking and have an adverse impact on small and independent carriers.[66] A representative of the Eastern Apple Growers' Council testified before the House of Representatives:

> [W]ith the passage of this bill and the ultimate carrying out of all of the provisions … you are going to eliminate the small independent truck owner and turn the truck transportation over to large transportation companies ….
>
> You take, for instance, now we have common carrier lines running out of the smaller cities in Virginia and all over the country, supplying storekeepers and merchants throughout the country that have no railroad facilities. Those trucks run regularly, on regular routes, and haul the goods out and the produce out under intrastate regulations.

---

mutually interdependent – transportation improvements stimulate economic growth, and that growth, in turn, increases the demand for transportation.' The converse is also true." (quoting Abdussalam A. Addus, *Subsidizing Air Service to Small Communities*, 39 TRANSP. Q. 537, 552 (1985))); *see also* Paul Stephen Dempsey, *Transportation: A Legal History*, 30 TRANSP. L. J. 235, 237–38 (2003) ("As the gateways to an increasingly global market, transportation corridors are the arteries through which everyone, and everything everyone consumes, flow …. As a fundamental component of the infrastructure upon which economic growth is built … a healthy transportation system serving the public's needs for ubiquitous service at reasonable prices is vitally important to the region and the nation it serves …. [A] community with poor, declining or deteriorating access to the established and prevailing transportation networks will wither like a human limb or organ starved of oxygen by an artery made impassable by a tenacious blood clot.").

[64] *National Transportation Policy, supra* note 44, at 308–09.

[65] Paul Stephen Dempsey, *Rate Regulation and Antitrust Immunity in Transportation: The Genesis and Evolution of This Endangered Species*, 32 AM. U. L. REV. 335, 344 (1983).

[66] Representative Paul H. Maloney introduced telegrams opposing the bill, arguing in identical language, "Should trucks be under the Interstate Commerce Commission transportation costs will be increased, which will affect adversely rural communities which are dependent on trucking facilities." *Regulation of Interstate Motor Busses and Trucks on Public Highways: Hearing on H.R. 6836 Before the H. Comm. on Interstate & Foreign Com.*, 73d Cong. 453 (1934).

Now, if you put them under Federal regulation it will finally raise the cost of transportation …. You are going to affect the price level of the purchases and the sales of every farmer in every rural community in the entire United States.

....

… I am a champion of the small and independent carrier, because he is the salvation of the rural section, so far as transportation costs are concerned. If we can keep him independent and unregulated, our transportation costs will be kept down.[67]

On the other hand, a representative of the Oneonta Chamber of Commerce and other Upstate New York organizations argued in favor of increased regulation. His region's economic activity largely depended on rail, and he argued that "communities where railroads and railroad employees are important factors … are all interested in overcoming the handicaps put on railroad transportation by unregulated carriers by water and motor trucks."[68] He insisted that this was a "vital" question for "agricultural sections of the country."[69] Similarly, a representative for Southern grain shippers argued that "our business is in jeopardy on account of unregulated" transportation, and that the ICA was a success "because we do not have to worry about giving a big dinner party, or having a poker party, or something of that sort, in order to get a rate" in rail transportation.[70]

The MCA ultimately seemed to attempt to reconcile competing rural interests. It provided that common carriers by motor vehicle needed to secure a certificate of public convenience and necessity from the ICC in order to operate, and that such providers could not engage in unjust discrimination among localities.[71] But it automatically grandfathered in carriers operating before June 1, 1935.[72] The Act also excluded "motor vehicles controlled and operated by any farmer, and used in the transportation of his agricultural commodities and products thereof, or in the transportation of supplies to his farm" and "motor vehicles used exclusively in carrying livestock, fish (including shell fish), or agricultural commodities[.]"[73]

According to transportation law expert Paul Stephen Dempsey, the MCA, like the ICA, succeeded in providing equitable rural access to these transportation services. After the MCA's passage, destructive competition abated, and during the half-century which followed, motor carrier service was ubiquitously available

---

[67] *Regulation of Interstate Motor Carriers: Hearing on H.R. 5262 and H.R. 6016 Before a Subcomm. of the H. Comm. on Interstate & Foreign Com.*, 74th Cong. 299 (1935) (statement of W.S. Campfield).

[68] *The Water Carrier Act, 1935: Hearing on H.R. 5379 Before H. Comm. on Merch. Marine & Fisheries*, 74th Cong. 156–57 (1935) (statement of William Capron).

[69] *Id.* at 158.

[70] *To Amend the Interstate Commerce Act: Hearing on S. 1629, S. 1632, and S. 1635 Before the S. Comm. on Interstate Com. and the Merch. Marine Subcomm. of the S. Comm. on Com.*, 74th Cong. 714–15 (1935) (statement of Harry A. Volz).

[71] Motor Carrier Act of 1935, Pub. L. No. 74-255, §§ 206(a), 216(d), 49 Stat. 543, 551, 558.

[72] Motor Carrier Act § 206(a).

[73] Motor Carrier Act § 203(a)(21)(b).

throughout the nation at a price which was "just and reasonable."[74] "Service was safe and dependable to large and small communities throughout the nation," Dempsey explains."[75] And urban support of rural access was a relatively uncontroversial part of the system.[76] "[T]here was some measure of 'cross subsidization' performed under the regulatory umbrella of the ICC ... with more lucrative, denser traffic lanes paying a premium above marginal costs to subsidize rural and small community service."[77]

Congress continued its pattern of intervention with the Civil Aeronautics Act of 1938 (CAA).[78] In advocating the legislation's passage, aviator Colonel Edgar Gorrell, one of the law's most ardent advocates, argued in testimony before Congress that smaller airlines required protection against stronger, larger lines.[79] He contended that by "reaching out into the regions of light-density traffic and developing smaller communities, the small lines have performed an incalculable service to the country."[80] To keep providing that service, they needed assurance through "an opportunity to protect themselves against even the possibility of oppressive competition."[81] The CAA was passed, and "entry regulation was imposed upon the infant airline industry, in part, so that small communities would have access to this emerging mode of transport."[82]

Congress once again continued on the path of intervention with the Transportation Act of 1940.[83] This was the first federal effort to craft a comprehensive national transportation policy,[84] and the first time "a national transportation policy governing all agencies subject to the Interstate Commerce act [sic] ha[d] been enacted."[85] Its "chief feature" was "further extension of unified and centralized control of domestic transportation," including the addition of water carriers to the ICC's purview, setting additional rates and permit requirements, and establishing a Board of Investigation and Research to study each mode of transportation.[86] Overall, transportation policies culminating with the 1940 Act

---

[74] Paul Stephen Dempsey, *Interstate Trucking: The Collision of Textbook Theory and Empirical Reality*, 20 TRANSP. L. J. 185, 187 (1992).

[75] *Id.*

[76] *Cf. id.* (describing how a half century later, the system would be perceived as "wasteful and hateful").

[77] *Id.*

[78] Civil Aeronautics Act of 1938, Pub. L. No. 75-706, 52 Stat. 973 (codified at 49 U.S.C. §§ 401-722).

[79] *Aviation: Hearing on H.R. 5234 and H.R. 4652 Before the H. Comm. on Interstate & Foreign Com.*, 75th Cong. 90 (1937) [hereinafter *Aviation Hearing*]; *see also* Paul Stephen Dempsey, *The Rise and Fall of the Civil Aeronautics Board – Opening Wide the Floodgates of Entry*, 11 TRANSP. L.J. 91 (1979).

[80] *Aviation Hearing*, *supra* note 79, at 90.

[81] *Id.*

[82] Dempsey, *supra* note 37, at 449; *see also* Dempsey, *supra* note 79, at 92–95 (discussing Congress's creation of the Civil Aeronautics Board and subsequent dismantling of it).

[83] Transportation Act of 1940, Pub. L. No. 76-785, 54 Stat. 898.

[84] *Id.*

[85] Ralph L. Dewey, *The Transportation Act of 1940*, 31 AM. ECON. REV. 15, 15 (1941).

[86] *Id.* at 16, 23.

"reflect[ed] a strong congressional policy that the public in rural areas be protected against pricing and service discrimination."[87]

As with transportation, regulatory policy of the era embraced the idea that geographically equitable access to telecommunications services was necessary. After the advent of the telephone in 1876, Alexander Graham Bell's use of his patented technology helped him establish the American Telephone and Telegraph Company (AT&T) in 1895, which initially had a monopoly.[88] With the expiration of the patents just after 1900, AT&T encountered competition from independent companies.[89] Theodore Vail, then-president of AT&T, "pressed for universal service and government regulation to curb what he saw as wasteful competition."[90] AT&T was then brought under the jurisdiction of the ICC with the Mann–Elkins Act of 1910, which amended the ICA.[91] The Act applied "to telegraph, telephone, and cable companies (whether wired or wireless) engaged in sending messages from one State, Territory, or District of the United States, to any other … who shall be considered and held to be common carriers."[92] It excluded from the Act "the transmission of messages by telephone, telegraph, or cable wholly within one State."[93] The Act provided that all charges made for "the transmission of messages by telegraph, telephone, or cable … shall be just and reasonable"[94] and that rates and charges for telegraph and telephone transmissions could not be "unjust or unreasonable or unjustly discriminatory."[95]

The Radio Acts of 1912 and 1927 also held major implications for rural access to telecommunications. The former placed radio communications under the jurisdiction of the ICC.[96] The latter created the Federal Radio Commission and established the standard that radio stations, in order to receive a license, needed to show that the "public interest, convenience, or necessity would be served by the granting" of the license.[97] In advocating passage of the Radio Act of 1927, Congressman Johnson of Texas commented that his rural constituents had requested that Congress intervene with anti-monopoly, antidiscrimination measures:

> The people of Texas are interested in legislation on this subject …. I want to quote from [a letter] which I received … from a farmer who lives in an inland rural community in my home country …. [T]he writer says:

---

[87] Dempsey, *supra* note 37, at 449.

[88] Paul Stephen Dempsey, *Adam Smith Assaults Ma Bell with His Invisible Hands: Divestiture, Deregulation, and the Need for a New Telecommunications Policy*, 11 HASTINGS COMMC'NS & ENT. L. J. 527, 531–32 (1989).

[89] *Id.* at 532.

[90] *Id.*

[91] Mann-Elkins Act, Pub. L. No. 61-218, sec. 7, § 1, 36 Stat. 539, 544–47 (1910).

[92] *Id.*; *see also* Dempsey, *supra* note 88, at 532.

[93] Mann-Elkins Act sec. 7, § 1.

[94] *Id.*

[95] Mann-Elkins Act § 15.

[96] Radio Act of 1912, Pub. L. No. 62-264, 37 Stat. 302.

[97] Radio Act of 1927, Pub. L. No. 69-632, § 11, 44 Stat. 1162, 1167.

["]Please use your influence in keeping corporations from getting control of the air by a series of chain stations, high-power stations, purchase of wave lengths, or any other monopoly that would create further disturbances which will interfere with our listening in on other closer-in stations. The combination of the eight large stations in the northeast[] ... are very annoying to people in Texas."[98]

Congress subsequently enacted the Communications Act of 1934 and modeled it after the ICA.[99] As with the Transportation Act of the same period, rural interests were mixed, with some advocating protections and universal service and others arguing that small, independent rural service providers and their constituents would be better off left alone.[100]

Many rural communities were served by small, independent phone companies with just a few dozen to a few hundred customers.[101] Their representatives insisted that complying with additional federal regulations would impose costs on companies that were already struggling to survive and serve their constituents.[102] On the other hand, some remained concerned about rural access to quality radio communications, particularly since rural communities were disproportionately dependent on radio.[103] Texas Congressman Thomas Blanton, in advocating for protecting rural access to radio communications, argued, "every congressional district of the United States is entitled to a small local station, and I want to see every Congressman here have at least a small local station in his home town. The people are entitled to this."[104]

The Communications Act of 1934 created the Federal Communications Commission (FCC) and tasked it with ensuring "so far as possible, to all the people of the United States a rapid, efficient, Nation-wide, and world-wide wire and radio communication service with adequate facilities at reasonable charges."[105] Like the

---

[98] 67 CONG. REC. 5,558 (1926).

[99] *See* Dempsey, *supra* note 88, at 530, 533; Paul J. Larkin, Jr., *Turning Points in Telecommunications History*, 29 J. MARSHALL J. COMPUT. & INFO. L. 513, 530 (2012).

[100] *See* Dempsey, *supra* note 88, at 530, 533; Larkin, *supra* note 99, at 530.

[101] *See Federal Communications Commission: Hearing on S. 2910 Before the S. Comm. on Interstate Com.*, 73d Cong. 184 (1934) (mentioning existence of thousands of "little telephone companies, cooperative lines, and farmer lines" which would be challenged to comply with new federal requirements).

[102] *See, e.g., Federal Communications Commission: Hearing on H.R. 8301 Before the H. Comm. on Interstate & Foreign Com.*, 73d Cong. 273 (1934).

[103] *See* 75 CONG. REC. 3,698–99 (1932). One reason for the Act involved opposition to the Federal Radio Commission. Congressman Sirovich characterized it as "autocratic and tyrannical," and claimed that they had "ridden ruthlessly over the small stations of the country." *Id.* at 3,699. He proposed "to stop their nefarious conduct" by abolishing the Commission and transferring their work to the Department of Commerce. *Id.*

[104] *Id.* at 3698.

[105] Communications Act of 1934, Pub. L. No. 73-416, § 1, 48 Stat. 1064, 1064 (codified as amended at 47 U.S.C. § 151); *see also* Larkin, *supra* note 99, at 530. Electrification was also a concern. In the early 1930s, 90 percent of city dwellers and only 10 percent of rural residents had access to reliable electricity. To bridge this gap, the Roosevelt administration pushed the Rural Electrification Act (REA) of 1936 through Congress. Debra C. Jeter et al., *Democracy and Dysfunction: Rural Electric Cooperatives and the Surprising Persistence of the Separation of Ownership and Control*, 70 ALA. L. REV. 361, 365 (2018).

MCA, it seemed to try to reconcile competing rural interests. The Act specifically excluded from its purview any intrastate communications or any wire communications already regulated by a state commission.[106] This would have excluded small, independent, locally focused telephone companies. But the Act's mandate for universal service was broad, meaning that those rural communities without service would be able to receive it under the Act, which provided:

> It shall be the duty of every common carrier engaged in interstate or foreign communication by wire or radio to furnish such communication service upon reasonable request therefor; and, in accordance with the orders of the Commission, in cases where the Commission, after opportunity for hearing, finds such action necessary or desirable in the public interest, to establish physical connections with other carriers, to establish through routes and charges applicable thereto and the divisions of such charges, and to establish and provide facilities and regulations for operating such through routes.[107]

The Act required that charges for services be "just and reasonable" and prohibited common carriers from making "any unjust or unreasonable discrimination."[108] Its goal of achieving universal service meant that "subscribers in rural, isolated and high-cost areas ... should have access to services at comparable rates to those available in urban areas."[109]

The tensions surrounding telecommunications service provision, access, and pricing mirrored those surrounding transportation.[110] In the 1950s, telephone

---

[106] Communications Act §§ 2(b), 3(e).

[107] Communications Act § 201 (a).

[108] Communications Act §§ 201(b), 202(a).

[109] Nadine Irène Kozak, On the Last Mile: The Effects of Telecommunications Regulation and Deregulation in the Rural Western United States and Canada 18 (2010) (Ph.D. dissertation, University of California San Diego) (on file with the University of California eScholarship).

[110] FCC Commissioner Craven gave a particularly passionate argument in favor of increased protections for rural access to radio in a 1942 House hearing to consider amendments in the Communications Act of 1934:

> the proposed bill suggests correctly that the distribution of radio broadcasting facilities remains a problem .... [I]t is unthinkable that any section of the Nation's population should be deprived of radio service or that we should willingly permit a degradation of existing service to any area .... [T]he forcing of unsound competition in the field of radio will nullify the directions of Congress to distribute radio broadcasting facilities fairly and equitably among the various States and communities. Moreover, the forced application of the doctrine of unlimited economic competition will result in a further concentration of competitive stations in the large cities and a dearth of facilities in the smaller communities throughout the Nation. Likewise, if too many stations are forced into the large cities, the net result will be impaired program service to the entire Nation .... with the consequence that rural radio listeners may be sacrificed for a regulatory theory in which the commercial aspects of radio broadcasting are overemphasized and the public service aspects are neglected .... The population residing in rural areas is entitled to receive as much improved radio service as people in cities. There should be no discrimination.

> *Proposed Changes in the Communications Act of 1934: Hearing on H.R. 5497 Before the H. Comm. on Interstate & Foreign Com.*, 77th Cong. 981–83 (1942).

companies requested rate increases, but were denied by the Public Utility Commissions that oversaw them, in part due to the public policy objective of universal service.[111] Instead of increasing rates, agencies developed a policy of subsidizing local rates by making long-distance rates more expensive, thereby making local rates more affordable for average users.[112] This meant that "the generous profits earned on heavily trafficked, densely populated (urban) routes subsidized less profitable, thin (rural) markets."[113] This substantial revenue-shifting system persisted for several decades. As late as 1983, "the average monthly price charged for local residential service was about $11, while the average monthly cost of providing the service was approximately $26."[114]

Although perhaps less profitable for the service providers, these approaches were effective. Telephone access went from 40 percent of U.S. households in 1930 to more than 90 percent in 1970.[115] Rural access to radio, alongside the rural electrification pursued in the same era, is credited with modernizing the American countryside. Like transportation, affordable access to telecommunications is an essential part of economic vitality.[116] Specifically, "the availability of telecommunication services reduces isolation, increases business viability, improves farming productivity, and improves access to educational and medical services."[117] The availability of quality telecommunications infrastructure can help rural communities attract other resources and thrive, while on the flip side, the absence of effective telecommunications may doom a region to economic stagnation.[118]

In general, the regulatory approach for public utilities in this era sought to reduce competition for several reasons. Certain service providers were deemed to have natural monopolies, or markets where high costs of entry would result in "economic waste" if competition were allowed by making customers pay multiple times for fixed costs of infrastructure, such as stringing telephone wires.[119] Thus, policymakers actively advocated for barriers to entry and unification of services in order to allow the service provider in question to achieve an economy of scale.[120] But the question

---

[111] Dempsey, *supra* note 88, at 534.

[112] *Id.* at 535.

[113] *Id.*

[114] *Id.*

[115] *Id.* at 535–36; *US Household Penetration of Telecommunications, 1920–2015, in* JEAN-PAUL RODRIGUE, THE GEOGRAPHY OF TRANSPORT SYSTEMS (5th ed. 2020), https://transportgeography .org/?page_id=1706 [https://perma.cc/C5YY-QASX].

[116] *See* Peter L. Stenberg et al., *Rural Areas in the New Telecommunications Era*, 12 RURAL DEV. PERSPS. 32 (1997); Steve Craig, *"The More They Listen, the More They Buy": Radio and the Modernizing of Rural America, 1930–1939*, 80 AGRIC. HIST. 1, 2 (2006) ("As radio helped dispel rural isolation, it also served to convey and reinforce the notion of a single, American national identity.")

[117] Stenberg et al., *supra* note 116, at 32.

[118] *Cf.* UTAH COAL COUNTRY STRIKE FORCE, EXECUTIVE SUMMARY 5, 7 (2019) (identifying high-quality regional broadband as economic asset that can be used to pursue large-scale revitalization).

[119] Dempsey, *supra* note 88, at 536.

[120] *Id.* at 536–37.

of rural access also revealed that competition needed to be curtailed for another reason. If small, independent rural service providers – like telephone companies, radio stations, and truck companies – were forced to compete with large corporate companies, the rural service providers were going to lose, which would also likely mean a drop in quality of service to rural communities. Further, if competition remained unfettered, more rural communities risked not being served at all.

From the passage of the ICA through the 1940s, the regulatory frameworks that governed the transportation and telecommunications industries served the goal of securing, enhancing, or protecting rural service in four main ways. First, those frameworks removed barriers from rural access to services by forcing companies to be responsive to rural service requests through principles of nondiscrimination.[121] Second, they protected existing rural services by excluding or protecting small, independent, intrastate service providers from regulation and by protecting existing providers from competition so they could achieve economies of scale.[122] Third, they limited service providers' ability to abandon rural service by requiring administrative justifications to do so and by refusing requests if those justifications did not comport with public interest standards.[123] And fourth, they helped make rural services affordable through measures such as subsidizing rural rates with profits from less expensive regions and by imposing the "just and reasonable" standard for rates.[124]

---

[121] The ICA, the MCA, the Telecommunications Act, and other major statutes included explicit mandates to this effect. Telecommunications Act of 1996, Pub. L. No. 104-104, § 104, 110 Stat. 56, 86; Motor Carrier Act of 1935, Pub. L. No. 74-255, § 202(a), 49 Stat. 543, 543; Interstate Commerce Act of 1887, Pub. L. No. 49-104, § 2, 24 Stat. 379, 379–80.

[122] For example, small, local phone lines were excluded from telephone regulations; small, independent radio stations were given special treatment; and small, independent truckers were excluded from trucking regulations in order not to burden rural communities. *See* Communications Act of 1934, Pub. L. No. 73-416, § 2(b), 48 Stat. 1064, 1065 ("[N]othing in this Act shall be construed to apply or to give the Commission jurisdiction with respect to … intrastate communication service of any carrier."); Communications Act § 221(b) (excepting from Act any services or facilities "where such matters are subject to regulation by a State commission or by local governmental authority"); Communications Act § 307(b) (allowing Federal Communications Commission to issue special radio licenses for stations not exceeding 100 watts of power if deemed necessary); Motor Carrier Act § 203(a)(21)(b) (excluding various kinds of motor vehicles from statute's purview, including those controlled and operated by farmers to transport products to and from their farms, those used exclusively to carry livestock, fish, or agricultural commodities, and "casual, occasional, or reciprocal transportation of passengers or property"). Otherwise, natural monopolies, like phone service provision, were protected from competition by utility regulations. Communications Act § 214(a) ("No carrier shall undertake the construction of a new line or of an extension of any line … unless and until there shall first have been obtained from the Commission a certificate that the present or future public convenience and necessity require or will require … such additional or extended line"); *see also id.* (excluding from provision any "local, branch, or terminal lines not exceeding ten miles in length").

[123] Many service providers, like railroad and airline services, sought to abandon service to rural communities over the years, but their requests were denied by state and federal agencies based on the likely effects to rural communities. Dempsey, *supra* note 37, at 450–55.

[124] Communications Act §§ 201(b), 202(a); Joseph D. Kearney & Thomas W. Merrill, *The Great Transformation of Regulated Industries Law*, 98 COLUM. L. REV. 1323, 1346–47 (1998).

Altogether, these protections created a framework that had a substantial impact in helping rural communities overcome the handicap of the diseconomies of scale that naturally arise with distance and population sparseness. As Sitaraman, Ricks, and Serkin observe, this regulatory order "promoted geographic dispersion in economic activity ... [and] helped construct an era of geographic convergence in the mid-twentieth century."[125] While regional wealth today tends to be concentrated in a handful of megacities, during this regulatory period, more wealth moved across geographic boundaries. This distributional geographic equity was in large part due to the efficacy of the regulatory apparatus in evening the playing field for disadvantaged localities that would have otherwise been what they are seen as today – "left behind."[126]

Of course, regulated industries mandated to provide nondiscriminatory access and fair rates to rural communities did not create rural utopias. Rural America was already transforming in the early twentieth century.[127] Agricultural economics were changing; populations fluctuated.[128] Economic regulation of infrastructure industries was not the only policy affecting rural communities. But as Chapter 5 shows, the transition to deregulating certain common carriers and public utilities inflicted a deep wound on rural communities – one that was easy to overlook from the vantage of the city, and one that made it all the harder for rural communities to recover from other shocks they would experience in the coming decades. In any event, given that this legal framework very much helped to sustain rural regions for decades, highlighting its longevity and efficacy casts doubt on the idea that rural communities are "unsustainable."

HOW THE REA FITS IN

Senator George W. Morris of Nebraska did not believe that rural communities were unsustainable just because they needed some help to access infrastructure everyone else enjoyed. By the 1930s, Senator Norris "had gained somewhat of a national reputation of being for the underdog and of trying to right the wrongs of those who had suffered."[129] Norris saw farmers – the stand-in for rural residents in those days – as among those underdogs. He believed that substantial public expenditures were worthwhile to bring the farmer "the comforts and happiness" of electrification, while also remedying the international embarrassment of other countries' superior

---

[125] Ganesh Sitaraman et al., *Regulation and the Geography of Inequality*, 70 DUKE L. J. 1763, 1767–68 (2021).

[126] *Id.* at 1765.

[127] Brian Thiede & Tim Slack, *The Old Versus the New Economies and Their Impacts*, in RURAL POVERTY IN THE UNITED STATES 231, 232 (Ann Tickamyer et al. eds., 2017) (noting nation was transformed in late nineteenth and early twentieth centuries by Industrial Revolution and urbanization, moving country from majority-agrarian-rural to majority-urban for first time in 1920).

[128] Harry K. Schwarzweller, *Migration and the Changing Rural Scene*, 44 RURAL SOCIO. 7 (1979).

[129] RICHARD LOWITT, GEORGE W. NORRIS: THE TRIUMPH OF A PROGRESSIVE, 1933–1944, at 6 (1978).

progress on electrifying their respective rural regions.[130] He also believed that securing "comforts and happiness" for those "down and out" could be reconciled with the non-wasteful and strategic deployment of resources and the creative structuring of public financing for rural electrification.

Senator Norris recognized market supremacy as the enemy of the rural underdog. In one instance, his colleagues in the Senate wanted to know whether there was even demand in rural regions for electricity. Many farmers, another senator pointed out, had the option to electrify their homes but had not yet done so.[131] Norris explained that electricity had been too expensive for those nonusers, and that nonuse was not a reflection of a lack of interest. "The rates charged were outrageous, so that a farmer could afford to buy but a very small amount. That is the reason why the electrification of farm homes by private utilities in the past 10 years," he said in 1936, "has been practically a failure."[132]

Norris also rejected the idea that the private sector stood to be an effective player in the REA's structure, in light of private utilities' longstanding failure to electrify the countryside. Another senator asked whether the REA might extend its low-interest loans to these private companies so that "they could extend their transmission lines into areas that are not now being furnished with electric energy."[133] Norris was strongly opposed. He replied:

> [J]udging from my experience and, I think, from the experience of the country, the big power systems which have been holding up rural electrification ever since they had a grip on the country are in no position now to come to the Government of the United States and ask it to loan them money at 3 percent to go into investments for the purpose of making some more money.
>
> It is not the idea that any of these organizations will make a dollar. I would not be here advocating this bill if that were the purpose. It is not to enable anyone to make money out of these public funds, but to get the benefit of electricity and its comforts to people who do not now have those benefits. There is not going to be any profit making out of this.[134]

But Norris also understood that scale and efficiency were worthwhile aims, which could be achieved with the right strategies. He and the other drafters of the REA designed it so that systems of distribution of electricity would be "self-liquidating," meaning loans would earn back their original cost.[135] Cooperative organizations

---

[130] *Id.* at 128–29; 80 CONG. REC. 2819 (1936) ("It is fair on the subject generally of rural electrification to say that the United States is far behind other countries similarly situated.").

[131] 80 CONG. REC. 2822 (1936) ("Is the Senator aware of the fact … that there are today in the United States lines carrying electricity to rural areas, and that only one out of every four of the farmers contiguous to those lines was using electricity and had electrified his home?").

[132] *Id.*

[133] 80 CONG. REC. 2826 (1936).

[134] *Id.*

[135] 80 CONG. REC. 2755 (1936).

of farmers would incorporate themselves under state law. But they needed to be "sufficient in number and covering enough compact territory to make a system of distribution of electricity self-liquidating."[136] They would buy their power whole-sale, "either from a publicly owned plant in the vicinity or from a privately owned plant in the vicinity."[137]

Norris noted that "when most persons think of a rural state, they think first of the density of population."[138] But the structure of the REA, he explained, meant that "the density of population is not a controlling feature."[139] Density did not necessarily mean that a project would be self-liquidating because it did not guarantee adequate levels of consumption. The Rural Electrification Administration, the agency that implemented the REA, would "never loan any money until they are satisfied that a proposition is self-liquidating,"[140] he reassured other senators.

Norris proposed that farmers would consume high levels of electricity and would, therefore, make the projects worthwhile. "One farm that has all kinds of equipment in the house and all kinds of equipment in the barn ... is a great deal better cus-tomer than one that takes only light. If none of them took anything but light, it is very doubtful whether we could ever make this plan work."[141] But in any case, Norris argued, use mattered more than volume or density of users: "[A] few customers tak-ing a great deal of electricity are worth much more than many customers taking only a little electricity each."[142]

He acknowledged, "It would not be good business to build a generating system for a single farmers' organization. The expense in such a case would be too high, so that it would not be a self-liquidating proposition."[143] Addressing the skeptics, he acknowl-edged, "The question might justifiably be asked whether under the provisions of the bill it would not be possible to loan money to every little farm organization to build a gen-erating system, which might bring about the ruin of the project."[144] The REA, Norris explained, would mostly serve to build out transmission lines from existing generat-ing stations. But to remove authorization for construction of generating systems might "interfere with the establishment of some systems which would be a great success."[145]

Norris's advocacy of the REA thus also demanded that his colleagues in the Senate open their minds. When the bill was under consideration, he

---

[136] *Id.*

[137] 80 CONG. REC. 2820 (1936).

[138] *Id.*

[139] *Id.*

[140] *Id.*

[141] *Id.*

[142] *Id.*

[143] 80 CONG. REC. 2756 (1936). In another instance, he said, "[I]t would not be practicable to construct a farm line somewhere and build a generating plant for it; that would cost too much. A generating plant, to be efficient, would have to be sufficiently large to supply a number of farm lines."

[144] *Id.*

[145] *Id.*

acknowledged, "We have no real precedent in our country for what we propose to do, and to some extent, we are going without precedent."[146] Referring to farmer cooperatives buying their electricity wholesale, a colleague asked Norris whether he had "any illustrations showing the practicability of that sort of thing under the present act and under the present administration." Norris replied, "No; I have not in mind any concrete case."[147]

Norris also recognized that both universalism and variability could be achieved through the right strategic structure. He explained that the Rural Electrification Administration was already working in every state, "and in doing so they do not find any two States which are exactly alike."[148] He therefore insisted that the REA needed to be left vague in some respects in order to not limit the possibilities of its impacts.

The REA's impacts – problems with which are discussed in more depth in Chapter 7 – have been profound and long-lasting. The REA's authorization of low-interest, long-term, federal loans to Rural Electric Cooperatives (RECs or Cooperatives) transformed the American countryside:

> Today, these Cooperatives are still critical to the process of supplying electricity to rural consumers because they primarily serve sparsely-populated areas, which many [Investor-Owned-Utilities] have historically considered unprofitable and are thus hesitant to serve. Without RECs, consumers in these rural areas could face higher electricity rates or have to do without power altogether.[149]

As of 2019, "rural electric cooperatives provide[d] electric power to forty-two million people in over twenty million residences, businesses, farms, and schools across forty-eight states … [and] own approximately 40% (over two million miles) of the nation's electric distribution lines."[150]

The REA's unique structure and ambitions are illustrative for a variety of purposes. First, the question underlying the prospect of such investments once again emerges: What are the practical and ethical drivers of how laws, policies, and institutions distribute resources across landscapes and populations? In this instance, Norris and his allies saw rural electrification as the obligation of government. The Senate at the time recognized the public's need for public investment in public goods – and the effort succeeded in large part by one senator's insistence against the primacy of corporate profit.

---

[146] 80 CONG. REC. 2750 (1936). He later said again, "There is not any guide or precedent established that we can follow except perhaps the meager information we have from rural electrification organizations which have been set up and are doing business, and have been for several years, in different parts of the United States." *Id.* at 2753–54.

[147] 80 CONG. REC. 2820 (1936).

[148] 80 CONG. REC. 2826 (1936).

[149] Zachary Brecheisen, *Green Acres: How Bringing Pennsylvania Rural Electric Cooperatives under the Full Provisions of the Alternative Energy Portfolio Standard Can Boost Renewable Energy Growth in Pennsylvania*, 19 PENN ST. ENV'T L. REV. 333, 337 (2011).

[150] Alexandra B. Klass & Gabriel Chan, *Cooperative Clean Energy*, 100 N.C. L. REV. 1, 12 (2021).

The REA shows how public investments can pursue efficiency goals without abandoning these ethical obligations. The REA held communities accountable. It was not mere charity, and its benefits were not bestowed randomly on passive actors with no skin in the game. Rural cooperatives had to take responsibility for securing the REA's benefits and managing them. That community accountability helped ensure the REA's efficacy not only by making the communities responsible for their loans but also by helping the REA be implemented in the fashion necessary for each unique locality.

Skeptics of rural interventions are often concerned about un-strategic policies haphazardly and wastefully trying to "save" every distressed or underserved rural area. The REA, much like other rural investment policies, such as the Department of Housing and Urban Development (HUD)'s Community Development Block Grants, provides a model for interventions that are federally supported but community driven. Major federal investments can provide communities the tools to thrive. Communities, in turn, can do their part to take those tools and use them in context. RECs' staying power seems to suggest something about the "sustainability" of such investments, and about population-sparse communities' willingness to put in the effort to sustain themselves if the right tools are made available. This model, in turn, raises questions about community capacity and the tools needed to actually leverage the other tools. Chapter 8 explores these questions in more depth.

5

The Myth of Rural Decline

In 2018, economics reporter Eduardo Porter penned a *New York Times* op-ed entitled "The Hard Truths of Trying to 'Save' the Rural Economy."[1] Porter wrote pessimistically, "One thing seems clear to me: nobody – not experts or policymakers or people in these communities – seems to know quite how to pick rural America up."[2]

Porter is not alone in thinking about rural communities this way. Economist David Swenson makes a similar point in a 2020 piece in *The Conversation*. Referring to candidates for President, he says, "[W]hat to do about rural economic and persistent population decline is the one area that has always confounded them all."[3] He continues, "The facts are clear and unarguable. Most of the nation's smaller urban and rural counties are not growing and will not grow .... Academics are good at isolating the causes and the consequences of rural decline, but we have yet to figure out what to do about it."[4] Swenson's piece links to a 2019 *New York Times* essay by columnist and economist Paul Krugman, entitled "Getting Real about Rural America: Nobody Knows How to Reverse the Heartland's Decline," in which he also describes southern Italy as "backward."[5]

Porter, Swenson, Krugman, and many others attribute diminishing rural prosperity to rural "decline." Population decline – and its associated decline in jobs and infrastructure – they propose, stems from changes in automation, other

---

[1] Portions of this chapter were excerpted from Ann M. Eisenberg, *Distributive Justice and Rural America*, 61 B.C. L. Rev. 189 (2020) [hereinafter Eisenberg, *Distributive Justice*], *Economic Regulation and Rural America*, 98 Wash. U. L. Rev. 737 (2021) [hereinafter Eisenberg, *Economic Regulation*], and *Rural Disaffection and the Regulatory State*, 126 Penn State L. Rev. 739 (2022) [hereinafter Eisenberg, *Rural Disaffection*].

[2] Eduardo Porter, *The Hard Truths of Trying to 'Save' the Rural Economy*, N.Y. Times (Dec. 14, 2018), www.nytimes.com/interactive/2018/12/14/opinion/rural-america-trump-decline.html.

[3] David Swenson, *Most of America's Rural Areas Are Doomed to Decline*, The Conversation (May 7, 2019), https://theconversation.com/most-of-americas-rural-areas-are-doomed-to-decline-115343 [https://perma.cc/LH7D-FPXX].

[4] *Id.*

[5] Paul Krugman, *Getting Real about Rural America: Nobody Knows How to Reverse the Heartland's Decline*, N.Y. Times (March 18, 2019), www.nytimes.com/2019/03/18/opinion/rural-america-economic-decline.html [https://perma.cc/877B-533M].

technological advances, and outsourcing. According to this line of thinking, rural communities have *declined*, from causes that are framed as inexorable tidal waves. Forces of nature. As such, we as a society lack any agency to do anything about them.

Of course, these economists' views on rural obsolescence and hopelessness are shaped by some unspoken assumptions. They assume that automation and technological advances mean that a reduced regional workforce automatically and naturally follows and that such a reduced workforce is morally neutral. They assume outsourcing and liberalized trade are facts of life now, and are both morally neutral and permanent. They assume not to question the modern landscape of consolidated, industrialized agriculture as the status quo. So the problem becomes a relatively narrow one. Rural America is dying a mysterious death and there seems to be no cure. So the response becomes a question of how to react and adjust to these static conditions. Or how to best mourn and grieve. Perhaps most egregiously, they assume, with certainty, that *every intellectual discipline and all non-academics* lack a solution or a vision for making life more balanced, sustainable, and prosperous outside major urban centers.

Yet, if we listen to views like these – and it's hard not to, given their prominence in national discourse – we are bound to get the story wrong. Centrally, I take issue with the word "decline." If someone poisoned your friend John, you wouldn't say, "John's health declined." The search for solutions requires a search for accountability, not merely the categorization of forces of nature. Collecting on the debts owed across the country necessitates asking who poisoned John, how, and why.

The myth of rural decline allows those who helped drive the decline to be absolved of their responsibility. These half-stories hurt rural communities by indirectly suggesting that rural marginalization is natural and inevitable, self-driven by rural backwardness somehow, precluding more meaningful discussions of better approaches. Rural regions' prospects are also hurt by a lack of imagination, just as Senator Norris recognized when he proposed a novel financing scheme for rural electrification. An imagined "multiverse" has proliferated over the past several years in popular culture, TV shows, movies, and books. The multiverse refers to the idea that there are infinite parallel universes or alternate timelines where slight changes or different outcomes lead to massive butterfly effects. I suspect our collective imaginary's preoccupation with contemplating the multiverse stems from our sense that things in the world have gone horribly wrong. We would like to believe that different decisions would have taken humanity down a better path.

It is helpful to think about the path not taken in rural communities – the policy that could have been but never was, or the law that might never have been passed if things had worked out differently. Imagining a different timeline reveals different possibilities that could have shaped our past. But it can also reveal different possibilities for the future. The people who can tell us what the parallel universe might have looked like include the populations, workers, and protesters who desperately resisted subjugation, demanding an alternative future. Yet, those rural resisters have often fought only to have their movements crushed and driven out by the demands of market supremacy – the political–economic system that advantages the most power-ful corporations and their insatiable lust for extraction. This is so often the true story of rural "decline," the intentionality and cruelty of which remains largely invisible to urban consumers.

HOW FEDERAL AND STATE LAW AND POLICY HAVE UNDERMINED RURAL LIVELIHOODS

The discussion now turns to the law and policy frameworks that have shaped three key economic sectors that once helped sustain rural life: agriculture, natural resource extraction, and manufacturing. I argue that an examination of the evolu-tion of these frameworks can help fill in the picture of who poisoned John, how, and why. In other words, the following attempts to complicate the "decline" narrative by showing how decision-makers in federal and state institutions actively undermined rural welfare, often in the face of social resistance, often knowing what the negative consequences would likely be for rural life. Or, when the negative consequences of those decisions became more apparent, decision-makers failed to take adequate action in response.

The discussion ultimately demonstrates how utilitarian thought embodied in decision-making processes effectuated a grand sacrifice of rural communities in the name of other priorities – complicating the idea of rural "decline." Rural communi-ties have not so much "declined" as they have been traded for other things perceived as more valuable.

For each of those three sectors, this discussion highlights (1) major legal devel-opments of the past several decades; (2) how those legal developments imposed or overlooked concentrated economic losses and reduced opportunities that burdened rural people and places; and (3) how these policies that undermined rural welfare were rationalized by service to "the greater good," yet did not result in gains for soci-ety's most vulnerable or adequate mitigation for the affected communities.

This sacrifice was justified rhetorically by the pursuit of aggregate welfare. Policymakers often insisted that what they were doing was better for everyone. Concerning each of the respective sectors discussed, promises were made about cheap and abundant food, cheap or clean energy, a higher GDP, and better access to cheap goods. But in practice, these decisions were often most aggressively pursued in service of market supremacy, or a vision of "efficiency" that, in fact, advantaged the most powerful market participants. Aggregate welfare has thus consistently been framed in terms of efficiency, productivity, and liberated markets. In other words, market supremacy has been framed as the *same* as aggregate welfare – with an indif-ferent eye turned away from the profound losses imposed on discrete populations, in addition to overinflated claims of benefits to the public. In any event, the following account suggests that rural communities "declined" just as much as policymakers were willing to sacrifice, undermine, and neglect their livelihoods.

FACILITATING CONSOLIDATED, INDUSTRIALIZED AGRICULTURE
IN THE NAME OF A MARKET-SUPREMACIST "GREATER GOOD"

Even if the traditional small farm has never been the romanticized version seen on TV, commentators focusing on the nexus of the agricultural sector's evolution and community economic development tend to agree on one thing: Farm consolidation and industrialization from the mid twentieth century to the present has not been a positive development for farming communities as a whole.[6] What's more, the consolidation and industrialization of twentieth-century agriculture was not a passive, inevitable phenomenon. Rather, these trends have been facilitated and supported by a diverse set of catalysts in law and policy, often linked to rhetoric about efficiency and productivity.

The 1933 Agricultural Adjustment Act (the first "Farm Bill") started the wheels turning toward dramatic farm consolidation over the next ninety years – tilting the scale in favor of large agribusiness.[7] The Farm Bill has been renewed every five years

---

[6] Mary Jane Angelo, *Corn, Carbon, and Conservation: Rethinking U.S. Agricultural Policy in a Changing Global Environment*, 17 GEO. MASON L. REV. 593, 602 (2010) (explaining that "[f]rom an economic and social standpoint, nonlabor intensive industrial agriculture has led to fewer farmers producing the vast majority of crops, the virtual disappearance of the traditional family farm, high-risk working and living conditions for farm laborers, increased production costs; and a decline of economic and social conditions in rural communities"); Jonathan W. Coppess, *High Cotton and the Low Road: An Unraveling Farm Bill Coalition and Its Implications*, 23 DRAKE J. AGRIC. L. 353, 370 (2018) (noting a complex set of shifts in farm consolidation as the most notable development since the last major farm economic crisis in 1980s); Neil D. Hamilton, *Harvesting the Law: Personal Reflections on Thirty Years of Change in Agricultural Legislation*, 46 CREIGHTON L. REV. 563, 567 (2013) [hereinafter Hamilton, *Harvesting the Law*] (describing the "Big Ag" period stemming from the 1980s to the present, with some present-day evolution toward food localism, as with Community-Supported Agriculture programs); Neil D. Hamilton, *Myth Making in the Heartland – Did Agriculture Elect the New President?*, 13 J. FOOD L. & POL'Y 5, 10 (2017) [hereinafter Hamilton, *Myth Making*] (discussing how "structural shifts – in land tenure, farm consolidation and livestock production – are often facilitated by public programs such as farm income support, crop insurance, the RFS, and farm lending practices"); Bekah Mandell, *Feasts of Oz: Class, Food, and the Rise of Global Capitalism*, 20 S. CAL. INTERDISC. L.J. 93, 101 (2010); (observing that the U.S. Department of Agriculture Secretary Butz's focus "on the mechanization, industrialization, and commoditization of agriculture required larger investments in capital than traditional farming" and that "[t]he increasing need to invest heavily in equipment, fertilizers, pesticides, and herbicides in order to stay competitive meant that only farmers with access to capital could remain competitive under the new system"); Christopher D. Merrett & Cynthia Struthers, *Globalization and the Future of Rural Communities in the American Midwest*, 12 TRANSNAT'L L. & CONTEMP. PROBS. 33, 36 (2002); Nathan A. Rosenberg & Bryce Wilson Stucki, *The Butz Stops Here: Why the Food Movement Needs to Rethink Agricultural History*, 13 J. FOOD L.& POL'Y 12, 13 (2017).

[7] Rosenberg & Stucki, *supra* note 6, at 14; Erin Morrow, *Agri-Environmentalism: A Farm Bill for 2007*, 38 TEX. TECH L. REV. 345, 369 (2006). Morrow notes,

> The farm bill does not subsidize all farmers. Farm bill provisions provide little assistance for or entirely exclude many fanners, crops, regions, and even entire industries within agriculture. Meanwhile, corporate agriculture receives the bulk of farm bill funds, putting additional pressure on farm policy intended to preserve small family farms. The farm bill, in an arbitrary case of line-drawing, focuses on a few commodity crops.

Morrow, *supra* note 7, at 369–70.

since its enactment.[8] Although initially intended as a modest intervention into crop markets, the Farm Bill is now entangled with nearly all aspects of rural community development.

For years, critics have argued that the Farm Bill serves to subsidize expansion of mega farms that put family farmers out of business.[9] Even in early Farm Bills, "farmers, tenants, and sharecroppers were 'shoved aside in the rush toward bigger units, more tractors, and less men per acre,'" reducing the number of farmers of all races by approximately one-third by 1945.[10] By 1970, 90 percent of Black farmers, who had primarily been located in the South, were forced out of their agricultural livelihoods and driven northward in the Great Migration in large part because the U.S. Department of Agriculture facilitated farm consolidation, mechanization, and various forms of discrimination, such as withholding loans.[11]

President Nixon's Secretary of Agriculture, Earl Butz, is often portrayed as the champion of modern farm consolidation, agricultural industrialization, and the high-volume cultivation of monoculture cash crops.[12] Others point out, though, that the programs associated with Butz – such as cutting production controls for corn or weakening supply management that helped control commodity prices and support farm livelihoods – in fact predate his time in office.[13] In any case, the 1970s saw continued federal support for agricultural industrialization and consolidation, which arguably became more mainstream during that era.

Then, the 1980s farm crisis brought a substantial turning point in the evolution of modern agriculture, during which institutions' manipulation of the farming sector cleaved deep wounds in the countryside. First, in the 1970s, the USDA, bankers, and

---

[8] JIM MONKE, CONG. RSCH. SERV., R45210, FARM BILLS: MAJOR LEGISLATIVE ACTIONS, 1965–2018, at 1 (2018).

[9] Daniel Imhoff, *Overhauling the Farm Bill: The Real Beneficiaries of Subsidies*, ATLANTIC (Mar. 21, 2012), www.theatlantic.com/health/archive/2012/03/overhauling-the-farm-bill-the-real-beneficiaries-of-subsidies/254422/ [https://perma.cc/LF6W-UTBC].

[10] Rosenberg & Stucki, *supra* note 6, at 15; *see also* Warren Whatley, *Labor for the Picking*, J. ECON. HIST. (DEC. 1983).

[11] Rosenberg & Stucki, *supra* note 6, at 15. Rosenberg and Stucki further explain:

> As the civil rights movement gathered steam, assaults on black farmers intensified. By the 1950s, "any program for small, poverty-ridden farmers in the South became entangled with the civil rights movement." The founder of the Citizens' Council drew up a plan to remove 200,000 African-Americans from Mississippi by 1966 through "the tractor, the mechanical cotton picker … and the decline of the small independent farmers." As government-funded mechanization continued apace, "tens of thousands" of poor farmers were forced out of agriculture …. Black farmers who held onto their land used their independence to support civil rights workers, which often made them targets for lynch mobs and local elites. Throughout the South, USDA agents withheld loans black farmers needed to operate – amid other discrimination – which continued after the Civil Rights Act. From 1959 to 1969, black farmers declined by over two thirds, almost triple the rate of white farmers.

> *Id.* at 16 (footnotes omitted).

[12] *See, e.g.*, Mandell, *supra* note 6, at 101.

[13] Rosenberg & Stucki, *supra* note 6, at 18.

university extension offices told farmers that they must either "get big or get out."[14] Because the rate of inflation was running higher than interest rates, institutional lenders, including government lenders like the Farm Home Administration (FmHA), advised farmers to borrow as much as possible to invest in farmland.[15]

By the 1980s, though, the bubble had burst. The Federal Reserve abruptly reversed course on its lending practices and dictated high interest rates on loans that the average small farmer simply could not repay.[16] This might not have destroyed so many small farms on its own, but coupled with reduced crop subsidies and increased competition from multinational food monopolies' domination of markets, small farmers were no longer positioned to survive.[17]

The fallout from the farm crisis was devastating and widespread. During the worst period between 1986 and 1987, almost one million Americans were displaced from their farms.[18] The years before and after that peak saw between 500,000 and 600,000 farm foreclosures.[19] From 1981 to 1988, "more farmers died from suicide than from any other unnatural cause."[20] Rates of alcoholism and domestic abuse also rose dramatically. Despite the rise in mental health issues among farmers spurred by the farm crisis, provisions for rural mental health services decreased during the same period.[21]

The farm crisis – which many rural residents blamed on public institutions such as the FmHA – reshaped middle-class rural communities, whose requests for federal help went unheeded.[22] In 1979, 5 percent of rural counties had an unemployment rate of over 9 percent.[23] In a mere five years, that rate ballooned: 50 percent of rural counties had unemployment rates exceeding 9 percent.[24]

As the rural farm town unraveled, it was simultaneously being transformed into something else: the staging site for industrialized agriculture. The number of farms in the United States dropped by two-thirds between 1935 and 2012, while the average farm size more than doubled.[25] The centrality of the Farm Bill, the FmHA, the

---

[14] JOEL DYER, HARVEST OF RAGE: WHY OKLAHOMA CITY IS ONLY THE BEGINNING 15 (1997).

[15] *Id.*

[16] *Id.* at 2, 15 (explaining how Federal Reserve Chairman Paul Volcker contributed to the 1980s farm crisis by raising interest rates to temper inflation, which had negative effects for farmers who had just borrowed substantial amounts to buy additional farmland).

[17] *Id.* at 2.

[18] *Id.* at 15. Rosenberg and Stucki point out, however, that earlier decades had seen substantial displacement of small farmers, but they came from more marginalized populations and, therefore, received less attention. Rosenberg & Stucki, *supra* note 6, at 19.

[19] DYER, *supra* note 14, at 15.

[20] *Id.* at 4.

[21] *Id.* at 5.

[22] *Id.* at 25 (discussing the Oklahoma governor's failed efforts to secure federal assistance to "investigate the actions of the farm lenders and provide additional money for rural mental health").

[23] *Id.* at 17.

[24] *Id.*

[25] Roberto A. Ferdman, *The Decline of the Small American Family Farm in One Chart*, WASH. POST (Sept. 16, 2014), www.washingtonpost.com/news/wonk/wp/2014/09/16/the-decline-of-the-small-american-family-farm-in-one-chart/ [https://perma.cc/SXB3-5U7H].

Federal Reserve, and other federal policies to these trends illustrates how public institutions facilitated the destruction of this longstanding way of life. Some commentators have even proposed that the events of the 1980s planted the seeds for anti-government militia movements among rural populations.[26]

States have also facilitated the rise of industrialized, consolidated agriculture. In particular, the proliferation of state right-to-farm laws over the past several decades has contributed to the dominance of agribusinesses over small farms and farming communities.[27] Right-to-farm laws limit nuisance suits involving agriculture.[28] Initially, the laws' stated rationale was to preserve farmland. To do so, they raised evidentiary burdens for bringing nuisance actions against farmers. Specifically, "many of the laws adopted a 'coming to the nuisance' concept whereby activities that were not a nuisance when commenced would not become a nuisance due to the changed land uses of neighbors."[29] Yet, since their inception, observers have lamented that right-to-farm laws "provide too much protection for agricultural pursuits and other activities at the expense of neighboring property owners."[30] Right-to-farm laws have evolved to serve as a legal shield of sorts for industrial agriculture, affording agribusiness an advantage in legal rights compared to neighbors.

The agribusiness industry's relationship with rural communities is problematic. Small, family-run farms are often economically challenging to run and are far from immune from ethical concerns such as poor conditions for farmworkers. Nonetheless, they are likelier to have more reciprocal relationships within communities.[31] The presence of more farms run by more diversified farmers provides more work opportunities, affords farmers more independence, supports families that have children in schools, and generally benefits the socioeconomic health of a community.[32] In other words, the relationship between small farms and their surrounding socioeconomic environments can be understood as symbiotic: Each feeds the other.

Large agribusiness operations, by contrast – almost all of which are owned by white men – have more parasitic, extractive relationships with their host communities.[33]

---

[26] *See, e.g.,* DYER, *supra* note 14, at 1–7. This theory has been tested empirically and yielded mixed, unclear results. *See* JOSHUA D. FREILICH, AMERICAN MILITIAS 110–23 (2003).

[27] *See generally* Loka Ashwood et al., *Property Rights and Rural Justice: A Study of U.S. Right-to-Farm Laws*, 67 J. OF RURAL STUD. 120 (2019).

[28] Terence J. Centner, *Governments and Unconstitutional Takings: When Do Right-to-Farm Laws Go Too Far?*, 33 B.C. ENVTL. AFF. L. REV. 87, 87 (2006)

[29] *Id.*

[30] *Id.* at 88.

[31] Bruce Weber & Kathleen Miller, *Poverty in Rural America Then and Now, in* RURAL POVERTY IN THE UNITED STATES 31 (Ann R. Tickamyer et al. eds., 2017).

[32] *See* Meredith Redlin & Brad Redlin, *Amendment E, Rural Communities and the Family Farm*, 49 S.D. L. REV. 787, 787, 792 (2004) (rural communities' viability and sustainability are connected to the form of agriculture that surrounds them). Communities with family farms have shown healthier local economies than those with large-scale corporate farms. *Id.*

[33] Rosenberg & Stucki, *supra* note 6, at 19.

They bring with them a "tide [of] adverse social, economic, and environmental impacts" that also reduce the small farmer's ability to compete. Eventually, the presence of agribusiness in a rural community has the effect of "replacing the independent farmer with disempowered sharecroppers and destroys the social fabric of towns."[34] As corporate landowners consolidate land, they also reduce the number of decision-makers contributing to community development, suffocating local autonomy.

Many defend the rise of consolidated, industrialized agriculture as necessary to scale agricultural production due to the supposed inefficiency of the small farm and agribusiness's "natural" market strength. In one sense, this theory confuses the chicken and the egg. It assumes that small farms have died off because they are naturally less able to compete. Small farms likely are less competitive in that sense, but publicly provided capital, subsidies, legal frameworks, and technological incentives have also heavily tilted the scale in favor of agribusiness.[35] It seems likely that the early twentieth-century model of U.S. agriculture – and its associated problems with poverty, economic precariousness, and racism – is not an ideal or sustainable model to return to. But it is also clear that modern agribusiness's extractive relationship with rural regions – in addition to the industry's failed promise to provide abundant, healthy, affordable food to "feed the world" without destroying the environment – raises serious concerns about equity and sustainability.[36]

The transformation of agriculture discussed here illustrates several points. First, this evolution involved public institutions making small, independent farmers worse off to the benefit of corporate farms. Farm families throughout the twentieth century – especially farmers of color, but also the vast majority of white farmers – bore a substantial and disproportionate economic loss compared to the rest of society. Governmental policies drove them off their land and out of the countryside to the benefit of industrialized agriculture. Certainly, some people willingly migrated to cities. But for the most part, agricultural policy has been detrimental to rural communities as a whole. The "decline" narrative fails to recognize legal institutions' role in redistributing the wealth and land of small farmers to large agribusinesses. These measures have often been justified in the name of cheaper food to "feed the world." But the main beneficiary seems to be corporate agriculture, lightly disguised under the veil of market efficiency and productivity.

---

[34] Randolph C. Canney, *Amendment E: A Personal Perspective on Defending Its Constitutionality*, 49 S.D. L. Rev. 777, 778 (2004).

[35] Rosenberg & Stucki, *supra* note 6, at 20–21; *see* Angelo, *supra* note 6, at 593 (quoting Michael Pollan, *Farmer in Chief*, N.Y. Times Mag. (Oct. 12, 2000), www.nytimes.com/2008/10/12/magazine/12policy-t.html [https://perma.cc/DA6U-E9NM]).

[36] *See* Neil D. Hamilton, *Moving Toward Food Democracy: Better Food, New Farmers, and the Myth of Feeding the World*, 16 Drake J. Agric. L. 117, 134 (2011).

A BRUTAL COAL EXTRACTION REGIME, AND ITS ABANDONMENT, IN THE NAME OF A MARKET-SUPREMACIST "GREATER GOOD"

Natural resource extraction was historically another major source of economic activity for rural communities. In recent decades, this sector has contracted, contributing to socioeconomic challenges for regions that depended on it.[37] Although extractive industries are diverse – including industries such as forestry, fishing, natural gas and oil drilling, and gold mining – the Appalachian experience with coal provides a clear illustration of how market supremacist policies made regional residents worse off and contributed to the conditions now understood as "decline." The issues seen in Appalachia are reflected in other rural communities, including coal communities elsewhere and rural communities reliant on other extractive industries.

The complicity of the state and federal legal apparatus in Appalachian problems, and the many benefits the country has reaped from Appalachian exploitation, speak to the burdens Appalachia has borne in the name of aggregate welfare, to the advantage of exploitative corporate actors. In his book, *Ramp Hollow*, historian Steven Stoll argues that the subjugation of Appalachia was neither an accident nor an unfortunate tragedy along the way to industrialization.[38] He characterizes the nineteenth-century "scramble for Appalachia" as embedded in "the idea that historical progress required taking land away from agrarians and giving it to others."[39]

Residents of Appalachia in the nineteenth century were mostly, but not uniformly, subsistence farmers of European descent. These agrarians – who contributed to displacement of the region's Indigenous population – often did not own the land they used for survival. Politicians living in the North and East owned the titles to large stretches of Appalachian land and, for a time, turned a blind eye to the tens of thousands of squatters that claimed adverse possession to subsections of those many acres.[40] Motivated by a burgeoning anti-"mountain people" sentiment, however, and supported by the courts, elite title holders were mostly able to evict residents from the land on which they had built homes, cultivated farms, and formed communities.[41]

Appalachians have since experienced consistently limited access to ownership interests in the land they worked and lived on or nearby to.[42] Even this

---

[37] *See generally* Eisenberg, *Distributive Justice, supra* note 1.
[38] *See generally* STEVEN STOLL, RAMP HOLLOW: THE ORDEAL OF APPALACHIA (2017).
[39] *Id.* at xiv–xv.
[40] *Id.* at 10 (explaining that "[a]s long as political elites pretended not to see the flaunting of private property and constitutional authority, they could continue to believe that the interests of the backwoods aligned with those of the nation-state").
[41] *Id.* at 9–16.
[42] *See, e.g.,* BETH SPENCE ET AL., W. VA. CTR. ON BUDGET & POL'Y, WHO OWNS WEST VIRGINIA? 7 (2013), https://d3n8a8pro7vhmx.cloudfront.net/wvcbp/pages/468/attachments/original/1511177697/land-study-paper-final3.pdf?1511177697 [https://perma.cc/4CAE-7KQJ].

early evolution bore environmental justice implications, as regional residents had already lost autonomy and the prospect of self-determination.[43] Some commentators continue to point to Appalachia's geographic isolation as an explanation for its persistent regional poverty.[44] But this isolation narrative discounts other key factors that have shaped Appalachian poverty, namely, this initial land dispossession and the subsequent arrival of extractive industries.[45]

Those regional residents who were able to acquire land remained vulnerable to the loss of another form of property: Mineral rights. The agents of nineteenth-century speculators in natural resources were "men of great guile and charm" who would take advantage of regional residents' limited literacy and access to information.[46] Due to this unequal bargaining power, regional residents' interests in their timber and minerals "were virtually given away."[47] With so much land and so many minerals owned by powerful out-of-state actors, the stage was thus set by the mid nineteenth century for a corporate takeover of Appalachia.[48]

Appalachian coal mining began in earnest in the nineteenth century. The state and federal legal apparatus, in turn, served to funnel local residents into the coal labor machine. Those systems gave the coal industry a mandate to pollute freely and deprived local residents of opportunities for redress.[49] The Battle of Blair Mountain in 1921 illustrates the federal government's role in facilitating the coal industry's domination. Coal miners, growing intolerant of inhumane working and living conditions, rose up against mine operators when their efforts to

---

[43] *Cf.* Brigham Daniels et al., *Just Environmentalism*, 37 YALE L. & POL'Y REV. 1, 64–65 (2018). The loss of autonomy like that seen in Appalachia is among the themes shaping rural environmental injustice. New Mexico, for example – currently considered the poorest state in the nation – experienced a similar land grab in the nineteenth century, when unscrupulous speculators used similar tactics to dispossess residents of their land. Ann M. Eisenberg, *Land Shark at the Door? Why and How States Should Regulate Landmen*, 27 FORDHAM ENVTL. L. REV. 157, 179 (2016). Parallels also exist with the experience of African-American farmers in the South and Native Americans removed by the U.S. government. The loss of control over land renders communities vulnerable to outsiders shaping the future of their land uses and socioeconomic development. *See generally* STOLL, *supra* note 38 (arguing that the enclosure of land and land dispossession are central to the history of capitalism and the rise of socioeconomic inequality).

[44] STOLL, *supra* note 38, at 17; Nicholas F. Stump & Anne Marie Lofaso, *De-Essentializing Appalachia: Transformative Socio-Legal Change Requires Unmasking Regional Myths*, 120 W. VA. L. REV. 823, 825–29 (2018).

[45] *See generally* STOLL, *supra* note 38.

[46] HARRY M. CAUDILL, NIGHT COMES TO THE CUMBERLANDS: A BIOGRAPHY OF A DEPRESSED AREA 63 (1963).

[47] *Id.* at 73–75; *see* STOLL, *supra* note 38, at 35 (describing a West Virginia farmer and civic leader lamenting that "this great natural wealth went into the hands of syndicates for a nominal sum and was lost to the people").

[48] *Cf.* STOLL, *supra* note 38, at 27 (describing "the industrial invasion of Appalachia" as "slow violence that brought an end to agrarian autonomy in places like West Virginia").

[49] *See* Brandon Nida, *Demystifying the Hidden Hand: Capital and the State at Blair Mountain*, 47 HIST. ARCHAEOLOGY 52, 54 (2013).

unionize were suppressed. After federal troops intervened, the miners alone were tried, dealing a long-lasting blow to organized labor in the coalfields.[50]

In more recent history, the Surface Mining Control and Reclamation Act of 1977 (SMCRA) involved a "broken promise" to protect coalfield communities.[51] Before the Act, unregulated mining practices exacted significant environmental harms in Appalachia.[52] During those years, mining states engaged in a race to the bottom, with states such as West Virginia generally beholden to industrial interests.[53] In response to public outcry, the SMCRA introduced a set of federal regulations designed to address problems associated with mining and also created the federal Office of Surface Mining.[54] The SMCRA reduced the disastrous effects of mining pre-1977, but not enough, even today, to fully mitigate the adverse environmental, economic, and social impacts the industry has imposed on coalfield communities.[55] In fact, Judah Schept observes, the SMCRA "created the legal infrastructure for strip mining's most violent form, mountaintop removal, to take hold" and "enabled mountaintop removal to expand significantly."[56]

Another prominent example of policymakers' failure to address Appalachian environmental injustice is the law's treatment of black lung. According to relatively recent investigative reports, black lung – a preventable but often fatal disease – has seen a resurgence among coal miners.[57] Reporters argue that both the coal industry and federal oversight of safety regulations have failed to protect miners from

---

[50] *Id.* at 63.

[51] Patrick C. McGinley, *From Pick and Shovel to Mountaintop Removal: Environmental Injustice in the Appalachian Coalfields*, 34 ENVTL. L. 21, 54 (2004); *see* Nicholas F. Stump, *Mountain Resistance: Appalachian Civil Disobedience in Critical Legal Research Modeled Law Reform*, 41 ENVIRONS: ENVTL. L. & POL'Y J. 69, 107–14 (2017) (describing acts of civil disobedience by Appalachians in response to the Surface Mining Control and Reclamation Act).

[52] McGinley, *supra* note 51, at 48–49. McGinley writes,

> The most visible adverse impacts of coal strip mining were the scars gashed in Appalachian mountainsides. Surface mining strips away forest vegetation, causing erosion and attendant stream sedimentation and siltation, accompanied by negative impacts on aquatic life and drinking water supplies. In some coalfield regions, iron-laden sulphuric acid mine drainage pollution from underground mining produces red-orange stained stream beds and renders watercourses ecologically sterile.... [M]ining contaminated or depleted underground aquifers that provide domestic and farm water supplies to many coalfield families. Loud noise and dust from blasting and earth-moving activities disturb nearby communities and wildlife.... Landslides caused by indiscriminate dumping of mine spoil downslope on steep Appalachian mountainsides buried cars, homes, and sometimes killed people. *Id.*

[53] *Id.* at 50; Nida, *supra* note 49, at 54.

[54] McGinley, *supra* note 51, at 307.

[55] *Id.* at 54.

[56] JUDAH SCHEPT, COAL, CAGES, CRISIS: THE RISE OF THE PRISON ECONOMY IN CENTRAL APPALACHIA 76, 87 (2022).

[57] Heather Willard, *Black Lung Cases Soar, Senators Seek to Curb Rise*, LOGAN DAILY NEWS (Aug. 28, 2018), www.logandaily.com/news/black-lung-cases-soar-senators-seek-to-curb-rise/article_3f27bd80-50e1-5af6-bdd3-d2eaadel341a.html [https://perma.cc/7XPM-YF2J].

the coal dust that causes black lung.[58] Despite this failure, the federal government has historically approved a mere 7.6 percent of miners' applications for black lung benefits.[59]

Prior to mainstream attention to climate change, coal production was often lauded for its collective benefits due to its utility as a cheap energy source. The American industrial revolution was powered by coal from West Virginia, Pennsylvania, and Kentucky. Coal-fired power accounted for virtually all manufacturing on the eastern seaboard after 1850.[60] Coal continues to comprise a substantial portion of the U.S. energy mix, and many still view it as a cheap source of energy with a handful of regrettable consequences.[61] Government's support for the coal industry, then, has often been understood as critical to economic progress – a market-supremacist perspective that has discounted coal's many environmental, economic, and human costs in coal country.

To understand coal country's current socioeconomic challenges, then, it is first necessary to understand the rise of coal. Coal was able to dominate central Appalachia because state and federal laws and institutions embraced worker suppression and lax safety and environmental regulations. Framing coal as an organically cheap energy source discounts the public sector's role as a catalyst in the manipulation of coal markets, while also diminishing the industry's externalized costs imposed on the region and beyond. Coal, therefore, was positioned to dominate because market supremacy necessitated prioritizing coal extraction and industrial development over the welfare of the Appalachian region.

While Appalachian coal country was sacrificed for the production of coal, it has also been sacrificed to coal's decline. As exploitative as coal production is, regional livelihoods and communities predictably evolved over decades to be reliant on the industry. Just as commentators have long celebrated coal as being "cheap" by virtue of energy markets, similar commentary today observes that coal has "declined" for innate, market-driven reasons. Many point to lowered costs of extracting natural gas – one of coal's main competitors – with the advent of high-volume hydraulic fracturing technology.[62] But the claim that coal's decline "just happened" rings hollow when viewed in the context of public involvement in energy markets. Congress exempted natural gas from every major environmental statute, paving the way for a drilling frenzy.[63] This decision to barely regulate natural gas was intentional. It also

---

[58] Howard Berkes, *As Mine Protections Fail, Black Lung Cases Surge*, NPR (July 9, 2012), www.npr.org/templates/transcript/transcript.php?storyId=155978300 [https://perma.cc/B2ME-QCZY].

[59] Brian C. Murchison, *Due Process, Black Lung, and the Shaping of Administrative Justice*, 54 ADMIN. L. REV. 1025, 1027 (2002).

[60] STOLL, *supra* note 38, at 34.

[61] McGinley, *supra* note 49, at 307.

[62] Richard L. Revesz, *Regulation and Distribution*, 93 N.Y.U. L. REV. 1489, 1550 (2018); *see* RICHARD L. REVESZ & JACK LIENKE, STRUGGLING FOR AIR: POWER PLANTS AND THE "WAR ON COAL" 141, 146–54 (2016).

[63] Eisenberg, *Distributive Justice*, *supra* note 1, at 207–08.

created a market advantage for natural gas that predictably undermined coal's competitiveness, in turn leaving coal-reliant communities in the lurch.

Environmental law scholarship has begun to acknowledge that strengthened environmental regulations have also played a role in undermining the coal industry, contributing to adverse economic consequences for discrete populations. These acknowledgements reflect a loosened grip on the political and rhetorical entrenchment associated with "jobs versus environment" debates. Interestingly and troublingly, those who support a policy of reducing carbon emissions have often insisted that coal has declined and will decline for reasons other than environmental regulations – such as automation and competition from natural gas. This insistence that the pain to coalfield communities is acceptable if markets are to blame reflects an undercurrent of market supremacist rhetoric in clean energy advocacy. But the full story of where coal stands today also involves increased environmental regulations. For instance, Richard Revesz has acknowledged that "the Transport Rule, Mercury Air Toxics Standards, and the Clean Power Plan" have indeed had an effect on the coal industry.[64] Such observations help model how environmental advocates can address decarbonization's trade-offs to carbon-reliant communities head-on, rather than denying those trade-offs' existence.

Because of these intertwining factors, coal's market share of U.S. electricity generation dropped from 50 percent in 2009, to 34 percent in 2012, to 20 percent in 2022.[65] Patrick McGinley concludes "that few in the conservation/environmental community, the coal and power industries, nor leaders of any political stripe are advocating planning and action to address the reality of declining coal production in central Appalachia and what it portends for coalfield communities."[66]

In sum, coal's decreased relevance to energy markets cannot simply be attributed to natural causes. Rather, government policies allowed – and at times actively contributed to – the industry's initial regional dominance, and to its subsequent decline. It is possible to recognize this decline as a difficulty for coalfield communities while also celebrating the decline's implications for better carbon emissions policy. But failing to acknowledge the role of public decision-makers in both creating and abandoning the coalfields removes any accountability for the creation of these conditions – and indeed, perpetuates the harmful notion that Appalachians are to blame for their own circumstances. Coal communities have, in fact, been sacrificed, first to produce energy, then anew in the name of clean(er) energy.

Although the Appalachian story might be a particularly extreme example, other rural communities have been trapped in similar relationships with extractive

---

[64] Revesz, *supra* note 62, at 1550; *see* REVESZ & LIENKE, *supra* note 62, at 141, 146–54.

[65] McGinley, *supra* note 49, at 308–11; Isabella O'Malley, *Electricity Generation from Renewables Surpassed Coal in the U.S. Last Year*, PBS NEWS HOUR (Mar. 28, 2023), www.pbs.org/newshour/science/electricity-generated-from-renewables-surpassed-coal-in-the-u-s-last-year [https://perma.cc/YF6G-C2A].

[66] *Id.*

industries, growing dependent on the very industries harming them.[67] In turn, laws and public institutions are very much capable of driving both the rise and the contraction of those industries. The rise and fall of coal has involved public drivers, not merely private ones.

Such public involvement can also be seen in other instances, as with the infamous story of the spotted owl endangered species designation and its effects on the Northwestern timber industry.[68] Those who support these often-hazardous industries' phaseout will frequently insist that markets are organically driving decline, notwithstanding public interventions such as environmental regulations. This rhetoric, too, rings in market supremacy, insisting that if markets dictate an outcome, that outcome is acceptable – no matter the socioeconomic costs. To say these industries "decline" often discounts the public role in industry expansion and contraction – and also the public role in leaving rural communities in the lurch. This discussion is not meant to suggest that such measures are never necessary. But to say that coal communities and similarly situated regions "declined" discounts public institutions' involvement in crafting, exploiting, and abandoning those regions.

GUTTING RURAL MANUFACTURING IN THE NAME
OF A MARKET-SUPREMACIST "GREATER GOOD"

Manufacturing is a third sector that has historically been one of the few lifelines sustaining the rural way of life. Although deindustrialization has affected urban centers, rural communities have been disproportionately dependent on manufacturing and are more likely to lack other opportunities when plants close.[69] As is the case with natural resource extraction and agriculture, the law's treatment of the manufacturing sector over the past several decades has imposed losses and burdens on rural communities. Those losses and burdens have often been justified by an insistence that measures to make markets freer are better for everyone.

Much has been written about the rash of manufacturing plant closures in the 1980s and 1990s.[70] With the advent of the North Atlantic Free Trade Agreement

---

[67] *See* Karen Clay & Alex Weckenman, *When Are Resources Curses and Blessings? Evidence from the United States 1880–2012*, at 2, 4–7 (Dec. 2016) (unpublished manuscript) (on file with the author).

[68] *See generally* JENNIFER SHERMAN, THOSE WHO WORK, THOSE WHO DON'T: POVERTY, MORALITY, AND FAMILY IN RURAL AMERICA (2009).

[69] Michelle W. Anderson, *The Western, Rural Rustbelt: Learning from Local Fiscal Crisis in Oregon*, 50 WILLAMETTE L. REV. 465, 467–68 (2014); see Nico Thomas & Steve Campbell, *The Geography of Manufacturing: The Case of MEP and Rural Manufacturers*, NIST MFG. INNOVATION BLOG (Jan. 31, 2018), www.nist.gov/blogs/manufacturing-innovation-blog/geography-man-ufacturing-case-mep-and-rural-manufacturers [https://perma.cc/PF4X-VQCM] ("When there are downturns in manufacturing the economic impacts disproportionately affect rural communities.").

[70] *See, e.g.*, Fran Ansley, *Inclusive Boundaries and Other (Im)possible Paths toward Community Development in a Global World*, 150 U. PA. L. REV. 353, 415 (2001) [hereinafter Ansley, *Inclusive Boundaries*]; Fran Ansley, *Standing Rusty and Rolling Empty: Law, Poverty, and America's Eroding*

(NAFTA) under the Clinton administration – as well as other measures, such as the treaty creating the World Trade Organization – many longstanding manufacturing plants opted to relocate to places where labor was cheaper and regulations were laxer.[71] As this swift change spread throughout the country, mass layoffs displaced workers and, in some instances, entire towns.[72]

Yet, both then and now, the displacement issue has often been at the periphery of the narrative.[73] Ample commentary sums up this phase as historical background, with a handful of words – globalization, deindustrialization, or outsourcing of jobs, for instance. Today, discussions on rural distress rarely revisit ongoing ramifications of widespread deindustrialization, and the human agency that drove that deindustrialization, making it something that was done *to* rural communities. Especially within legal scholarship, modern studies rarely harken back to the specific measures that either caused or purported to address the large-scale displacement of the many workers and communities whose livelihoods had evolved over time around the manufacturing sector.[74] Yet, the federal legal measures implemented to minimize workers' losses could hardly be called a good-faith effort.[75]

One of those federal efforts was the Trade Adjustment Act of 1974 (TAA). The TAA purported to offset the effects of reduced trade restrictions on workers and communities.[76] The Act provided compensation for lost wages and job retraining for workers who could make a showing that their losses stemmed from international competition.[77] The Department of Labor still administers the TAA, and it continues

---

Industrial Base, 81 GEO. L.J. 1757, 1868 (1993).; Leslie Kay & Kevin Griffin, *Plant Closures: Assessing the Victims' Remedies*, 19 WILLAMETTE L. REV. 199, 199–200 (1983).

[71] *See* Sara Dillon, *Getting the "Message" on Free Trade: Globalization, Jobs and the World According to Trump*, 16 SANTA CLARA J. INT'L L. 1, 16–17 (2018).

[72] *See* Virginia L. Duquet, Note, *Advantages and Limitations of Current Employee Ownership Assistance Acts to Workers Facing a Plant Closure*, 36 HASTINGS L.J. 93, 93 (1984) (explaining that "[j]ob loss is a harsh reality or an ominous threat facing many American workers" and stating that "[i]n many instances, a plant closure not only affects individual employees, but also can devastate an entire community").

[73] *See* Dillon, *supra* note 71, at 14, 44 (explaining how commentators and writers did not focus on the problem of job loss caused by globalization, and faulting the "silence of elites" for allowing the perception in rural America that the country's leaders are indifferent to their hardship).

[74] UW-WHITEWATER FISCAL & ECON. RSCH. CTR. & REDEVELOPMENT ECON., THE ECONOMIC AND FISCAL IMPACT OF WISCONSIN'S BROWNFIELDS INVESTMENTS 19 (Nov. 2015) https://dnr .wi.gov/topic/Brownfields/documentsftsg/uwwreport.pdf [https://perma.cc/3K62-LWUG]. *But see* Dillon, *supra* note 71, at 2 (acknowledging that job losses are associated with a globalized economy).

[75] *See* Dillon, *supra* note 71, at 14 (arguing that "this explosive issue was broadly ignored" from the 1990s onward, and that elites such as trade law attorneys focused on technical legal questions that were a "side show" for regular people).

[76] Shana Fried, Note, *Strengthening the Role of the U.S. Court of International Trade in Helping Trade-Affected Workers*, 58 RUTGERS L. REV. 747, 749 (2006). President Kennedy's Trade Expansion Act of 1962 technically created the trade adjustment assistance program, but commentators agree that this was not a meaningful avenue for worker benefits until the 1974 amendment relaxed eligibility criteria. *Id.*

[77] *Id.* at 749–51.

to hear petitions from workers claiming displacement. Diverse industries are affected by international competition. But the vast majority of claims come from employers and workers in the manufacturing sector.[78] Since the start of the program, several million workers have taken advantage of it.[79]

Although preferable to inaction, the Act has been criticized as failing to provide adequate compensation for workers' and communities' losses. Economists disagree about its overall effects. Some argue that it is "reasonably effective as compensation," though perhaps not as a means for effective retraining or relocation assistance.[80] Critics cite studies illustrating that, by transitioning to the program, the average worker loses approximately 30 percent of his or her wages. These workers are also unlikely to ever find jobs that pay as well or have benefits comparable to the work they lost.[81] Of importance to the aging rural population, the program proves least effective for older workers who have been in their particular industry for an extended period.

In the 1980s and 1990s, a social movement arose in response to the large-scale displacement that accompanied trade deregulation. This movement was due, at least in part, to TAA's inability to account for all losses – particularly where entire communities were displaced.[82] Activists agitated for private and public recognition of the economic upheaval that plant closures effectuated.[83] Some modest judicial and legislative gains came from the plant-closure movement. But for the most part, deindustrialization was swift, and its fallout was only minimally addressed through law.[84]

Among those modest successes was the 1988 Worker Adjustment, Retraining and Notification Act (WARN Act) that was passed in response to widespread plant closures with the goal of aiding dislocated workers.[85] Yet, even from its inception, critics were skeptical that the WARN Act would meaningfully address the vulnerability associated with layoffs. The Act's language was vague and unclear, raising difficulties in application.[86] Perhaps most egregiously, the WARN Act only required that

---

[78] Tom DiChristopher, *Sizing up the Trade Adjustment Assistance Program*, CNBC (June 26, 2015), www.cnbc.com/2015/06/26/is-aid-to-trade-displaced-workers-worth-the-cost.html [https://perma.cc/N4JX-CGX9].

[79] *Id.*

[80] *Id.*

[81] *Id.; see* Kara Reynolds & John Palatucci, *Does Trade Adjustment Assistance Make a Difference?* 13 (Am. Univ. Dep't of Econ., Working Paper No. 2008-12, 2008) (stating that "TAA workers earned on average 30 percent less than they made at their previous job").

[82] *Cf.* Ansley, *Inclusive Boundaries, supra* note 70, at 415 (discussing the need for social movements to highlight issues of "economic justice and [that social movements are] capable of carrying on the best of what we began in the plant-closing campaigns of past decades, yet also capable of going significantly beyond the old [social movements] in their awareness of the highly asymmetrical global system and their openness to the claims of the excluded and oppressed").

[83] *See id.* at 367–69.

[84] *Id.* at 353–55; Dillon, *supra* note 71, at 12–14.

[85] Ethan Lipsig & Keith R. Fentonmiller, *A WARN Act Road Map*, 11 LAB. LAW. 273, 273 (1996).

[86] *Id.*

employers with 100 or more employees provide 60 days' advance notice of a planned closing or a "mass layoff" of 50 employees or more.[87]

Although the U.S. economy enjoyed a net boom from the swift and unmitigated measures that undermined this rural economic lifeline, many small communities dependent on one major employer were essentially destroyed.[88] Today's ghost towns – communities that have ceased to exist due to full-scale outmigration and abandonment – can often trace their deaths directly back to a plant closure. These losses were distributed to urban centers as well. But rural communities' dependency on manufacturing, lack of alternatives, and the subsequent proliferation of rural blight all suggest that rural communities bear a disproportionate burden of these economic losses. And these losses were generally justified in the name of "progress," or the aggregate welfare of the nation. Once again, aggregate welfare and market supremacy were celebrated as one and the same.

To summarize, the overall theme in the legal regimes shaping key rural livelihoods over the past several decades is a pattern of decision-makers choosing to trade rural welfare for some other perceived benefit. The Federal Reserve, the FmHA, Congress, and state legislatures opted to facilitate the rise of agribusiness to the detriment of the small farmer. These decisions concentrated economic losses on rural communities in the name of cheap, abundant food, which could purportedly be better furnished by larger, more "efficient" corporate producers. The SMCRA and natural gas regulations have been weak, while measures to mitigate the decline of extractive jobs have been minimal; the former measures were justified by cheap, reliable energy, while the latter inaction has been justified by environmental benefits, all of which are entangled with supposedly freely operating markets for coal and gas. And manufacturing plants were permitted to abruptly shut down despite entire towns' reliance on them.

This analysis shows that to declare that rural America has "declined" does not tell the full truth. Public institutions traded rural well-being for corporate advantage. Corporate advantage has been treated as synonymous with the greater good. Rural America has been sacrificed, its lifelines exchanged for other things.

HOW FEDERAL LAW AND POLICY HAVE UNDERMINED RURAL INFRASTRUCTURE IN THE NAME OF A MARKET-SUPREMACIST "GREATER GOOD"

Much of the conversation on rural marginalization has focused on jobs and lost economic activity. The first half of this chapter has illustrated how several

---

[87] 29 U.S.C. § 2102 (2018); *see* Ansley, *Inclusive Boundaries, supra* note 70, at 372 n.33 (recognizing that the passage of the WARN Act was a victory for the plant-closure social movement, but calling it an "extremely limited" protection for displaced workers).

[88] *See generally* Peter Cole, *A Tale of Two Towns: Globalization and Rural Deindustrialization in the U.S.,* 12 WORKINGUSA 539 (2009) (comparing the experiences of two rural communities that lost major employers after NAFTA and observing the range of small-town suffering from minimal to severe).

traditional rural economic lifelines have not simply been "lost" in a pattern of "decline." Rather, public decision-makers constructed frameworks in law, policy, and regulations that facilitated a large-scale trading of those jobs for other values, and in particular, for a depiction of societal welfare pitched as contingent on corporate autonomy, innovation, efficiency, and, ultimately, dominance. This trade-off operated to the detriment of diversified rural land ownership, workers' needs, local government viability, regional stability, and socioeconomic and geographic equality.

The discussion now turns to another piece of the story of policymakers' sacrifice of rural America: Infrastructure regulation. Just as policymakers traded rural jobs for other values, they have also traded rural infrastructure for a version of the collective good that is similarly infused with market-supremacist principles. Just as our collective conversation has forgotten about the farm crisis, government support for extractive industries, and trade liberalization, we have also forgotten about the era of deregulation. Yet, deregulation – a series of intentional steps taken by Congress in the name of corporate efficiency for everyone's sake – also challenges the narrative of "decline." The legal history of the deregulatory era instead reveals a series of knowing choices to trade rural welfare for other things. Congress's deregulation of transportation and telecommunications, in particular, bore severe consequences for rural vitality and prosperity.

As discussed in Chapter 4, prior to deregulation, common carriers and utilities – including most public transportation and telecommunications providers – were not allowed to simply stop providing service on a whim. They were prohibited from doing so, because they were viewed as necessary to the public interest. Most service providers operated under legal mandates to pursue universal service at just and reasonable rates to consumers. These requirements were overseen by a federal agency known as the Interstate Commerce Commission (ICC). But by the mid century, the ICC was under attack. And the deregulatory era started in earnest with the railroads.

The regulated national rail system was not doing well by the 1950s and 1960s.[89] Increasingly disgruntled rail companies used freight profits to subsidize struggling passenger lines.[90] By the late 1960s, train passengers experienced "poor service, schedules, and abrasive treatment" by railroads.[91] Rail companies supposedly had "deliberately downgraded standards and discouraged patronage" because of their desire to discontinue service on unprofitable lines.[92]

---

[89] *See* Laurence E. Tobey, *Costs, Benefits, and the Future of Amtrak*, 15 Transp. L.J. 245, 249 (1987) (explaining that after World War II, private cars, planes, and intercity buses largely displaced demand for rail service).

[90] See Paul Stephen Dempsey, *The Dark Side of Deregulation: Its Impact on Small Communities*, 39 Admin. L. Rev. 445, 452 (1987) [hereinafter Dempsey, *The Dark Side*].

[91] 116 Cong. Rec. 14,166 (1970).

[92] *Id.*

The Supreme Court set the stage for increased rates of discontinuing common carrier services with its 1964 decision in *Southern Railway Co. v. North Carolina*,[93] which tilted the scale in the decision-making process more heavily in favor of carrier profits over potential impacts of loss of service on local populations. *Southern Railway* and the ICC's evolving standards paved the way for railways to discontinue common carrier service. While 1929 saw a peak of 20,000 passenger trains, "the number of passenger trains fell by 60 percent between 1958 and 1970. By 1970, only 360 intercity trains were left."[94]

Demand grew in the mid century for Congress to address the "national disgrace" of the railroads.[95] The Rail Passenger Service Act of 1970 reflected Congress's effort to save passenger rail service with the creation of Amtrak.[96] Ironically, this law would usher in a new era of transportation deregulation that would deeply exacerbate rural isolation.[97] Yet, some advocates of rural interests saw themselves as having no other choice but to support it. Democratic Senator Frank Church of Idaho explained why he reluctantly planned to vote in favor of the Amtrak law:

> I have no confidence that this legislation will really solve the problems of providing clean, comfortable, and salable railroad passenger service ....
>
> ....
>
> ... The theory seems to be that the Union Pacific can improve its railroad passenger service by removing it altogether. Many passengers who have suffered the poor service, schedules, and abrasive treatment of the railroad may feel that way also.
>
> Yet there are other people in rural areas who still must rely on train transportation ....
>
> ... I will support the legislation. I hope that ... it will result in some measure of assistance to the people of my State of Idaho.[98]

Perhaps most significantly, the Act created the National Railroad Passenger Corporation, which superseded the ICC as the overseer of passenger rail service and continued the trend of chipping away at the ICC as protector of geographic equity in service provision.[99] As regulated private rail gave way to Amtrak, 500 additional communities lost intercity passenger train service.[100] As of the late 1980s, commentators observed that "with the exception of the heavily traveled Boston–Washington

---

[93] S. Ry. Co. v. North Carolina, 376 U.S. 93 (1964).

[94] Dempsey, *The Dark Side, supra* note 90, at 452 (footnote omitted).

[95] *Id.*

[96] Rail Passenger Service Act of 1970, Pub. L. No. 91-518, 84 Stat. 1327; Tobey, *supra* note 89, at 254.

[97] Ganesh Sitaraman et al., *Regulation and the Geography of Inequality*, 70 DUKE L.J. 1763, 1789 (2021) ("Deregulation prompted railways to discontinue service along many routes and to altogether abandon many rail lines. The results were devastating for many rural and smaller communities whose economic well-being depended on rail service.")

[98] 116 CONG. REC. 14,166 (1970).

[99] Tobey, *supra* note 89, at 255.

[100] Dempsey, *The Dark Side, supra* note 90, at 453.

corridor, service levels on American passenger trains are the worst in the world."[101] Meanwhile, throughout these developments, "thousands of small communities" were "pruned" from the passenger rail system.[102]

Airline deregulation followed shortly after rail deregulation. Legislators debating the Airline Deregulation Act of 1978 recognized the grave risks airline deregulation posed to rural communities. Some insisted that the bill included adequate protective measures. Kansas Republican Senator James Pearson explained that he:

> had some reservations ... related more to the problems of local air service in those rural parts of our country where rail passenger transportation no longer exists, where bus service is inadequate, and where in many instances the commuter service or local air service is really one of the last means of people achieving a sense of communication and doing their commerce and business as is necessary.
> ... I think [a change made to address that concern] adequately fills the needs of the local air carriers in a new and abbreviated certified manner with a new subsidy program.
> ... It is a phased deregulation. It is not total deregulation ....
> ... [M]y concern was for the small and isolated communities across the country. Communities that depend upon subsidized air service for economic growth and stability. But I now believe that the bill adequately protects such communities.[103]

In a similar vein, New Mexico Republican Senator Harrison Schmitt said during debates that his primary concern was "what would happen to the small communities of our country."[104] He said he believed that "small communities will be treated most fairly" because they would have a guarantee of air service for the first time.[105] He outlined the bill's provisions that would protect small communities, including direct subsidies, a guarantee of air service for ten years, a requirement for an airline wishing to abandon a small community to be replaced, and a new certification for local air carriers with more liberal regulations.[106]

Others were less optimistic. South Dakota Democratic Senator George McGovern characterized airline deregulation as a "grim scenario" with virtually immeasurable downstream effects on municipal airport investments and airline industry employees with specialized skills.[107] But "[t]he focal point" of his concern was "the air service for smaller communities."[108] He anticipated a mass exit of rural service providers and a deterioration of service where it still existed, emphasizing

---

[101] *Id.* (quoting William E. Thorns, *Clear Track for Deregulation American Railroads, 1970–1980*, 12 TRANSP. L.J. 183, 196 (1982)) (misquotation in original).

[102] *Id.*

[103] 124 CONG. REC. 10,649–50 (1978).

[104] *Id.* at 10,652.

[105] *Id.*

[106] *Id.*

[107] *Id.* at 10,660

[108] *Id.*

that policymakers should look to what would happen after the ten-year phaseout.[109] Advocates for small communities also testified before Congress, "provid[ing] example after example of the discriminatory fares and deteriorating service resulting from deregulation," trends which would fall disproportionately on small, remote localities across the country.[110]

As McGovern predicted, the airline industry followed in step with the passenger rail industry in curtailing service to rural communities. The Airline Deregulation Act of 1978 allowed "[a]ll but the last carrier in a market" to be free to discontinue service at will.[111] Congress did establish a ten-year program of federal subsidies to provide air service to impacted small communities, although it was generally "alleged that small communities had little to fear from deregulation" because of some policymakers' insistence that regional markets would adjust to meet needs.[112] Yet, 40 percent of small communities experienced a loss of air service after deregulation.[113] Meanwhile, ticket prices increased disproportionately for those communities, in addition to a rise in other convenience and safety concerns.[114]

With their next step in deregulation, Congress pursued the Staggers Rail Act of 1980 (SRA), which would become one of the legislative lynchpins of the deregulatory era. The SRA sought to free freight railroads from federal restrictions, further setting the stage for loosening federal oversight of other infrastructure industries.

While one might conclude that the abusive conduct of railroad companies warranted less freedom, rather than more, policymakers favoring the SRA saw increased private discretion as the key to a better transportation system.[115] Proposed measures to make rail companies more viable included giving "substantially reduced priority" to shipper (i.e., consumer) protection, reduced administrative control of potential monopolistic practices, and reduced commitment to maintaining specific services that would not otherwise be maintained.[116] The proposed solution to rail companies' letting their service deteriorate was to allow the companies to impose a surcharge on less profitable lines in order to cover the costs they would otherwise be expending.[117]

The prospect of deregulating the railroads was controversial, however, and as with airline deregulation, advocates for rural interests and small towns perceived

---

[109] *Id.* at 10,660–61.
[110] Dempsey, *The Dark Side, supra* note 90, at 457 (discussing impacts in California, the Midwest, the Dakotas, the Carolinas, Mississippi, New Mexico, Rhode Island, Tennessee, and West Virginia).
[111] *Id.* at 454.
[112] *Id.*
[113] *Id.* at 457.
[114] *Id.* at 455–57
[115] *See* Staggers Rail House Debates, 126 CONG. REC. H24,834 (daily ed. Sept. 9, 1980) (statement of Rep. Harkin) ("We must allow our railroads to have the flexibility to succeed. We must create a climate that will see railroads desiring to expand, not looking to get out of the business.").
[116] *See* L. Orlo Sorenson, *Impacts of Rail Deregulation on Rural Communities*, 15 POL'Y STUD. J. 760, 765 (1987) [hereinafter Sorenson, *Impacts of Rail Deregulation*].
[117] *See* 126 CONG. REC. 24,804, 24,840 (1980).

early on the risks posed to them if regulators weakened mandates for nondiscriminatory universal service at just and reasonable rates. During debates in the House of Representatives during the fall of 1980, Democratic Michigan Representative Donald Albosta raised poignant concerns about the SRA's potential impacts on various regions of Michigan. Albosta noted, first off, that giving the railroads more freedom was not necessarily the only and most obvious option for rail transportation reform, and that "we could buy all the track to be abandoned in the country for the price of 10 miles of urban subway."[118] Albosta characterized the SRA as "like major surgery: we are allowing railroads to cut off limbs to save the trunk. Yet we could someday have the need and the ability to go back and save those limbs."[119] He warned,

> We should cross off these tracks with caution, for we may never be able to bring
> them back, even in an emergency .... Why destroy them without at least waiting
> to see whether we truly need each limb, or whether we can save the health of the
> American railroad system and bring it back to a point where its arteries are full of
> life again, and the trunk can support the limbs again?[120]

Recognizing the potentially devastating regional effects of losing rail access, policymakers discussed the possible scope and nature of future rail line abandonments that would come with increased rail company discretion. For instance, Albosta commented,

> There is no question in the minds of any of the people on that railroad [from
> Cadillac to Grand Rapids, Michigan,] and there is no question in the minds of the
> people who have designed this particular bill that the shortline railroad's future
> could be jeopardized. It is the only railroad there and closing it will not only hurt
> the local economy of Michigan but affect this country's ability to bring rail traffic
> through another route besides the Chicago gateway.[121]

Concerns such as these were answered with reassurance that line abandonments would not become more likely. For instance, Democratic New Jersey Congressman James Florio pushed back against Albosta's worries, insisting that "we have more than fully addressed that problem in this legislation ... [with] a multitude of programs,

[118] *Id.* at 24,870.
[119] *Id.*
[120] *Id.*
[121] *Id.* at 24,840. Similar concerns had been raised on the floor of the Senate. South Dakota Senator George McGovern observed,

> Even from a purely social standpoint, ensuring the viability of the Nation's rail system is an
> essential step in preserving the vitality of rural America. Railroads determined the settlement
> patterns in much of the country, as elevators were built along branch lines, and settlements
> sprung up at key junctions. A century later, the economies of these rural towns still depend on
> their access to rail transportation. Preserving the rural rail system is an indispensable part of the
> effort to maintain rural vitality

126 CONG. REC. 7,247, 7,274 (1980).

branch line assistance programs, and a rail banking provision in the Amtrak Act ... dealing with the opportunities to stop inappropriate abandonments."[122] Similarly, Illinois Democrat Michael Madigan remarked that rail companies' ability to charge a surcharge for less profitable lines would help keep those lines running, and if not, that local commissions would still be able to hold rail companies accountable for reduced quality in service.[123]

Michigan Democrat John Dingell went further in his indictment of aspects of the SRA. One of the central tensions of legislative debate pitted a provision known as the Eckhardt amendment against a provision known as the Staggers–Rahall–Lee compromise. The Eckhardt amendment, according to a memo from Georgia Democrat Ronald Ginn to President Jimmy Carter appealing for help opposing it, would "gut" the deregulation bill by curtailing railroads' freedom to set their own rates.[124] The compromise, by contrast, would shift power back to the rail companies by removing geographic and product competition as considerations from determinations of market dominance – meaning railroads would be considered market-dominant less frequently, thereby triggering ICC intervention to regulate rates less frequently.[125]

In supporting the Eckhardt amendment, Dingell declared to his colleagues that they had before them "a clear choice. If you go with Staggers–Rahall–Lee, you will endorse a proposal written at the request of Conrail – and other larger railroads – and one which allows for blatant discrimination against small short line railroads, shippers, utilities and consumers."[126] Although Dingell agreed "that railroads ought not be forced to operate in the red," he believed the compromise would "solve the problem of a minor dislocation with major surgery" by creating "a system whereby larger railroads – the Conrails and the Southerns – can enrich their incomes."[127] But, Dingell opined, this was a Machiavellian scheme where the end attempts to justify the means:

> The provisions of the Staggers-Rahall-Lee compromise can be used in a discriminatory fashion to allow large railroads ... to force small shippers to use other modes of transportation to pay exorbitant rates thereby making them noncompetitive. At the same time, rates for competing traffic can be held down leaving shippers with no other alternative than to abandon the service of certain small short line railroads to the whim and caprice of a larger monopolistic railroad. The end result of this

---

[122] 126 CONG. REC. 24,804, 24,871 (1980). The Amtrak Act replaced the prior system of regulated passenger rail system with a more limited system run by Amtrak, a federally owned enterprise. *See id.*

[123] *See id.* at 24,840–41.

[124] *See* Memorandum from Congressman Ronald Ginn (Ga.), to President Jimmy Carter, 175 DAILY COMP. PRES. DOC. 2 (Sept. 4, 1980).

[125] *Staggers Rail Act: Oversight, Hearing Before the Subcomm. on Com., Transp., and Tourism of the Comm. on Energy and Com. H.R.*, 98th Cong. 13 (1983) [hereinafter Staggers Rail Act: Oversight] (Statement of Rep. Rahall).

[126] 126 CONG. REC. 24,804, 24,840–41 (1980).

[127] *Id.* at 24,841

arbitrary and offensively discriminatory rate manipulation is clear to me – whole-sale abandonment of hundreds of small short line rail carriers across the Nation, straight into the hand of the railroad monopoly.[128]

The House ultimately adopted both the Eckhardt Amendment and the Staggers–Rahall–Lee compromise, weakening the Amendment's provisions and shifting the balance of power back toward the rail companies.[129] Concerns about rural vitality notwithstanding – likely having been reassured by the protections built in for rural communities – 95 percent of congressional representatives voted in favor of the SRA in its final form.

By the time the prospect of deregulating intercity bus service was before Congress merely one year later, representatives of rural districts seemed even more skeptical. They had by then seen both airline and rail deregulation play out on the ground after being promised that rural communities would not be hurt.[130] Legislative conversations surrounding what would ultimately become the Bus Regulatory Reform Act of 1982 exhibited similar themes, with legislative debate starting just a few months after the election of Ronald Reagan to the presidency. One of the bill's proponents characterized it as "a natural extension of our efforts … to promote flexibility in the regulatory structure surrounding the Nation's transportation industries."[131] Another proponent said the bill was "a responsible effort that meshes both the philosophy of deregulation with the practicalities of the federal–state climate in which the inter-city bus industry has developed during the past half century."[132] The proposed bill would relax entry requirements into the interstate bus industry, permit a higher volume of intrastate busing, permit bus companies greater leeway in abandoning their operations, and reduce federal oversight of prices charged.[133]

Noting "the unorthodox manner in which this bill has been handled and rushed through," Missouri Republican Representative Gene Taylor remarked:

---

[128] *See id.* He continued, "I reiterate that my colleagues have a choice. You can support the Eckhardt amendment which provides for a fair and expedited rate proceeding in rate division cases of rate divisions between railroads or you can accept the Staggers-Rahall-Lee Conrail compromise which promotes arbitrary rate discrimination, demise of smaller railroads, and wholesale abandonments of short line carriers." *Id.*

[129] *Id.; see also* Staggers Rail Act: Oversight, *supra* note 125.

[130] *See* 127 CONG. REC. 28,181 (1981) ("West Virginia and many rural parts of our Nation have indeed been impacted by airline deregulation, trucking deregulation, or loss of train service through elimination of many Amtrak routes, and in many parts of this country roads are very difficult and very expensive, if not downright impossible to build. So for much of rural America the bus company is the only game in town. For many of our 14,000 small towns across America, this is the only game left in town.").

[131] *Id.* at 28,175 (statement of Rep. Anderson).

[132] *Id.* at 28,177–78 (statement of Rep. Clausen).

[133] *See id.* at 28,175. Debate in House of Representatives about Bus Regulatory Reform Act of 1981, Nov. 19, 1981, p. 28175. For abandonment procedures, "State denials of the carrier's application to discontinue its intrastate service over the same route are presumed to be unreasonable burdens on interstate commerce and not in the public interest." *Id.*

I do believe it is time that we slow down our urge to deregulate and try to calm our deregulation fever. Rural America, especially, has been hurt by our efforts at airline deregulation, and many Members have personal experience with the inability of the airline industry to serve small towns and small communities. In this regard, we were assured several years ago by the administration and by the committee at that time that small cities and towns would be served by commuter and charter airlines since the big scheduled airlines had left their communities. That simply has not happened, and I doubt that it ever will. Now the committee comes to the floor in a heated rush with a bill that could cause further damage to rural America's transportation systems. We have no airplanes in small towns and cities, and we will soon have fewer interstate and intercity buses …. Many people in this Nation, especially in rural areas isolated from big population centers and in small towns between major population centers, rely on well-regulated bus transportation systems. Most of these people, by the way, are our senior citizens, those who would have to pay the high cost of airline travel, and who cannot afford it even if airline travel were still available…. I think it is time for us to take a look and see whether in our passion for deregulation fever we are in fact penalizing rural America especially in serving their transportation needs[134]

Texas Democrat Abraham Kazen of Texas thanked Taylor for raising these "flashing red lights," observing that,

[I]f this bill passes today in the form that it is written, we are going to wake up tomorrow, those of us who represent rural districts, and find out that we have no transportation whatsoever. Airlines do not stop, the train does not stop, and now they are going to take the bus stops away from us. You know, I heard a while ago a Member say the old refrain about how are you going to keep them down on the farm. This is the way you are going to keep them there, because they are not going to have any way of getting out.[135]

Kansas Republican Charles Patrick Roberts pointed out that it had become cheaper for him to fly from New York to Miami than the far shorter trip from Dodge City to Wichita, and that trucking deregulation had made it more costly to procure supplies for rural hospitals.[136]

Skeptics were once again given reassurance that the bill contained enough safeguards to ensure service to rural areas and small towns.[137] One congressman said of the safeguards, "[R]ural America has been hurt by deregulation. I realize the bill

---

[134] *Id.* at 28,172 (Debate in House of Representatives about Bus Regulatory Reform Act of 1981). At the beginning of debates, he said, "I would certainly urge everyone from the rural areas to be here to listen to this, to be sure that you are adequately protected by these safeguards that will be described by the Members who will be handling this bill on the floor, because I think it is important that you satisfy yourselves that these protections are there." *Id.* at 28,173.

[135] *Id.*

[136] *See id.*

[137] *See id.* at 28,181.

contains 'safeguards' designed to protect rural communities but we have been down that road before."[138]

Republican Congresswoman Virginia Dodd Smith of Nebraska raised concerns about the bill's provision to permit the ICC to preempt state decisions on rates and rules.[139] She explained,

> If airline deregulation is the model for this legislation, then rural Nebraska has nothing to hope for in terms of adequate and reasonably priced transportation. Already, certain bus lines that have served my State in the past are abandoning service to small communities. In most cases, these bus companies were the sole source of public transportation .... I make this point to show how eager these bus companies are to abandon service to small communities and to show how inadequate the so-called protection for small communities provisions in this bill will be if they ever become law.[140] ...
>
> We were assured that rail deregulation was all taken care of with full protection for communities that already had air service. But it has not worked out that way. We have had no end of trouble. We have had hearings. We have had hearings on subsidies. We have small airlines that have gone out of business, they have gone broke. We have had delays in getting answers. We have much poorer service than we did before. I am now very much afraid that we will have less and less bus service. We do not have air service and we do not have Amtrak. We cannot leave rural America without service .... I urge a 'no' vote.[141]

By 1980, "[w]ith the passenger trains having vanished from rural America, and with commercial aircraft no longer landing at many small town airports, the only means of public intercity transport left was the bus."[142] But, following in step, the Bus Regulatory Reform Act of 1982 expanded carriers' ability to abandon or discontinue service and raise fares. Local residents could attempt to forestall abandonment by proving that a closure would leave them without alternative means of public transport. Yet, the ICC consistently sided with companies, prompting the New York Department of Transportation to claim that the ICC showed "a total disregard and lack of concern for the welfare of the riding public."[143]

---

[138] *Id.* at 28,173 (statement of Rep. Roberts of Kansas).

[139] *See* 127 CONG. REC. 28,181, 28,183 (1981). "The major opposition was found in the ranks of legislators from rural states who feared loss of service to small towns and cities without air or rail passenger service. These fears [we]re justified .... The [new] one-sided appeal process for carriers mean[t] virtually unrestrained freedom to exit markets." William E. Thoms, *Unleashing the Greyhounds – The Bus Regulatory Reform Act of 1982*, 6 CAMPBELL L. REV. 75, 97 (1984).

[140] 127 CONG. REC. 28,184 (1981).

[141] *Id.* Congressman Roberts of South Dakota stated, "I have severe reservations about the deregulation of the intercity bus industry .... Complete deregulation ... is detrimental to the well-being of rural America." *Id.*

[142] Dempsey, *The Dark Side, supra* note 90, at 459.

[143] *Id.* at 460 (quoting *Household Goods Transportation and Bus Regulatory Reform Oversight: Hearing Before the Subcomm. on Surface Transp. of the S. Comm. on Com., Set, & Transp.,* 99th Cong. 145 (1985) [hereinafter *Household Goods Hearing*] (statement of John K. Mladinov)).

A mere eleven months after deregulation, 1,294 locations in forty states lost or were proposed to lose service, 776 of whom lost intercity service entirely.[144] Most of those communities had populations of less than 10,000. In short, "[i]n less than [one] year, almost [one] million people lost their bus service."[145]

Common carrier exits contributed to a demonstrable downward cycle for these communities, and many of these trends came before the ten-year federal subsidy to ensure air service to small communities ran out.[146] Regional access to commerce is in large part dependent on regional access to affordable transportation; for instance, the vast majority of major businesses at the time indicated in a survey that they would not locate in an area without access to air transportation.[147] With a national shift away from manufacturing in the 1980s toward the service sector, large employers began to require sophisticated communications and information systems, including high-quality air service, which had come to be viewed as a comparable necessity to electricity and telephones – prompting some to argue that air service should be treated as a public utility.[148] Just as discontinued rail service led to some western ghost towns, a bankrupt airline could yield the same results. While some praised these deregulatory efforts as laudable moves toward efficiency, other commentators at the time lamented the retreat of critical public protections.[149]

In 1991, Congress passed the Intermodal Surface Transportation Efficiency Act (ISTEA), which formally devolved highway planning to the states.[150] In 1998, the Transportation Equity Act for the 21st Century mandated statewide transportation planning, which included some of the first planning initiatives for rural areas.[151] Yet, today, rural communities remain isolated from national transportation networks.

Anyone who has sought to take a bus, train, or plane to a remote or small town has experienced the expense and inconvenience associated with modern rural transportation access.[152] In Chapter 2, I raised the question of whether my hometown of Ithaca, New York, has characteristics of rurality. I regularly think about Ithaca as a case study in transportation deregulation. I still travel to and from Ithaca frequently,

---

[144] *Id.* at 461 (citing *Household Goods Hearing, supra* note 143, at 2 (statement of Sen. Larry Pressler)).

[145] *Id.*

[146] Timothy Meyer, *Misaligned Lawmaking*, 73 VAND. L. REV. 151, 219 (2020) ("Not surprisingly, carriers began to drop service on unprofitable routes. Direct subsidies failed to stem the tide of rural retrenchment. The result has been the well-documented isolation of rural communities." (footnotes omitted)).

[147] Dempsey, *The Dark Side, supra* note 90, at 458.

[148] *Id.*

[149] *Id.* at 459 ("[S]ome measure of public protection is more than justified. And who else but a public agency can serve as the ultimate arbiter, stabilizing the kind of erratic market conditions that brought about the creation of these agencies in the first place?" (quoting SUSAN J. TOLCHIN & MARTIN TOLCHIN, DISMANTLING AMERICA: THE RUSH TO DEREGULATION 250 (1983))).

[150] Intermodal Surface Transportation Efficiency Act of 1991, Pub. L. No. 102-240, 105 Stat. 1914.

[151] Transportation Equity Act for the 21st Century, Pub. L. No. 105-178, 112 Stat. 107 (1998).

[152] *See* Susan Stellin, *Small Airports, Left Behind*, N.Y. TIMES (Feb. 28, 2011), www.nytimes .com/2011/03/01/business/01airports.html [https://perma.cc/3GUZ-YQ2H].

and with each passing year, it seems to become more challenging and more expensive. As of this writing, I am living in Pittsburgh, Pennsylvania, a roughly six-hour drive from Ithaca. As prosperous as Ithaca may be, it did not stop American Airlines from announcing in 2022 that it was ending all service, after decades of operations there, to and from this small municipality.[153] The airline blamed a pilot shortage for the service discontinuation. Ithaca only has two direct flights left now: one to New York City and one to Newark. Pittsburgh does not have a single direct flight to Upstate New York. The fastest option for a bus trip from Pittsburgh to Ithaca will take 13 hours and go through Newark. An online search for Amtrak travel from Pittsburgh to Ithaca or Syracuse reveals the message, "This trip cannot be booked. We do not have any travel options between the stations entered."

TELECOMMUNICATIONS DEREGULATION
AND THE DIGITAL DIVIDE

The deregulation of rural telecommunications mirrored the deregulation of rural transportation and had similarly deleterious effects, although the legal pathway was a bit different. In the 1940s, AT&T's size and dominance drew the attention of the U.S. Department of Justice, which argued as early as 1949 that AT&T was in violation of the Sherman Act and that its lack of competition undermined the goals of public regulation.[154] AT&T agreed in a 1956 consent decree that it would limit its activities to the telecommunications sector, license its technologies to competitors, and subject itself to competition from other firms.[155] It jostled for power with competitors in judicial and agency processes for the next twenty years when the political tides were turning even further away from the regulated natural monopoly model and toward greater competition. In 1984, the largest corporate dismantling in the history of antitrust took place, when AT&T was forced to divest itself of Bell operating companies.[156] Divestiture coincided with deregulatory interventions, which shifted telecommunications generally toward a competition model.

---

[153] Caitlin Holtzman, *American Airlines Ending Ithaca Service Despite Objections*, Ithaca Voice (June 21, 2022), https://ithacavoice.com/2022/06/american-airlines-ending-ithaca-service-despite-objections/ [https://perma.cc/26N8-6LKB].

[154] 15 U.S.C. §§ 1-3; United States v. Am. Tel. & Tel. Co., 552 F. Supp. 131, 135–36 (D.D.C. 1982) ("On January 14, 1949, the government filed an action … against … the American Telephone and Telegraph Company, Inc. … alleging] that the defendants had monopolized and conspired to restrain trade … in violation of sections 1, 2, and 3 of the Sherman Act …."), *aff'd*, 460 U.S. 1001; see also Allocation of Frequencies in the Bands Above 890 MC, 27 F.C.C. 359 (1959); Hush-A-Phone Corp. v. United States, 238 F.2d 266 (D.C. Cir. 1956).

[155] Paul Stephen Dempsey, *Adam Smith Assaults Ma Bell with His Invisible Hands: Divestiture, Deregulation, and the Need for a New Telecommunications Policy*, 11 Hastings Commc'ns & Ent. L.J. 527, 539 (1989).

[156] Am. Tel. & Tel. Co., 552 F. Supp. at 226–27; Dempsey, *supra* note 155, at 531, 552 (describing breakup of AT&T as "most significant single event in American telecommunications history").

As with transportation, deregulation of the telecommunications sector was disproportionately hard on rural communities, despite some continued protections. Specifically, Dempsey wrote in 1989:

> Deregulation … affected rural telephone bills as telephone companies passed on more of the actual service cost to their customers. In the past, federal regulation supported rural subsidies. Under rate-averaging requirements, the FCC required telephone companies to charge urban and rural customers the same for service, despite the fact that fewer customers were available to cover fixed costs ....
> Adequate telecommunications services at a reasonable price are essential for economic growth ....
> [R]ural telephone bills have increased. The process of deregulation could hasten depopulation of rural areas and further the congestion of urban areas because of the greater availability and lower costs of essential services in urban areas.[157]

Universal service is still a legal mandate for phone service providers today, both wired and cellular.[158] Yet, rural communities have been left behind in this sector as well. Dempsey observed in his writing thirty years ago that rural communities were being left out of the "technology revolution"; that rural communities might "never be strung to the national fiber optics system"; and that generally, "whatever benefits urban regions of the nation may enjoy in terms of new technology and increased competition, these benefits appear not to be trickling down to the rural regions of the nation."[159]

Replacing the Telecommunications Act of 1934, the Telecommunications Act of 1996 brought "[t]he cornerstone of telecommunications deregulation in the United States."[160] The Act reduced the role for the FCC's oversight, making way for more competition in service provision.[161] It also broke up traditional regulated phone monopolies and gave state public utility commissions responsibility for ensuring universal service and overseeing pricing, decentralizing regulation from federal agencies to state ones. The Act mandated funding for rural schools, libraries, and healthcare facilities' telecommunications technology. But it "left out low-income households and high cost regions, including rural areas."[162] As a result of relaxed regulations, some rural regions were left "with antiquated telephone technology" that technically met modern federal requirements for universal service, but still "provide[d] a menu of services far below those available in urban areas."[163]

---

[157] Dempsey, *supra* note 155, at 580–81 (footnotes omitted).
[158] *Universal Service*, FCC, www.fcc.gov/general/universal-service [https://perma.cc/2JUB-BPTV].
[159] Dempsey, *supra* note 155, at 581–82.
[160] Telecommunications Act of 1996, Pub. L. No. 104-104, 110 Stat. 56; Nadine Irène Kozak, On the Last Mile: The Effects of Telecommunications Regulation and Deregulation in the Rural Western United States and Canada 17 (2010) (Ph.D. dissertation, University of California San Diego) (on file with the University of California eScholarship).
[161] Kozak, *supra* note 160, at 17 (footnote omitted).
[162] *Id.* at 19 (citing CORNELIA BUTLER FLORA & JAN L. FLORA, RURAL COMMUNITIES: LEGACY AND CHANGE 216 (2d ed. 2004)).
[163] *Id.*

Ironically, then, the telecommunications sector was turned loose just as the seeds were planted for the internet to grow into one of the most important fundamental services of modern society. The rise of broadband internet as a basic public need came at an unfortunate time in the arc of utilities regulation, given its coincidence with enthusiasm for maintaining competitive markets in private sector service provision.[164] The FCC has been the main federal agency tasked with deploying broadband to underserved areas. Yet, its efforts to do so have not yet achieved the vision of a universally connected America.[165] Advocates have coalesced around two obvious solutions to this ongoing digital divide: either do for broadband now what the Rural Electrification Act of 1936 did for electricity,[166] or regulate internet service provision as a public utility.[167] Bills attempting the former goal have failed to pass in Congress. Regulations attempting the latter have ended up in court, although the FCC seems poised to revisit the possibility as of this writing.[168]

Many of today's challenging rural conditions can be traced back to deregulation. This chapter focused on transportation and telecommunications deregulation. But similar trends affected other sectors, such as agriculture and trade, and arguably, the delay in universal broadband deployment. Distressed rural regions have experienced socioeconomic deterioration as populations have migrated to cities, regional employers have shuttered, local governments have lost tax revenue, and infrastructure has aged. This downward cycle of economic nondevelopment is precisely what policymakers and rural advocates have feared since the debates over the Interstate Commerce Act: When necessary infrastructure services are not required to provide service to less profitable places, they cease to do so. The move toward service providers' discretionary service provision has contributed to the concentration of services in densely populated geographic areas, regional economic turmoil, the depopulation of the countryside, and exacerbated geographic wealth inequality.

Deregulation of these sectors can be understood as the retreat of government from rural regions. Where once there were protections, now there is a vacuum. Given the priorities that policymakers chose despite the trade-offs – a mass contraction of infrastructure industries, to the detriment of geographically disadvantaged regions – the

---

[164] *Cf.* Jonathan E. Nuechterlein, Howard Shelanski, *Building on What Works: An Analysis of U.S. Broadband Policy*, 73 FED. COMM. L.J. 219, 220 (2021) (discussing embrace of private sector investment and skepticism of price controls in 2010 FCC National Broadband Plan).

[165] *See generally* Christopher Ali, FARM FRESH BROADBAND: THE POLITICS OF RURAL CONNECTIVITY (MIT PRESS, 2021).

[166] Amie Alexander, *Utility Law-All Hands on Deck: Bringing Broadband Home to Rural Arkansas*, 40 U. ARK. LITTLE ROCK L. REV. 401, 411 (2018).

[167] Ann Eisenberg, Jessica A. Shoemaker, & Lisa R. Pruitt, *5 Ways Biden Can Help Rural America Thrive and Bridge the Rural-Urban Divide*, THE CONVERSATION (Jan. 21, 2021), https://theconversation .com/5-ways-biden-can-help-rural-america-thrive-and-bridge-the-rural-urban-divide-150610 [https://perma .cc/82RP-GEDM].

[168] *FCC Seeks Comment on Safeguarding and Securing the Open Internet*, Federal Communications Commission (Sept. 28, 2023), www.fcc.gov/consumer-governmental-affairs/fcc-seeks-comment-safeguarding-and-securing-open-internet [https://perma.cc/E627-BEAW].

deregulatory era should be understood as a decision to do less for rural communities in order to do more for service providers, urban and suburban consumers, and other perceived interests. While there might have been some wisdom or necessity behind some of these trade-offs, commentary on rural socioeconomic marginalization should at least recognize this development as a choice pursued with some knowledge of the risks. Viewed holistically, this era involved a massive retreat of an important component of the regulatory state from rural America. This was not merely "decline."

Before deregulation, rural communities were folded into the scope and protections of this form of protective regulation; they were a central part of the economic regulatory fabric. Post-deregulation, rural America became aberrant – a special exception to this part of the regulatory system, warranting special assistance, special reports, and special protections. In addition to the tangible negative effects of deregulation and those effects' downstream impacts – such as widespread loss of intercity bus service making already struggling places less attractive and viable – rural America was pushed to the periphery of the regulatory state's protections. In other words, the regulatory state's retreat from rural America reflected government's reduced concern with rural space, physically, socially, and legally – a form, that is, of structural exclusion.

Deindustrialization and deregulation were both large-scale trends with far-reaching impacts. They were also both large-scale trends driven by human beings who made the decisions to pursue them. Deindustrialization and deregulation made rural regions less livable. This is not a story of decline, but a story of deprivation.

6

The Myth of Rural Radicalism

In December 2021, I relocated temporarily from South Carolina to an Airbnb in the Capitol Hill neighborhood of Washington, DC. In January 2022, I started a seven-month fellowship at the Kluge Center at the Library of Congress.[1] It was an exciting opportunity to focus on research. I'd be using it to wrap my head around the complicated world of rural broadband policy while also making progress on this book. Rural broadband is, they say, the new rural electrification, which meant the Rural Electrification Act of 1936 had something to tell me – and you – about rural broadband.

This fellowship was also, it occurred to me, the longest amount of time I had spent living in an actual major coastal urban center. Walking Capitol Hill's chilly, historic streets just before Christmas, the breathtaking townhomes laden with magical, bright lights, I had a slightly surreal sense of being in Disney World. I was also surprised to feel a slight twinge of envy as I scanned the elegant Christmas trees displayed in the bay windows of these more than a century-old homes. Sure, I am a coastal, urban liberal elite. But I'm not *that* elite.

In the spring, the neighborhood would become all the more idyllic. Lincoln and Stanton Parks filled with strollers and golden doodles, cyclists, joggers, and older people power walking in pairs. Most everyone looked slender and healthy in their high-quality athleisure. I frequented a café with an outdoor walk-up window where I could go with my dog and people-watch, conjuring images of Paris.

Lincoln Park on a temperate Saturday was like paradise. But how many people get to have this life that's so advantageously urban? Walking everywhere helped keep us skinny. Fresh and healthy food was available at any number of cafes and restaurants in walking distance if you lived nearby. Wide boulevards, safe parks, and just the right population density made running and dog-walking fun and safe. The air and the water were clean. The public transportation was cheap and relatively close.

---

[1] Portions of this chapter were excerpted from *Rural Disaffection and the Regulatory State*, 126 PENN STATE L. REV. 739 (2022).

But my functional little Airbnb in Capitol Hill was stretching my budget pretty thin. It was almost twice as expensive as my mortgage payment in South Carolina. Many of my friends had left DC or New York because they could no longer afford to live comfortably in those cities once they had kids. Most people around Capitol Hill, except those in service positions, were white, though certainly not everyone. I sometimes felt a pang of grief walking around Capitol Hill, knowing how few people get to live like this. Those service workers' commutes to their jobs were probably pretty long, their actual neighborhoods probably less idyllic. So, sure, the handful of big cities in the U.S. can give you a healthy, harmonious lifestyle ... if you have a lot of money.

Outside of my research, the only time rurality was brought to my attention during my time in DC was when I went to see a production of Oklahoma! at the Kennedy Center. I grew up on Oklahoma! My local high school did a production of it in the late 1990s and my parents loved the 1955 movie version. The version put on at the Kennedy Center was ... different. The director had reworked it to be some kind of commentary on the rural plight. I think. No cowboys danced across the stage, no surrey with a fringe on top was trotted out. No, these Oklahomans spent two hours drinking Bud Light at picnic tables, strumming the occasional guitar. Heavy women with tattoos in too-small jeans shorts played Ado Annie and Gertie Cummings. The main antagonist, local undesirable Jud Fry, was not killed in self-defense by the hero Curly, just brutally murdered by him. All that was missing was a backdrop of a trailer. I remember thinking, "I guess this is ... good?"

I wondered as I walked the Capitol Hill streets over and over again for more than half a year: Is anyone sitting in one of these two million-dollar townhomes on a laptop right now, penning an op-ed about how people in West Virginia are the problem with the country, or how West Virginians need to "get real" about the loss of their way of life?

With everything that I have learned over the past decade – including how the rural way of life actually *has* been under attack by legislators and other powerful decision-makers,[2] and that so many rural places and environments have historically been treated as mere sites of extraction to fuel urban consumption – I am sympathetic to the resentment toward so-called elites, self-proclaimed intellectuals, urbanites, government, and whoever else gets lumped into that category. I have heard enough city dwellers casually dismiss blows to rural livelihoods with a wave of the hand that I think, if I were rural, I would take that pretty personally. I would take the loss of my wages, identity, community, pension, regional prosperity, and certainty about my children's future pretty personally. I would take it personally if a stream I fished in were filled in with toxic coal ash and no one seemed to care. I imagine I would not find it to be much consolation for people in DC to watch a play full of faux-country people pretending to drink Bud Light.

---

[2] *See* Chapter 5, *supra*.

I often think back to a wedding I attended full of New York lawyers when I had been living in West Virginia for about a year. An environmental attorney I sat next to gave me a soapbox lecture about the necessity of not using air conditioning and of only taking public transportation in the interest of fighting climate change. He was clearly very proud of himself for making these sacrifices and felt everyone else should do their part by making them, too. I explained to him that public transportation wasn't really an option in most of West Virginia, and parts of the South could get so hot that people would be at risk without air conditioning.

It struck me in that moment: This guy and a lot of other people like him have no idea what it's like to live someplace other than here. It's easy to brag about taking public transportation in a place that has a great public transportation system. It also reminded me of my Midwestern mother's theory, developed in response to New Yorkers treating her as unsophisticated: that New York City is plenty provincial in its own way, as evidenced by the Manhattanites she used to work with who could keep straight only that she was from "one of the 'I' states" (Illinois).

Meanwhile, the people walking their dogs and strollers around the nicest parts of DC and New York are not only wealthy but powerful. More than one in ten DC residents works for the federal government, and the federal government is the largest single employer in the area. It does not seem implausible to me that decisions have been made by the Lincoln Park golden doodle owners that affect people in far-off places. And it does not seem implausible to me that those decisions might not always be good for those affected.

So I have come to sympathize with many rural complaints, some of which do not fall squarely in the neat and clean boxes of poverty and infrastructure neglect. This sympathy prompted me to ask whether the "antigovernment sentiment" supposedly seen at higher rates throughout rural communities is really driven by an ideological commitment to small government, as it is so often portrayed. As I dug into the question, I concluded that an important, overlooked thread of rural antigovernment sentiment is not just reactionaries railing about conspiracy theories. Some rural antigovernment sentiment is just a rational reaction to the federal government doing a less than optimal job. And sometimes that job is done less than optimally because federal actors do not always know or care about what life is like in rural communities. One can't deny the rise of extremist rhetoric and polarization throughout the country. Nonetheless, I have come to think of the portrayal of rural complaints as mere ideological gripes, notwithstanding those complaints' basis in reality, as the myth of rural radicalism.

To answer my question about rural antigovernment sentiment, I dug into the literature in sociology and rural sociology on rural sentiments toward federal agencies. This review included the books that were making headlines around 2016, such as Hochschild's *Strangers in Their Own Land* and Cramer's *The Politics of*

Resentment, as well as others that received less attention.[3] I found consistent themes across this literature. And those themes were generally not ideological, or talking points detached from reality. The themes, rather, were that rural populations often perceive the regulatory state – meaning federal agencies and the rules they promulgate and enforce – as antithetical to dignity, inclusion, and survival in one way or another. In fact, a deep dive into rural populations' perceptions of the regulatory state seems to confirm common concerns in other areas of literature about the regulatory state's structure, and even its fundamental legitimacy as a part of government.

Legitimacy theory turns on questions of populations' acceptance of, and compliance with, government.[4] The idea of legitimacy is premised on the assumption that people subject to laws and governance are invariably not going to be happy with every decision that government makes. The crux of legitimacy, though, is that even where governed populations are dissatisfied or disagree with governmental decisions, if the institution, law, or decision in question is perceived as legitimate, people will accept and comply with outcomes based on their trust of, and deference to, the relevant institutions – and not merely because of the threat of force or other forms of coercion. A particular governing body has a strong incentive for itself and its decisions to be perceived as legitimate because ensuring compliance by force or coercion is substantially more costly than when a population complies voluntarily.

Binding decisions, laws, institutions, and governments perceived as illegitimate will encounter resentment, resistance, and outright disobedience. Scholarly conversations on legitimacy tend to converge around key conditions that give rise to a particular law or institution's legitimacy or lack thereof.[5] Three of the conditions commonly understood to give rise to legitimacy include: (1) a population's sense of procedural inclusion, respect, and fair treatment; (2) a sense that, even if outcomes are not favorable, they are nonetheless rational, reasonable, or at least not arbitrary;

---

[3] ARLIE HOCHSCHILD, STRANGERS IN THEIR OWN LAND: ANGER AND MOURNING IN THE AMERICAN RIGHT (2016) (examining opposition to federal government in Louisiana); KATHERINE J. CRAMER, THE POLITICS OF RESENTMENT: RURAL CONSCIOUSNESS AND THE RISE OF SCOTT WALKER (2016) (articulating theory of rural political consciousness and anti-government resentment based on ethnographic study conducted in Wisconsin from 2007 to 2012); JENNIFER SHERMAN, DIVIDING PARADISE: RURAL INEQUALITY AND THE DIMINISHING AMERICAN DREAM (2021) (investigating community in Washington state experiencing gentrification and inequality); LOKA ASHWOOD, FOR-PROFIT DEMOCRACY: WHY THE GOVERNMENT IS LOSING THE TRUST OF RURAL AMERICA (2018) (studying relationships in rural Georgia community hosting nuclear plant); JILL LINDSEY HARRISON, PESTICIDE DRIFT AND THE PURSUIT OF ENVIRONMENTAL JUSTICE 131 (2011) (examining political conflict in California over pesticide drift).

[4] Tom R. Tyler, *Psychological Perspectives on Legitimacy and Legitimation*, 57 ANNU. REV. PSYCHOL. 375, 376 (2006).

[5] *See generally* Monica C. Bell, *Police Reform and the Dismantling of Legal Estrangement*, 126 YALE L.J. 2054, 2065 (2017); Victor D. Quintanilla, *Human-Centered Civil Justice Design*, 121 PENN. ST. L. REV. 745, 764 (2017); Emily Hammond & David L. Markell, *Administrative Proxies for Judicial Review: Building Legitimacy from the Inside-Out*, 37 HARV. ENVTL. L. REV. 313, 320 (2013)

and (3) for a particular community or group, a sense that the institution or law serves them in addition to other members of society; or in other words, the presence of a nonantagonistic relationship and the absence of a sense that the institution or law in question is merely a locus of power for another group's interests.

A synthesis of literature on rural populations' perceptions of the regulatory state suggests a crisis of legitimacy. Specifically, rural communities' disaffection with the regulatory state closely mirrors the conditions giving rise to legitimacy problems, which are often explored through a variety of angles in administrative law scholarship.[6] An analysis of the literature on rural views reveals that rural communities experience procedural injustice in their involvement with the regulatory state, that they are often frustrated with the regulatory state's substantive outcomes that affect them, and that they generally view the regulatory state through an "us versus them" lens.

The discussion that follows applies these conditions for legitimacy to the question of rural communities' relationships with the regulatory state. This analysis involved a review of prominent works of sociology[7] and rural sociology,[8] drawing out any mentions of perceptions of federal agencies; a review of literature on Westlaw based on key word searches for mentions of perceptions of the regulatory state among rural populations, with a focus on including rural populations of diverse racial and ethnic backgrounds; and additional searches in online databases for literature discussing rural sentiments toward federal agencies and their activities.

This analysis includes studies focused on such diverse places as Georgia, Louisiana, New Mexico, Washington State, and Wisconsin. Those studies also included the views of diverse groups, including Black, Native American, Latinx, and white rural populations. And the studies assessed those views in relation to multiple federal agencies affecting rural lifestyles and livelihoods, including the U.S. Department of Interior's (DOI) Fish and Wildlife Service (FWS) and Bureau of Land Management (BLM), the U.S. Department of Agriculture (USDA), the Nuclear Regulatory Commission (NRC), and the U.S. Environmental Protection Agency (EPA).

Generalization is, of course, challenging. The grievances addressed in the discussion that follows are not all considered to be moral equivalents. A Native American tribe's displacement from public lands is simply not the same as white ranchers

---

[6] *See generally* Cass R. Sunstein, *Chevron As Law*, 107 GEO. L.J. 1613, 1617 (2019); Emily Hammond, *Chevron's Generality Principles*, 83 FORDHAM L. REV. 655, 660 (2014); Gillian E. Metzger, *Administrative Law As the New Federalism*, 57 DUKE L.J. 2023, 2091 (2008).

[7] These include Hochshild, *supra* note 3; Cramer, *supra* note 3; ROBERT WUTHNOW, THE LEFT BEHIND 5 (2018); STEPHANIE A. MALIN, THE PRICE OF NUCLEAR POWER: URANIUM COMMUNITIES AND ENVIRONMENTAL JUSTICE S (RUTGERS UNIV. PRESS, 2015); and JILL LINDSEY HARRISON, PESTICIDE DRIFT AND THE PURSUIT OF ENVIRONMENTAL JUSTICE (MIT PRESS, 2011).

[8] These include JENNIFER SHERMAN, THOSE WHO WORK, THOSE WHO DON'T: POVERTY, MORALITY, AND FAMILY IN RURAL AMERICA (2009) [hereinafter Sherman, *Those Who Work*]; JENNIFER SHERMAN, DIVIDING PARADISE: RURAL INEQUALITY AND THE DIMINISHING AMERICAN DREAM (2021) [hereinafter Sherman, *Dividing Paradise*]; and Ashwood, *supra* note 3.

facing restrictions on grazing permits, for instance. Yet, the common outcomes across these experiences in perceptions of the regulatory state as foe rather than friend to a rural way of life seem worth highlighting to better contextualize the myth of rural radicalism. The common themes across diverse populations, places, and agencies undercut the idea that dissatisfaction with federal governance is merely an ideological phenomenon among rural white conservatives.

RURAL PERCEPTIONS OF PROCEDURAL INJUSTICE IN THE REGULATORY STATE

The first condition necessary to afford a particular institution legitimacy is a perception of procedural justice. Procedural *injustice* may be defined as "experiences in which individuals feel treated unfairly" by government, perceptions that government actors have behaved disrespectfully, and perceptions of a dismissive stance on the part of government toward community members' rights and concerns.[9] Other literature on procedural justice emphasizes the importance of rights of participation, opportunities to voice concerns regarding binding decisions, and acceptance of decisions' soundness or substantive accuracy, at least to a reasonable degree.[10] The literature on rural populations' perceptions of the regulatory state seems to include a component of perceived procedural injustice.

One of the most prominent themes influencing rural feelings toward the regulatory state is a sense of powerlessness in relationships with federal agencies and the federal government more broadly. This sense of exclusion has even been characterized as feeling bullied or belittled in interactions with federal agencies. For instance, rural sociologist Jennifer Sherman's 2014 study of longtime residents of pseudonymized Paradise Valley, Washington, a declining farming and ranching community, elicited many of these themes from those she interviewed. Sherman did not, unlike other researchers, hear "talk of either moral outrage or minorities having cut the line."[11] Instead, "much of the frustration that old-timers [longtime local residents] expressed had to do with the experience of being unimportant or unheard," especially in their relationships with federal agencies, including the U.S. Forest Service and Bureau of Land Management.[12] Many residents "connected antigovernment sentiments to concrete experiences of vulnerability or abuse at the hands of these larger entities."[13]

In an earlier study by Sherman in the northern California timber community of "Golden Valley," she found a similar sense of disempowerment among residents.

[9] Monica C. Bell, *Police Reform and the Dismantling of Legal Estrangement*, 126 YALE L.J. 2054 (2017).
[10] Lawrence B. Solum, *Procedural Justice*, 78 S. CAL. L. REV. 181, 320 (2004) (articulating the theory of procedural justice as an essential prerequisite for legitimacy).
[11] SHERMAN, *Dividing Paradise*, *supra* note 3, at 176.
[12] *Id.* at 176–180.
[13] *Id.*

Sherman conducted the study from 2003 to 2004, just over a decade after the Fish and Wildlife Service listed the spotted owl as a protected endangered species in 1990. This federal governance decision saw substantial local opposition at the time and had severe subsequent economic ripple effects. Sherman observed irony in the national media coverage of the controversy as one of "owls versus loggers" because "both owls and loggers were affected populations that had little to no agency in the decisions."[14] She noted that, "While loggers had major stakes in the outcome, ultimately they were just workers within the forest industry .... They were unable to influence the outcome in any area except the public's imagination."[15] This sense of powerlessness in turn fueled locals' perception of the listing as an unwarranted attack on their way of life.

These feelings of exclusion and belittlement at the hands of federal agencies have been observed in diverse rural communities. For instance, complaints about procedural exclusion have been raised in the context of federal agencies' obligations to consult with Native American tribes and local governments in the West that have been affected by large public land holdings. Rowe, Finley, and Baldwin argue that, while some federal consultations with tribes comport with best practices and often meet the legally required procedural minimums, "consultations usually meet the letter of the law while providing tribes with little opportunity to meaningfully shape agency decisions."[16] This has led to "a widespread perception among tribes" that consultation processes fail "to adequately and substantively incorporate tribes' concerns in the planning process."[17] Others report that agencies do not necessarily comply with legal requirements due to a lack of enforceability. Thus, "tribal officials understandably become disillusioned and the federal-tribal relationship suffers long-term damage."[18]

Sociologist Loka Ashwood found similar sentiments surrounding public meetings that the Nuclear Regulatory Commission (NRC) conducted in a community of Black and white residents in Burke County, Georgia. These meetings were perceived as "scripted actions defined by bureaucratic rules."[19] White and Black residents alike in Burke County felt hopeless, even threatened, in their relationships with the local nuclear power plant that the NRC was perceived to support to the severe detriment of the community. If local residents went up against "the system" – the joint powerhouse of the plant and the NRC – it was understood that there would be backlash, such as lost jobs. Local activist Reverend Samuel Franklin attempted to

---

[14] *Id.* at 35.
[15] *Id.* at 36.
[16] Matthew J. Rowe et al., *Accountability or Merely "Good Words"? An Analysis of Tribal Consultation under the National Environmental Policy Act and the National Historic Preservation Act*, 8 ARIZ.J. ENV'T L. & POL'Y 1, 19 (2018).
[17] *Id.* at 5.
[18] Colette Routel & Jeffrey Holth, *Toward Genuine Tribal Consultation in the 21st Century*, 46 U. MICH. J. L. REFORM 417, 467 (2013).
[19] LOKA ASHWOOD, FOR-PROFIT DEMOCRACY: WHY THE GOVERNMENT IS LOSING THE TRUST OF RURAL AMERICA 167 (2018).

support the efforts of white activists who came from out of town to advocate reform, but "ma[d]e it clear that he had little hope in the efficacy of their go-through-the-government ways."[20] Ashwood highlights "a simple truth relied on by those perpetually disinherited in the Burke County [B]lack community: God, not government, would deliver justice."[21]

In the local government context, many local government officials, especially in the West where federal agencies manage large amounts of public land, have complained about agencies' "highly variable planning processes" and the use of "technocratic language that means very little to local communities,"[22] exacerbating local feelings of exclusion and powerlessness. As one scholar states,

> when larger governmental units, like the federal government, ignore issues raised by smaller units, like state and local government, it appears as though the larger units are dismissing rural communities and their concerns …. By failing to account for the issues raised by smaller governmental units, larger governmental units effectively disregard rural communities.[23]

RURAL POPULATIONS' DEEP FRUSTRATION WITH SUBSTANTIVE OUTCOMES

The second condition necessary to create legitimacy is, where a population is subject to an institution's decisions, the population perceives those decisions as fair, or at least rational. Yet, rural residents have also expressed disillusionment or frustration with the substantive outcomes of federal agency decisions that affect them. Rural commentary tends to characterize federal agencies as capricious, unpredictable, and failing to serve local needs, if not actively harming residents. Overall, federal regulatory processes are perceived as detached, heartless, and meaningless, seeking to impose uninformed plans on rural communities through one-size-fits-all frameworks with little regard for local conditions and needs. Two common themes among rural frustrations with substantive outcomes emerged in this analysis: (1) A perception that agency outcomes make it harder to make a living; and (2) a perception that agency outcomes fail to protect rural residents from environmental threats.

---

[20] *Id.* at 159; JILL LINDSEY HARRISON, PESTICIDE DRIFT AND THE PURSUIT OF ENVIRONMENTAL JUSTICE 131 (2011) (explaining that residents complaining of pesticide poisoning were dismissed by regulatory officials).

[21] ASHWOOD, *supra* note 3, at 158.

[22] Michelle Bryan et al., *Cause for Rebellion? Examining How Federal Land Management Agencies & Local Governments Collaborate on Land Use Planning*, 6 J. OF ENERGY & ENV'T L. 1, 20 (2015), https://gwjeel.com/wp-content/uploads/2015/07/jeel_vol6_issue2_bryan.pdf; *see also* Rick Su, *Democracy in Rural America*, 98 N.C. L. REV. 837, 867, 873 (2020) (observing that unlike local governments, federal agencies are not directly responsive to local constituents and agencies tend to use "top-down" approach in rural communities).

[23] Holly Firlein, *Continental Divides: How Wolf Conservation in the United States and Europe Impacts Rural Attitudes*, 45 ECOLOGY L.Q. 327, 341 (2018).

A PERCEPTION THAT AGENCY OUTCOMES
MAKE IT HARDER TO MAKE A LIVING

Threats to livelihoods are a prominent theme in the literature on rural sentiments toward the regulatory state. Perceptions of those threats range in degree and depend upon who is asked. On one end of that spectrum, sentiments may involve relatively mild frustrations with agency decisions that seem inconvenient or unwise. On the other hand, sentiments may involve a deep sense of betrayal and oppression. The experiences of Black farmers at the hands of the U.S. Department of Agriculture provide a particularly egregious illustration of a federal agency crushing a rural population's livelihoods while also failing to offer protection from threats, a theme discussed later. Through its support of discriminatory county commissioners who undermined Black farmers' access to essential credit and benefit programs, and its failure to investigate subsequent civil rights complaints, the USDA's role in the massive dispossession of Black-owned farmland over the past several decades helped the agency earn its reputation as "the last plantation" among Black rural populations.[24]

Diverse rural populations continue to perceive the regulatory state as a danger to livelihoods and economic well-being. For instance, certain Native American tribes have expressed fears about the regulatory state threatening local economic dependence on coal extraction. Tribes have also struggled to maintain subsistence livelihoods due to a lack of control over public lands they have historically depended on for survival. As one example, Anderson describes "widespread dissatisfaction among the Alaska Native community with the limited nature of the federal subsistence program" managed by the Department of Interior.[25]

Predominantly white residents in extractive and land-based industries often see the regulatory state as a threat to their livelihoods. The Fosters, a married couple interviewed by Sherman in her Paradise Valley study, expressed the perception that agencies made their way of life harder. "[L]ike a number of other farmers and ranchers in the area," Sherman observed, the Fosters "experienced the government as an outside force whose whims were unpredictable and seldom responsive to their needs."[26] The law itself was considered an unpredictable barrier to making a living. Interviewees working in farming and ranching "often faced overwhelming challenges related to changing regulations. In addition to labor laws and water regulations, grazing permits were a major source of frustration for a number of old-timers

---

[24] *See* Pigford v. Glickman, 185 F.R.D. 82, 85–89 (D.D.C. 1999), aff'd, 206 F.3d 1212 (D.C. Cir. 2000); Angela P. Harris, *(Re)integrating Spaces: The Color of Farming*, 2 SAVANNAH L. REV. 157, 179 (2015) (attributing 98 percent decrease in Black farmers between 1920 and 1997 to partition suits and "credit discrimination perpetrated by the federal government itself through the USDA").

[25] Robert T. Anderson, *Sovereignty and Subsistence: Native Self-Government and Rights to Hunt, Fish, and Gather after ANCSA*, 33 ALASKA L. REV. 187, 215 (2016).

[26] SHERMAN, DIVIDING PARADISE, *supra* note 3, at 182.

in the cattle industry, many of whom complained at length about the decrease in public land available to them."[27]

The Fosters explained that "over the years government regulations and interventions had repeatedly challenged their livelihood."[28] They added, "We had to get out of the orchard industry because [of] regulations ... [W]e couldn't keep up with ... what the government wanted to do .... [I]t was ridiculous, but it was the law."[29] The couple said that "changing labor regulations made it difficult" to continue in the orchard business, and "they also struggled with changing rules regarding irrigation."[30] Changes in conservation priorities "contributed to their experiences of loss and betrayal."[31] In general, the sense of powerlessness felt by locals in Paradise Valley "was exacerbated by the feeling that those same agencies [the Forest Service, Bureau of Land Management, and state Department of Ecology] gave back little to the community, abandoning local populations while continually imposing new obstacles."[32]

Agency decisions are also often considered detached from local needs and knowledge. One rancher:

> described fighting with the Fish and Wildlife Agency over grazing rights to public lands, explaining that it failed to recognize that grazing was only detrimental to ecosystems when cows were fenced in too tightly. [She said,] "[T]hey have attorneys writing these things up, and attorneys answering why you shouldn't graze, but they don't address animal health or biosecurity or things that are important .... They kind of harassed us and it's unbelievable .... We had to sell a lot of cows because we just had our private land to graze them on."[33]

In her Paradise Valley study, Sherman found that antigovernment discourse on the news mirrored rural residents' "personal trials, including individual experiences with seemingly capricious agencies, institutions, and agendas that had negatively impacted their lives and livelihoods[,] ... [exhibiting] raw frustration with specific agencies and interventions that impacted their daily existence and way of life."[34] Even an employee of the U.S. Forest Service described it as top-down, bloated, and useless, stating, "we all agree that we [the Forest Service] do nothing."[35]

Another study highlighted rural residents' frustrations with conservation initiatives that were perceived as an imposition of disproportionate local burdens based on detached or uninformed urban priorities. In response to Fish and Wildlife efforts to conserve wolf populations, a rancher in New Mexico stated,

---

[27] *Id.* at 183.
[28] *Id.*
[29] *Id.* at 181–82
[30] *Id.* at 182.
[31] *Id.* at 184.
[32] *Id.* at 180.
[33] *Id.* at 184.
[34] *Id.* at 179.
[35] *Id.* at 180; CRAMER, *supra* note 3, at 150–51, 189.

People in the East view this part of the country as empty public lands and think
it should stay that way. They don't have a clue what it's like. All this is done on a
whim. Why should ranchers be prepared to take losses just so some New York City
guy can sleep well knowing there's wolves in the wild?[36]

Another rancher said, "Take the wolves and plant em in Central Park, cause they
impose it on us to have these goddamn wolves!"[37] In a similar vein, in Sherman's
study of California's Golden Valley, she found that locals universally blamed the
Fish and Wildlife Service spotted owl listing for "the sudden and devastating deterioration of their town and the local labor market."[38]

A PERCEPTION THAT AGENCY OUTCOMES FAIL TO PROTECT LOCALS FROM ENVIRONMENTAL THREATS

Many rural residents crave greater protection from – or remediation of – threats,
including severe environmental and public health hazards. This desire for protection comes in a variety of forms. Unexplained cancer clusters and inedible fish
surrounding polluted sites in Louisiana, Georgia, and Utah, for instance, drive residents' sense of a need for action. Yet those residents, too, often find reason to question whether the regulatory state has their best interests in mind.

African American U.S. Army Lieutenant General Russel Honoré, a Louisiana
resident interviewed by sociologist Arlie Hochschild, remarked how the U.S.
Environmental Protection Agency "passes the buck" to the industry-captured state
government of Louisiana, leaving residents vulnerable to private sector whims and
hazardous pollution.[39] Black residents interviewed by Ashwood in Burke County,
Georgia, expressed similar views: They desperately wanted protection from hazards
associated with the local nuclear plant, but the NRC was regularly perceived to side
with industry over locals.[40]

In the predominantly white town of Monticello, Utah, where two Superfund
sites were designated in 1989 due to legacies of uranium processing, environmental
sociologist Stephanie Malin found that the federal government was perceived as
having abandoned local residents after using them for decades of energy production. The Superfund sites "have been linked to ongoing, contested, and under-
addressed environmental and health issues," including cancer clusters.[41] However,
multiple federal agencies, including the Department of Energy and the Agency for

---

[36] Firlein, *supra* note 23, at 339.
[37] *Id.* (internal quotations omitted).
[38] JENNIFER SHERMAN, THOSE WHO WORK, THOSE WHO DON'T: POVERTY, MORALITY, AND FAMILY IN RURAL AMERICA 35 (2009).
[39] HOCHSCHILD, *supra* note 3, at 59.
[40] ASHWOOD, *supra* note 3, at 167.
[41] STEPHANIE A. MALIN, THE PRICE OF NUCLEAR POWER: URANIUM COMMUNITIES AND ENVIRONMENTAL JUSTICE 60 (2015).

Toxic Substances and Disease Registry, "did not conclude that the cancer clusters were related to uranium exposure, despite noting elevated rates of various cancers in the community."[42] This has led to community members feeling "ignored by federal agencies and scientists, reporting ... that they did not receive satisfactory responses to their public health concerns."[43] This dissatisfaction spurred the growth of a local activist group devoted to holding federal agencies accountable "because they were tired of seeing neighbors suffer illnesses without explanation and felt they deserved more honesty from the federal government," and that they should "make the federal government right the wrong they did to the community."[44]

In sociologist Jill Lindsey Harrison's California-based study examining the phenomenon of "pesticide drift" – the problem of hazardous pesticides moving through the air into residential areas – interviewees were similarly disillusioned with federal regulatory institutions. Activists interviewed in the study included "a diverse array of Latino/a farmworkers and their family members, other low-income agricultural community residents of color, and White, middle-class, and upper-middle class professionals."[45] Interviewees expressed the belief that cooperative tactics with federal and state regulatory officials (as well as with industry) "have failed to protect residents from pesticide exposure," motivating activists to adopt more confrontational tactics with government institutions.[46]

In general, a notable feature of rural concerns about both economic and environmental precarity, and the role of federal agencies in relation to both, is that the industries upon which locals economically depend may well also be the industries that pose the greatest threats to local ecologies and public health. Due to rural regions' relative isolation and lack of economic alternatives, this tension can result in a unique alchemy influencing rural sentiments toward industry and the regulatory state, which may strike outsiders as contradictory.

Specifically, many residents remain loyal to the polluting industries that employ them or those they know, while other residents take up environmental justice fights and advocate for the polluting industries to leave. Race, class, and views of federal agencies interact with these factors. For instance, although white rural workers and residents may bear environmental injustice burdens, they are more likely than communities of color to enjoy some of the hazardous industries' economic benefits.[47] These interacting factors help explain white rural populations' propensity to want

---

[42] *Id.* at 63. The Agency for Toxic Substances and Disease Registry is an agency of the U.S. Department of Health and Human Services. *See Agency for Toxic Substances and Disease Registry*, ATSDR, https://bit.ly/3DuCPXa [https://perma.cc/KB6R-VZBH].

[43] MALIN, *supra* note 7, at 63.

[44] *Id.*

[45] HARRISON, *supra* note 7, at 22.

[46] *Id.* at 172,

[47] *See, e.g.*, Thomas E. Shriver and Gary R. Webb, *Rethinking the Scope of Environmental Justice: Perceptions of Health Hazards in a Rural Native American Community Exposed to Carbon Black*, 74 RURAL SOC. 270, 272 (2009).

less government intervention despite perceiving industry's threats, and their tendency to side with industry over the regulatory state. At least industry has something to offer them – unlike agencies, which are perceived to be ineffectual anyway. These disparities also help explain rural minorities' greater desire for protection through the regulatory state rather than wanting agencies to simply leave them alone, because they are often excluded from local industries' economic benefits. Yet, many remain hopeless or disillusioned that such protection is attainable.[48]

RURAL POPULATIONS EXPERIENCE A COMMUNITY-LEVEL SENSE OF TENSION WITH THE REGULATORY STATE

The third component of legitimacy theory I address in this analysis concerns collectively antagonistic relationships between communities and institutions. Legitimacy literature often connects an individual's perception of poor treatment by government actors to that individual's perception of illegitimacy. However, members of a community may perceive mistreatment targeted toward others as a sign that the community as a whole stands in tension with a particular institution.[49] These vicarious negative experiences can "feed into a more general, cultural sense of alienation," making perceptions of illegitimacy emerge from "the cumulative, collective experience of procedural and substantive injustice."[50] Communities may develop "collective memory" of interactions with government actors, or a "cultural conception of what it is like to interact" with government actors "that emanates in part from membership in a group or identity category."[51] In short, this component of illegitimacy involves a sense of distrust of institutions and their activities not because "they do bad things to me," but because "they do bad things to us."

This factor also emerges as a theme in the literature on rural relationships with the regulatory state. In particular, there is a collective sense of the regulatory state as frequent antagonist in an "us-versus-them" relationship. Rural populations often express resignation to the fact that agencies serve some group or population other than them.[52]

The "us" tends to connote a place-based identity under attack – local, rural, or industry-related, for instance – although it also intersects with overlapping identities,

---

[48] See ASHWOOD, *supra* note 3, at 158; Thomas E. Shriver and Gary R. Webb, *Rethinking the Scope of Environmental Justice: Perceptions of Health Hazards in a Rural Native American Community Exposed to Carbon Black*, 74 RURAL SOC. 270, 278, 284–85 (2009) (describing Native American interviewees in rural environmental justice community as perceiving "an institutionalized system of racism, neglect, and denial" and lack of assessment or standards by EPA, the Centers for Disease Control, OSHA, and in particular the Oklahoma state environmental agency to address severe local contamination).

[49] Bell, *supra* note 5, at 2105.

[50] *Id.*

[51] *Id.* at 2106.

[52] See, e.g., Sherman, *Dividing Paradise*, *supra* note 3, at 180–81.

such as race and class.[53] The "them," or the populations or entities agencies are perceived to serve to the detriment of rural residents, tend to include urban residents
and corporations.[54] The antagonistic relationship, then, is that rural residents often
perceive the regulatory state's service to corporate interests and urban elites as an
attack on rural ways of life. For rural communities of color, these perceptions are
also intertwined with the understanding that the regulatory state systematically prioritizes the interests of white people.[55]

The regulatory state's perceived fealty to concentrated corporate interests, in
general, is a regular theme among diverse rural residents' views. For instance, in
Sherman's Paradise Valley study, she observed that "[m]any old-timers ... found
federal rules and regulations capricious, serving large and outside interests while
oppressing and impoverishing small-scale operations."[56] This concern about joint
corporate-regulatory antagonism may involve more of an urgent sense of immediate violence, as with agencies' perceived failure to address problems of worker
abuse, pesticide poisoning, and other forms of industry exploitation in Harrison's
pesticide drift study.[57] A central theme of Ashwood's several years of fieldwork in
Georgia revolved around both actual and perceived regulatory fealty to corporate interests in the system Ashwood calls "for-profit democracy."[58] A local former
NRC regulator who Ashwood spoke to emphasized the importance of plant profits and balanced budgets in the short-term over safety and long-term planning to
NRC decision-making. He stated, "Industry is the biggest stakeholder, with the
most influence .... It is not the public. It is not Congress, because industry influences them."[59]

The regulatory state's perceived fealty to urban elites often emerges as a parallel theme. The discussion earlier of rural disappointments with agency decision-
making illustrates this view: Conservation initiatives, in particular, are often viewed
as uninformed urbanites imposing an impractical and oppressive vision on regions
they neither care about nor understand. Although "jobs versus environment" tensions are a classic example, the perception of urbanites imposing their priorities on

---

[53] *See, e.g.*, Ashwood, *supra* note 3, at 69 (quoting several local residents characterizing nuclear plant
as a "they" threatening local landownership, aesthetics, and traditions in interest of greed); Sherman,
Those Who Work, supra note 8, at 35.

[54] *Cf.* Sherman, *Those Who Work, supra* note 8, at 38 (describing Northwestern loggers' sense that spotted owl controversy was "a clash of urban versus traditional rural cultures, with the latter being over-
whelmed and devalued by the former"); James R. Rasband, *The Rise of Urban Archipelagoes in the
American West: A New Reservation Policy?*, 31 Env't L. 1, 44 (2001) (suggesting that urban newcomers
to Western archipelagos advocating preservation and recreation on public lands ought to recognize
interests of communities that preceded them in Western land uses).

[55] *See, e.g.*, Ashwood, *supra* note 3, at 173 (quoting a Black local resident describing the local nuclear
plant as "white authority").

[56] SHERMAN, *supra* note 3, at 181.

[57] *See* Harrison, *supra* note 20.

[58] ASHWOOD, *supra* note 3, at 69.

[59] *Id.* at 16.

rural regions through the regulatory state is not limited to that conflict. For instance, one study documented rural educators' belief that federal education laws, administered through the Department of Education, are "designed primarily for urban and suburban districts and poorly suited for rural districts."[60]

Across studies, scholars have described rural residents' perceptions of the regulatory state's effect on their lives as the feeling that their very way of life is being taken from them.[61] This sense of attack may have to do with the disappointment in substantive outcomes discussed earlier. Losses of livelihoods and environmental destruction can each represent the deterioration of a regional culture. But many rural residents also lament the destruction or enclosure of both private and public local landscapes that they had once engaged with more intimately, freely, safely, and meaningfully.[62] Federal agencies are often viewed as culpable in this enclosure, whether as landowners that newly restrict access or as supporters of dominant industry players. Thus, many rural residents view federal agencies as playing a role in helping take away their childhoods, landscapes, memories, and folkways.[63]

Importantly, as Ashwood observes, the sense of us-versus-them is not as simple as cohesive rural populations on the one hand versus federal agencies and their real beneficiaries on the other.[64] For instance, both Black and white residents of Burke County, Georgia, including those who worked for the nuclear plant, viewed the NRC and the nuclear power plant as a dominating threat. But racial segregation and tension remained poignant in the community such that Black and white residents did not see themselves to be united as one force of opposition against the plant. Black residents, in fact, attempted to recruit Ashwood (who is white) during her field research to reach out to white locals to protest construction of new reactors. Thus, while rural marginalization is common across both of these communities, experiences and reactions vary based on other intersectional identities. Both populations viewed the regulatory state through the lens of hopelessness and powerlessness. Their respective responses to that feeling, though, broke down along racial lines. White locals, Ashwood observed, turned to right-wing politics. Black locals turned to the church.[65]

---

[60] Lars D. Johnson et al., Bellwether Educ. Partners, Federal Education Policy in Rural America 16 (Dec. 31, 2014), https://bellwether.org/wp-content/uploads/2014/12/ROCI_2014FedEdPolicy_Final.pdf. [https://perma.cc/6JWF-7KJS]; Deena Dulgerian, *The Impact of the Every Student Succeeds Act on Rural Schools*, 24 Geo. J. on Poverty L. & Pol'y 111, 112 (2016).

[61] See Erin Morrow, *Agri-Environmentalism: A Farm Bill for 2007*, 38 Tex. Tech L. Rev. 345, 348 (2006).

[62] See, e.g., Sherman, *Those Who Work*, supra note 38, at 35; see also Steven Stoll, Ramp Hollow: The Ordeal of Appalachia (2017) (examining the history of Appalachian land dispossession and coal extraction).

[63] See Ashwood, supra note 3, at 8–10, 69.

[64] Id. at 232.

[65] Id. at 14 (describing local residents as "turning to guns and God" as an "outlet for justice and the retribution denied by what Karl Polanyi called the market society").

Rural communities of color are often certain that the regulatory state operates in service of white supremacy, providing small- and large-scale material benefits to white populations to the severe detriment of rural minorities.[66] The explanations for this view often involve egregious stories of federal agencies' complicity in racial marginalization. For instance, one study involving interviews with Black farmers in the Mississippi Delta revealed that "[t]hey believed that the [USDA lending agency] Farmers Home Administration (FmHA) ha[d] intentionally tried to drive them out of business by not providing loans in a timely manner and by foreclosing on their operations."[67] Native American communities' distrust toward the federal government and its agencies has been characterized as centuries old, informed by the trauma of displacement, genocide, and other forms of violence.[68]

To be clear, some rural populations have expressed enthusiastic sentiments about federal agencies' aspirations and activities. For instance, one New Mexico rancher, despite his skepticism of the Endangered Species Act, described it as "a thing of beauty."[69] I have also written about the inclusive and intimate planning processes pursued by the Fish and Wildlife Service at the Malheur Wildlife Refuge as an example of effective, multi-stakeholder collaboration on complex questions of land use.[70] Instances such as these exist throughout the country.

Nonetheless, the evidence explored here is ample and concerning. Throughout the country and across demographics – despite important variations – scholarly investigations have found themes of hopelessness, powerlessness, disappointment, frustration, betrayal, and antagonism in rural populations' perceptions of the regulatory state. These themes are largely in alignment with the conditions giving rise to perceptions of government illegitimacy. The widespread nature of these views, alongside their consistency with problematic conditions described in legitimacy literature, suggests that the problem might not lie so much with oft-critiqued aspects of rural culture and politics. The problem might lie with the regulatory state itself.

---

[66] *See, e.g.*, Malin, *supra* note 7, at 140 (describing activists' views on environmental racism and the regulatory state's complicity therein).

[67] Spencer D. Wood & Jess Gilbert, *Returning African American Farmers to the Land: Recent Trends and a Policy Rationale*, 27 Rev. of Black Pol. Econ. 43, 57 (2000).

[68] *See* Amy Head, *The Death of the New Buffalo: The Fifth Circuit Slays Indian Gaming in Texas*, 34 Tex. Tech L. Rev. 377, 382 (2003); *see also* Nathan Munier et al., *Determinants of Rural Latino Trust in the Federal Government*, 37 Hisp. J. Behav. Sci. 420, 432–34 (2015) (connecting distrust of federal government in rural Latino population in Illinois to harsh federal measures taken against immigrants and sense that federal institutions ignore Latinos' concerns and "are incapable of taking their desires seriously").

[69] Erin Morrow, *The Environmental Front: Cultural Warfare in the West*, 25 J. Land Res. & Env't L. 183, 193 (2005).

[70] Ann Eisenberg, *Alienation and Reconciliation in Social-Ecological Systems*, 47 Env't L. 127 (2017) (discussing collaborative, multi-stakeholder planning process at Malheur Wildlife Refuge as example of success story).

RURAL SENTIMENTS' ALIGNMENT WITH OBJECTIVE
STRUCTURAL FEATURES OF THE REGULATORY STATE

Commentators might still be inclined to dismiss this literature. Rural sociologist Michael Carolan points out that there is a tendency to "ascribe irrationality" to rural behaviors and views, as with the inclination to accuse rural voters of being illogical with their voting patterns.[71] Yet, comparing and contrasting these rural sentiments with objective structural features of the regulatory state lends credibility to their views. The discussion now explores how feelings such as those examined earlier find a basis in objective structural aspects of the regulatory state.

ARE RURAL POPULATIONS STRUCTURALLY EXCLUDED FROM
AGENCY AVENUES FOR PUBLIC PARTICIPATION?

Rural residents' perceived voicelessness in relation to federal agencies is not particularly surprising viewed alongside the structure of, and literature on, avenues for public participation in agency decision-making. First, one of agencies' main activities is promulgating rules, a process which they commence by issuing a Notice of Proposed Rulemaking (NPRM) to the public, inviting public comment and participation. These processes are widely recognized to be inaccessible to average people.[72] The same barriers that marginalize individuals and populations in other ways – including race and class – act as barriers to participation in regulatory governance.

Geography, though, is likely an underappreciated barrier to participation in NPRMs. For instance, most comments on NPRMs are submitted online today. However, rural residents and tribes have substantially more limited access to the high-speed internet that would help make them equal participants in that process.[73] Even if a particular rural resident or under-resourced interest group had the means to participate in an NPRM, it is not clear that such participation would afford the meaningful "voice" associated with perceptions of procedural justice.

As to local collaborations between residents and agencies, the legal frameworks for these processes are highly variable and context specific. This suggests that whether a local public meeting is considered perfunctory or not could largely turn on an individual agency or bureau's professional culture and commitment to collaboration.[74] In any event, the rural sentiments expressed earlier are not unrealistic when compared to the structure and nature of processes for local–federal collaboration.

---

[71] *Cf.* Michael Carolan, *The Rural Problem: Justice in the Countryside*, 85 RURAL SOCIO. 22, 23, 50 (2019) (noting commentators' propensity to "ascribe irrationality" to rural behaviors and arguing that this tendency inhibits "mak[ing] sense of what is happening in the countryside").

[72] Michael Sant'Ambrogio & Glen Staszewski, *Democratizing Rule Development*, 98 WASH. U. L. REV. 793, 797 (2021).

[73] FED. COMMC'NS COMM'N, FCC-19-44, BROADBAND DEPLOYMENT REPORT 16 (2019).

[74] *See, e.g.*, Eisenberg, *supra* note 70.

ARE RURAL POPULATIONS SUBJECT TO UNFAVORABLE SUBSTANTIVE OUTCOMES OF AGENCY DECISIONS?

The two types of unfavorable substantive agency outcomes discussed earlier that are frequent concerns for rural communities include (1) agency decisions as a threat to livelihoods and (2) agency action (or inaction) providing inadequate protection from environmental threats. Aspects of agencies' decision-making processes may well help explain these rural fears.

REGULATORY TRADE-OFFS AND RURAL LIVELIHOODS

Cost–Benefit Analysis

A central component of agency rulemaking, cost–benefit analysis centers on a Clinton-era Executive Order's mandate to federal agencies that they must, upon

> recogniz[ing] that the private sector and private markets are the best engine for economic growth ... assess all costs and benefits of available regulatory alternatives, including the alternative of not regulating. Costs and benefits shall be understood to include both quantifiable measures ... and qualitative measures of costs and benefits that are difficult to quantify, but nevertheless essential to consider. Further, in choosing among alternative regulatory approaches, agencies should select those approaches that maximize net benefits (including potential economic, environmental, public health and safety, and other advantages; distributive impacts; and equity), unless a statute requires another regulatory approach.[75]

Agencies must adopt a regulation "only upon a reasoned determination that the benefits of the intended regulation justify its costs."[76] The executive Office of Management and Budget (OMB), through its Office of Information and Regulatory Affairs (OIRA), is directed to provide coordinated review of agency rulemaking.[77]

Ever since the advent of the environmental law canon in the 1970s,[78] resource-dependent communities have complained that environmental regulation poses unique risks to their livelihoods.[79] As discussed in Chapters 2 and 5, as of 1970, more than one-third of rural employment was based in manufacturing, mining,

---

[75] ExecOrder No 12,866, 58 Fed. Reg. No. 190 (Sept. 30, 1993), www.archives.gov/files/federal-register/executive-orders/pdf/12866.pdf [https://perma.cc/28UP-E4DN].

[76] *Id.*

[77] *Id.*

[78] *See* 42 U.S.C. § 7401 et seq.; 29 U.S.C. § 651 et seq.; 16 U.S.C. § 1531 et seq.; 33 U.S.C. § 1251 et seq.

[79] *See, e.g.,* Frederick H. Buttel, *Environmentalization: Origins, Processes, and Implications for Rural Social Change*, 57 RURAL SOCIO. 1, 24 (1992) (expressing hope that environmentalism "adds to rather than detracts from the quest of the majority of the world's population to earn an adequate livelihood, have economic security, and live in dignity"); Richard B. Stewart, *Pyramids of Sacrifice? Problems of Federalism in Mandating State Implementation of National Environmental Policy*, 86 YALE L.J. 1196, 1220 (1977) (observing that uniform federal emission limitations on new cars imposed high costs on rural areas while yielding few compensating benefits).

agriculture, forestry, and fishing.[80] These sectors have remained important lifelines for rural communities through the late twentieth century and today. These livelihoods have also often been among relatively few economic opportunities for rural communities for a variety of reasons, including distance from population centers, exploitative treatment by corporations, other drivers of a lack of economic diversification, and cultural attachments to traditional ways of life.[81] Thus, the potential trade-off with increased regulation is apparent: If someone makes a living from natural resources, and the law restricts the use of those natural resources, that person's livelihood seems positioned to suffer.[82]

Agency regulations are tasked with implementing federal legislation, and the political fights over environmental laws mirror some rural frustrations still being expressed today. During the period of active environmental legislating, legislators representing rural constituents expressed concerns not dissimilar to the concerns expressed over deregulation.[83] For instance, during 1976 debates over the possible expansion of the Clean Water Act 404 permit program and in response to *Natural Resources Defense Council, Inc. v. Callaway*,[84] holding that the Army Corps of Engineers had failed to implement the law properly, Representative Ichord, a Democrat from Missouri opined:

> the corps had to hastily draft regulations designed to fulfill the judicial order without even benefit of an environmental assessment or an environmental impact or inflation impact statement. The expansion of the 404 permit program created immediate and strong opposition in my own State of Missouri. My own personal view was that the rules forced by judicial edict represented a disastrous expansion of bureaucratic controls, a backdoor approach to land use planning, and an unconscionable harassment to many rural Americans who have enough to worry about without additional Federal red-tape and penalties.[85]

Ichord's advocacy to keep the "traditional," more limited conceptualization of the Army Corps' jurisdiction lost out under the Clean Water Act Amendments to the Federal Water Pollution Control Act of 1977.[86]

---

[80] *See* Ann M. Eisenberg, *Distributive Justice and Rural America*, 61 B.C. L. REV. 189, 206–07 (2020).

[81] *See* SHERMAN, *Dividing Paradise*, *supra* note 8, at 4.

[82] *See* Brigham Daniels et al., *Just Environmentalism*, 37 YALE L. & POL'Y REV. 1, 7–8 (2018) (describing zero-sum conflicts between livelihoods and environmental protections, such as "endangered predators" being "pitted against ranchers and river ecosystems against farming communities"); *Cf.* Wendy Lee Anderson, *Book Note*, 24 ECOLOGY L.Q. 377, 387 (1997) (reviewing THOMAS MICHAEL POWER, LOST LANDSCAPES AND FAILED ECONOMIES: THE SEARCH FOR A VALUE OF PLACE (1996)) (criticizing characterization of anti-environmental backlash as solely funded by corporations when local appeal seems apparent).

[83] *See* Chapter 5, *supra*.

[84] 392 F. Supp. 685 (D.D.C. 1975).

[85] 122 CONG. REC. 16,490, 16,542 (1976).

[86] *Evolution of the Meaning of Waters of the United States" in the Clean Water Act*, CONG. RSCH. SERV. %44585 R44585 at 11 (Mar. 5, 2019), https://crsreports.congress.gov/product/pdf/R/R44585/9 [https://perma.cc/49GY-UADT].

In 1977, during debates in the House over possible cost-sharing mandates for waste-water treatment plants under the Clean Water Act, Representative Smith of Nebraska, a Republican, observed the greater compliance difficulties for rural businesses:

> Under section 204(B)(1)(b) of Public Law 92-500, an industrial user is presently required to repay to the Federal Government his share of [wastewater] treatment plant installation costs. This is a payment in addition to the user fee for operation and maintenance of the plant. Although this might appear fair, it discriminates harshly against small rural businesses.
>
> The waste water treatment plant proposed for Stuart, Nebr., a town of 561, is an excellent example of this inequity. Stuart's sewer plant is designed to handle 67,000 gallons of waste water daily. The Stuart Locker Co., a small meatpacker, will generate about 0.5 percent of that total – 380 gallons – the Jack and Jill Market will generate about 0.2 percent – 160 gallons – and a small milk shipper will generate around 1 percent – 670 gallons. Despite this limited usage, [the law] will require Stuart Locker Co., and Jack and Jill Market to pay nearly $17,000 of the installation costs, and the milk shipper will be required to pay $36,000. Although these charges can be spread over several years, they are still a significant burden for a rural business with a tight profit margin. These same three businesses in a larger city would have little or no effect on a sewage treatment plan and, therefore, would have a much smaller [mandated] payment, or no payment.[87]

The final version of the law included a provision for the EPA Administrator to conduct a comprehensive investigation into rural sewage and associated costs.[88]

Rural stakeholders also testified about conservation initiatives' likely negative, unintended consequences for rural populations, including population loss, if certain restrictions or prohibitions were implemented. For instance, Abner Rice, President of the Oregon Sheep Growers Association, warned of a public lands predator control provision contained in the draft Endangered Species Act (ESA):

> [Federal] land intermingles with our private lands, and placing a ban on control methods now used, and having no alternative, no phase-out period, gives most growers no alternative except to get out.
>
> Most operations in Oregon are ranch-type, or family-type operations, trying to make a living in rural parts of the State .... The predator loss in these areas has been increasing in the past few years, and ranchers are unable to stand these losses. We need control for the safety of our livestock, the same as any other person is entitled to the protection of his private property, and this is all we are asking ....
>
> This bill can only add further chaos to our existing predator problems, forcing more rural people off of their land.[89]

---

[87] 123 CONG. REC. 10,359, 10,409 (1977).

[88] Federal Water Pollution Control Act Amendments of 1972, Pub L. No. 92-500, 86 Stat. 816, Sec. 101(q) (1) (1972).

[89] *Predatory Mammals and Endangered Species: Hearings Before the Subcomm. on Fisheries and Wildlife Conservation of the H. Comm. on Merchant Marine and Fisheries*, 92nd Cong. 341 (1972).

Ultimately, the ESA did not mention rural livelihoods or economics explicitly, but it did establish provisions for challenging regulations promulgated pursuant to it and for seeking one-year exemptions based on undue economic hardship or subsistence needs, with a specific exemption for Alaska Natives and residents of Alaska native villages.[90]

In some sense, environmental laws' approach to rural regions mirrored the approach seen in the deregulation statutes discussed in Chapter 5. Likely costs to rural regions were acknowledged. In some measures, they were accounted for: Special exceptions could be accessed and reports of study were promised. But the overall effect of both, arguably, was that the rural was made all the more peculiar in the law's view than the urban or suburban. Cities did not need special exceptions to airline deregulation, just as they did not need special help to adapt to the ESA. Rural regions were starting more and more during this time to seem like deviants, whose welfare was always an afterthought insisted upon after the needs of more mainstream society were prioritized.

Commentary on the effects of environmental regulations on employment regularly emphasizes that environmental regulations do not cause net, long-term job losses at a societal level and that job losses "tend to be dwarfed by the overall effects on public welfare."[91] This emphasis on net job losses arguably reflects the tacit view that cost–benefit analysis's prioritization of aggregate welfare is an adequate measure of a particular regulation's desirability. However, more recently, environmental legal scholarship has been reckoning with the fact that environmental regulations' effects on livelihoods in resource-dependent rural communities are meaningful and need to be taken seriously in the interest of fairness and in defusing rural disaffection's destabilizing force.[92]

Key aspects of cost–benefit analysis reveal why it would indeed be inadequate to ensuring full consideration of distributional needs in resource-dependent rural communities.[93] Centrally, cost–benefit analysis calculations do not traditionally or

---

[90] 16 U.S.C.A. §§ 1539(b), (e).

[91] *See* N.Y.U. Inst. for Pol'y Integrity, Does Environmental Regulation Kill or Create Jobs? (2017), https://bit.ly/32vMezA; Hochschild, *supra* note 3, at 284–85 (questioning trade-offs between environmental conservation and jobs, noting lack of regulatory effects on net employment and overall economic growth); Daniels et al., *supra* note 82, at 4 (arguing that "environmentalists often resist, ignore, or dismiss" the connection between environmental protection measures and their economic consequences, "even when the economic consequences of environmental protection are obvious and even when those consequences fall hardest on the poor and vulnerable."

[92] *Cf.* Richard L. Revesz, *Regulation and Distribution*, 93 N.Y.U. L. Rev. 1489, 1495, 1577–78 (2018).

[93] *Cf.* Ian Scoones, *Livelihoods Perspectives and Rural Development*, 36 J. Peasant Stud. 171, 172 (2009) (describing the "[l]ivelihoods perspective[]" common in rural development studies which examines "how different people in different places live," with particular emphasis on how people make a living using an approach in which one "look[s] at the real world, and tr[ies] [to] understand things from local perspectives"); Frederick H. Buttel, *Environmentalization: Origins, Processes, and Implications for Rural Social Change*, 57 Rural Socio. 1, 24 (1992) (remarking that environmentalism meant a new and dramatic reversal of rural "inconsequentiality," "bring[ing] rural societies and

formally include anticipated jobs to be lost as a result, directly or indirectly, of a proposed regulation.[94] Even where OIRA does consider job losses, it lacks a standard for "how many jobs must be lost for a regulation to be impermissible."[95] A likely explanation for the exclusion of a more formalized job-loss analysis is the common assumption among economists that regulation-driven shocks to labor markets will even out over time as displaced workers find new work.[96]

This approach poses unique problems for rural communities in two ways. First, rural labor markets are more limited. The reasoning that job markets will "clear" and recover may make some sense in those urban contexts where labor markets are relatively robust. But it overlooks key conditions in rural communities. A region's ability to be resilient in the face of a rash of job losses "will vary based on the population of the region and the economic diversity of the industries present in it."[97] But as has been demonstrated time and again with regular economic upheavals, rural labor markets are less resilient, often dependent on one industry, and less likely to bounce back from a shock, regulatory or otherwise. A shock to such a labor market will have profound ripple effects, going so far as to create the risk of regional fiscal collapse.[98]

Second, unique barriers impede displaced rural workers' capacity to start over again. As Masur and Posner observe, "Geographically isolated workers may find it harder to travel to another location or find a new job in the original location."[99] Regionally concentrated job losses generally make it more costly for the unemployed to find new work.[100] These barriers to mobility mean that a key assumption held by many economists and regulators – that a lost job is not all that dire because any given worker can find a new job – simply does not hold up in the rural context.[101]

Discrete, region-specific job losses stemming from regulation-driven industry contractions are indeed observable.[102] It may also be more difficult to measure

their environments center stage," and that environmentalization would "be crucial in determining whether the new forms of social regulation of the economy that emerge will either reinforce the growing inequality of the past decade or lead to new channels for the mobilization of subordinate class demands").

[94] Jonathan S. Masur & Eric A. Posner, *Regulation, Unemployment, and Cost-Benefit Analysis*, 98 Va. L. Rev. 579, 603–23 (2012).

[95] *Id.* at 582.

[96] *See id.* at 582–83.

[97] *Id.* at 632.

[98] *See generally* Adele C. Morris et al., Colum. Ctr. Glob. Energy Pol'y, The Risk of Fiscal Collapse in Coal-Reliant Communities (2019), https://brook.gs/3gCSAAD (detailing risks of fiscal collapse of coal's decline to coal-reliant communities).

[99] *Id.* at 620.

[100] *Id.*

[101] *Cf.* Hochschild, *supra* note 3, at 51 (observing that many workers in Louisiana petrochemical plants were torn between their love of local wilderness and their need to maintain jobs in polluting industries).

[102] *See* Marc A. C. Hafstead & Roberton C. Williams III, *Unemployment and Environmental Regulation in General Equilibrium*, 160 J. Pub. Econ. 50, 51 (2018) (acknowledging that "imposing a pollution tax causes a substantial employment drop in the polluting sector" and "a substantial shift

regulations' trade-offs in rural places than is typically acknowledged. As reflected in the discussion of wastewater cost-sharing, trade-offs are more complex than an easily quantifiable number of layoffs that can be attributed to a new regulatory provision.[103] What is the cost to a rural business owner of having to seek out more information about federal standards (likely with a worse internet connection), consult expertise on such standards (though lawyers and other experts, such as engineers, are far harder to find in rural regions), and then, if necessary, comply with the standards (at some expense that does not necessarily involve layoffs)?[104] A result that seems likely is that those with fewer resources will have to fall by the wayside while those with more resources can play the game by the new rules. Again, consolidation seems inevitable. The question, then, is whether rural workers are inevitably destined to bear disproportionate regulatory trade-offs in certain contexts because cost–benefit analysis assumes urban conditions and discounts suffering if it comes in smaller numbers.

Endangered Species Listing

Other regulatory processes minimize or overlook costs imposed on rural communities as well. For instance, in *The Costs of Critical Habitat*, Klick and Ruhl observe that the U.S. Fish and Wildlife Service (FWS), which is charged with implementing the ESA, currently takes the position that designating certain geographic areas as critical habitat for endangered species "entail[s] no incremental costs beyond those already triggered by the original listing of the species as endangered."[105] After assessing the effects of the critical habitat designation on home values in four Arizona counties, their study concludes that the designation reduced property values in those counties by between 3 percent and 4 percent.[106] They conclude that the FWS position is "in error," and that such effects, in fact, render the critical habitat designation to be "welfare reducing," due to FWS having underestimated the regulatory action's economic effects.[107]

Returning to the livelihoods theme, the listing of the spotted owl as an endangered species may no longer be breaking news, given that the heights of the controversy arose in the 1990s. But the regional ramifications of this listing for timber

---

in employment between industries"); *see also* Firlein, *supra* note 23, at 339 (quoting ranchers complaining of "[t]he disproportionate burdens placed on rural communities" by conservation efforts and how urban communities "are not the ones who bear the costs of such conservation").

[103] Ori Sharon, *Finding Eden in a Cost-Benefit State*, 27 GEO. MASON L. REV. 571, 581 (2020) (observing that "taken to the extreme, a wholly preservationist world is devoid of people").

[104] *Cf.* ROBERT WUTHNOW, THE LEFT BEHIND: DECLINE AND RAGE IN SMALL-TOWN AMERICA 101 (2018) (observing local officials' frustration with "unfunded mandates" from federal regulations, such as a requirement to install a new sewage treatment plant that communities could not afford).

[105] Jonathan Klick & J. B. Ruhl, *The Costs of Critical Habitat or Owl's Well that Ends Well* (U. Penn. Inst. L. & Econ. Rsch., Rsch. Paper No 20-57, 2020).

[106] *See id.*

[107] *See id.*

communities remain poignant. Sherman's study of Golden Valley centered on the listing's lasting aftermath. She explains:

> The 1990 listing of the northern spotted owl as threatened under the [ESA] would alter the economic landscape of Golden Valley irrevocably. The spotted owl decision … resulted in federally enforced bans on timber harvesting through much of the Pacific Northwest to preserve the owl's habitat. This decision affected all of the local public forests, which made up nearly 80 percent of the land in Jefferson County [where Golden Valley is located]. Timber harvests in the region dropped by 80 percent between 1989 and 1994 as a result.
>
> The spotted owl ruling was destructive to virtually all aspects of Golden Valley's economy…. Most residents who were there at the time remember the 1990s as a period of community-level depression, from which they are still struggling to emerge.[108]

The President's Northwest Forest Plan (NWFP) sought to offset some of these losses. "Yet, in all, 'the NWFP has been more successful in stopping actions thought to be harmful to conservation … than it has been in promoting active restoration and adaptive management and in implementing economic and social policies set out under the plan.'"[109] This intervention provides yet another example where rural concerns were recognized but not effectively addressed.

Recent commentary has observed that widespread unwillingness to fully acknowledge the potential costs of environmental regulations, such as those implementing the ESA, likely exacerbates public opposition to those regulations. Henson, White, and Thompson, deeming the ESA to be the "signature environmental law of the United States," argue that, while the ESA has achieved meaningful ecological successes, it continues to face opposition from substantial segments of the public, in part because of the unwillingness to acknowledge unintended consequences, including the perceived and actual costs borne by rural landowners.[110]

Again, two unique factors suggest that rural communities bear discrete consequences of these decision-making processes. First, rural residents have a greater tendency to be land rich but cash poor.[111] Rural livelihoods in ranching and farming,

---

[108] SHERMAN, *supra* note 38, at 31.

[109] Ann M. Eisenberg, *Just Transitions*, 92 S. CAL. L. REV. 273, 318 (2019) (quoting Jack Ward Thomas et al., *The Northwest Forest Plan: Origins, Components, Implementation Experience, and Suggestions for Change*, 20 CONSERVATION BIOLOGY 277, 283 (2006)).

[110] *See generally* Paul Henson et al., *Improving Implementation of the Endangered Species Act: Finding Common Ground through Common Sense*, 68 BIOSCI. 861 (2018), https://doi.org/10.1093/biosci/biy093 (arguing that ESA has been successful in meeting its core mission but improvements in implementation could lessen political controversy and make ESA more effective).

[111] Juhohn Lee, *Here's Why the Ultra-Wealthy Like Bill Gates and Thomas Peterffy Are Investing in U.S. Farmland*, CNBC (Aug. 20, 2021), www.cnbc.com/2021/08/20/heres-why-the-ultra-wealthy-like-bill-gates-investing-to-farmland.html [https://perma.cc/5KZJ-9U2Q] (noting that many farming families are asset rich but cash poor); Jon Christensen, *Land Rich, but Cash Poor, in the West*, N.Y. TIMES (Nov. 23, 1997), www.nytimes.com/1997/11/23/business/land-rich-but-cash-poor-in-the-west .html [https://perma.cc/ZU49-9DQE].

for instance, often involve a state of illiquidity, with all of a family's resources being "tied up in the land."[112] Thus, a phenomenon such as that observed by Klick and Ruhl bears unique implications for rural economic welfare in particular, given disproportionate rural reliance on land as both wealth and livelihood. And second, rural residents are more likely not only to have resource-dependent livelihoods, but also to be more "environmentally embedded," having more intimate and varied relationships with land and natural resources in general than non-rural residents.[113] Thus, restrictions on people's relationships with land and natural resources likely also represent unquantifiable losses in livelihoods, cultural norms, and ways of life.

REGULATORY DECISION-MAKING AND RURAL ENVIRONMENTAL INJUSTICE

The issues driving the oversight of the economic regulatory trade-offs borne by rural communities also help explain the regulatory state's limitations in addressing rural environmental injustice. The overarching issue is that regulatory decision-making emphasizes aggregate welfare, in turn embracing a utilitarian approach that justifies minority sacrifice in a system Ashwood labels "tyranny of the majority," drawing on Alexis de Tocqueville.[114] In other words, the regulatory state demonstrates a general lack of capacity (or political will) to meaningfully take distributional considerations into account.[115]

Jedediah Purdy offers an explanation for this failure: Environmental law and its associated regulatory decision-making apparatus were born during a period of relative national socioeconomic equality and prosperity.[116] It was, in fact, formed around the assumption that economic inequality was declining.[117] Questions of justice and distribution, then – including economic trade-offs and the siting of hazardous facilities – have been neglected by environmental agencies' decision-making processes.[118]

Features of the regulatory state both implicitly and explicitly designate rural populations as appropriate for sacrifice in the name of progress. For instance, the Code of Federal Regulations mandates that nuclear power plants must be located

---

[112] Jon Christensen, *Land Rich, but Cash Poor, in the West*, N.Y. TIMES (Nov. 23, 1997), www.nytimes.com/1997/11/23/business/land-rich-but-cash-poor-in-the-west.html [https://perma.cc/ZU49-9DQE]; Roger E. McEowen, *The Illiquidity Problem of Farm and Ranch Estates*, AGRIC. L. & TAX'N BLOG (Aug. 19, 2021), https://lawprofessors.typepad.com/agriculturallaw/2021/08/the-illiquidity-problem-of-farm-and-ranch-estates.html [https://perma.cc/KV3D-Q77L].

[113] ASHWOOD, *supra* note 3, at 190.

[114] *Id.* at 10.

[115] Sidney A. Shapiro & Robert R. M. Verchick, *Inequality, Social Resilience and the Green Economy*, 86 UMKC L. REV. 1 (2018).

[116] Jedediah Purdy, *The Long Environmental Justice Movement*, 44 ECOLOGY L.Q. 809, 810 (2018).

[117] *See id.* at 864.

[118] *Id.* at 810.

only in rural places.[119] While some would point out the logic in such an approach, such a practice can nevertheless help explain rural disaffection from the regulatory state. Numerous critiques highlight cost–benefit analysis's failure to address environmental injustice.[120] For rural communities of color – the "minority of minorities" – the regulatory state's structural disregard for environmental distributional concerns bodes particularly poorly.[121]

In Chapter 5, I argued that the deregulatory era involved the structural exclusion of rural regions from federal protections. This discussion has added to that picture by showing how, as the federal regulatory state retreated from protecting rural regions, it also began to intervene more aggressively in other ways, asking more of rural workers and landowners through increasing regulatory mandates. The evolution of the regulatory state helps contextualize a rural political consciousness that includes themes of voicelessness, frustration, and feeling antagonized. Rural populations do indeed have real, diverse reasons to feel betrayed and alienated from the federal government. These views are not political radicalism, but an understandable reaction to a government that has de-emphasized their needs in the interest of other pursuits. As Sherman concludes in her study of Paradise Valley, Washington:

> [I]t is important to focus not on why rural Americans are angry, frustrated, or delusional, but rather on the processes by which inequality is maintained through mechanisms that cause frustration, judgment, anger, and self-blame but not civic unrest or large-scale social change. The political realm has coopted these negative emotions to turn all of us against one another in ways that ultimately disempower and further disenfranchise the most vulnerable among us.[122]

---

[119] ASHWOOD, *supra* note 3, at 102 (citing Domestic Licensing of Production and Utilization Facilities, 10 C.F.R., pt. 50).

[120] Clifford Rechtschaffen, *Advancing Environmental Justice Norms*, 37 U.C. DAVIS L. REV. 95, 104 (2003); Frank Ackerman & Lisa Heinzerling, *Pricing the Priceless: Cost-Benefit Analysis of Environmental Protection*, 150 U. PA. L. REV. 1553, 1575 (2002) ("cost-benefit analysis rationalizes and reinforces" patterns of pollution being "dumped on the poor"); Catherine A. O'Neill, *Variable Justice: Environmental Standards, Contaminated Fish, and "Acceptable" Risk to Native Peoples*, 19 STAN. ENVT'L L.J. 3, 17 (2000); Joseph P. Tomain, *Distributional Consequences of Environmental Regulation: Economics, Politics, and Environmental Policymaking*, 1 KAN. J.L. & PUB. POL'Y 101, 110 (1991).

[121] ASHWOOD, *supra* note 3, at 172.

[122] Sherman, *Dividing Paradise*, *supra* note 8, at 196.

7

The Myth of Rural Whiteness

On a sunny, breezy afternoon in April 2019, two law students and I loaded into my Prius and set out on a three-hour drive. We were heading from Columbia, South Carolina's capital city and home to the law school, to St. Helena Island. St. Helena, with a population of roughly 8,400, lies just to the northeast of Hilton Head, on a neighboring sea island in Beaufort County. I had been to St. Helena once before and had by then taken many trips to other parts of the Lowcountry. West Virginia and the Lowcountry felt like two ends on a spectrum of the South. West Virginia sat high and cold, a world of craggy blue rock and dense trees playing home to a mostly white population. At the other end, the South Carolina Lowcountry sprawled open and out into the sea, its flat, damp marshes punctuated with clusters of live oaks. The Lowcountry hosts a substantial Black population, including members of the Gullah Geechee community.

The two young women and I were a bit giddy. We had a long evening ahead of us, as we were planning to make the return trip that same night. But it was also exciting to be giving a presentation at Penn Center. Named for its initial financing by Quakers in 1862, Penn Center continued to operate as a cultural and social services hub for the region's Gullah community, in addition to its status as a historic site of civil rights work.[1]

The Gullah community has a unique and compelling story of cultural heritage preservation in the face of severe adversity.[2] Europeans arrived to St. Helena Island (Figure 7.1) in the sixteenth century and spent the next several centuries forcing Native Americans and Africans to work on agricultural plantations. According to a historical account provided by Penn Center, "Due to the isolation of the Sea Islands, and the presence of relatively few landholders, these workers developed

---

[1] *Timeline of Penn Center History*, PENN CENTER, www.penncenter.com/history-v2 [hereinafter *Timeline*] (last visited May 9, 2023).

[2] Ladan Ghahramani et al., *Minority Community Resilience and Cultural Heritage Preservation: A Case Study of the Gullah Geechee Community*, 12 SUSTAINABILITY 2266 (2020), https://doi.org/10.3390/su12062266.

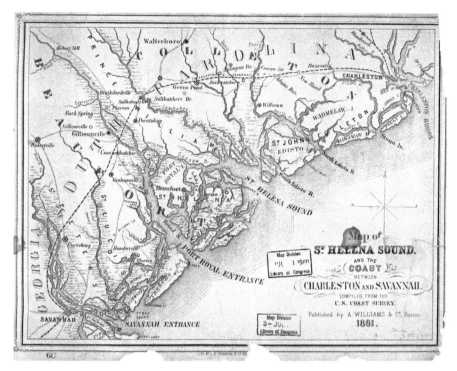

FIGURE 7.1 Map of St. Helena Sound, and the coast between Charleston and Savannah, A. Williams & Co., 1861, Library of Congress Geography and Map Division

their own creole culture and language unique to the region: Gullah."[3] The Gullah community may also be referred to as "Gullah Geechee" and includes communities with similar stories in Georgia.

Penn Center opened in 1862 as the first school for formerly enslaved people. The Sea Islands were occupied early by Union forces in the Civil War, making the school's operation possible. The Penn school continued operating through 1948, when it changed to a community services organization. In the 1960s, it became a hub of civil rights activities, hosting Reverend Dr. Martin Luther King, Jr. and other activists at retreats and interracial conferences. In 1974, the Penn Center campus was designated a National Historic Landmark District. In 1990, the Center adjusted its mission to specifically focus on promoting and preserving Gullah cultural assets. In 2017, President Obama included some of the Center's buildings in a Reconstruction Era National Monument designation, which in 2019 became a National Historic Park.[4]

---

[3] *Timeline, supra* note 1.
[4] *South Carolina: Penn Center*, NAT'L PARK SERV. (Feb. 24, 2023), www.nps.gov/places/south-carolina-penn-center.htm (last visited May 9, 2023).

Today, Penn Center and St. Helena Island face challenges that are not uncommon in rural communities and beyond. Central among those challenges is the difficulty of retaining young people to carry on traditions, steward resources, and generally keep a community alive. This is in addition to an issue facing all of the Southeast's low-lying coastal islands: sea level rise.[5]

Challenges notwithstanding, Penn Center remains an important local hub, and the students and I were eager to support them however we could. We had been asked to do a presentation for local residents about the risk of losing property during tax foreclosure. The students and I had spent the previous weeks preparing a sort of "know your rights" presentation, along with a handout detailing the steps in the state's tax foreclosure process.

The disproportionately high risk of losing property to tax foreclosure is one of the many ways in which our legal system imposes insecure land tenure on Black Americans and other marginalized populations.[6] But before turning to this aspect of rural life, I introduce the myth of rural whiteness that often serves to diminish, or render invisible, everything this chapter has discussed so far, albeit briefly: the ongoing presence and experiences of rural populations of color; the role of the rural South in civil rights advocacy; and the role law has played and continues to play in displacing and constraining rural racial and ethnic minorities and their opportunities for wealth creation and socioeconomic security.

The myth of rural whiteness interacts with several stereotypes about culture and the demographic makeup of rural regions. The most obvious of these harkens back to the Trump-country stereotype associated with West Virginia and other predominantly rural states. Rural is understood as synonymous with both white and conservative. This myth emerged, for example, when I expressed concern to an urbanite friend about rural South Carolina's vulnerability to hurricanes and flooding. Not knowing about rural South Carolina's racial and political diversity,[7] he said, "Eh, they voted for Trump anyway! They deserve what they get."

Obviously, this myth, while not entirely detached from real conditions in some places, is problematic in several ways. First, it erases the existence of substantial rural

---

5   Barry Gordener, *Rising Sea Levels Threaten the Lives and Livelihood of Those on a Fragile U.S. Coast*, NPR (Nov. 7, 2021), www.npr.org/2021/11/07/1051529051/rising-sea-levels-climate-change-south-carolina-coast.

6   *Cf.* Arionne Nettles, *Saving Black Homes Lost to Tax Inequity*, BOSTON GLOBE (Feb. 22, 2023), www.bostonglobe.com/2023/02/22/opinion/saving-black-homes-lost-tax-inequity [https://perma.cc/G3X3-BBX4] (discussing racial disparities in tax foreclosures in cities).

7   Surekha Carpenter & Sonya Ravindranath Waddell, *Analysis: The Connection between Race and Opportunity in Rural Parts of the 5th Federal Reserve District*, DAILY YONDER (Apr. 1, 2021), https://dailyyonder.com/analysis-the-connection-between-race-and-opportunity-in-rural-parts-of-the-5th-federal-reserve-district/2021/04/01/ [https://perma.cc/T72D-AXG6] (rural South Carolina 37 percent Black); *Population Estimates: Percent Distribution by Race*, S.C. REVENUE & FISCAL AFF. OFF. (2020), https://rfa.sc.gov/data-research/population-demographics/census-state-data-center/population-data/population-estimates-percent-race-2020 [https://perma.cc/LW9W-YPQL] (Saluda County, SC 15.6 percent Hispanic or Latino; Marlboro County, SC 4.9 percent Native American).

populations of color, who today comprise about one fourth of rural residents in the United States overall.[8] A failure to acknowledge the existence of rural populations of color means less attention to the challenges they face, including dramatically higher rates of concentrated, persistent poverty.[9] That erasure also minimizes the dynamism and sociocultural and political power of non-white rural populations, such as the key role Black rural voters played in Georgia and Indigenous voters played in Nevada and Arizona during the 2020 presidential election, or the story of Mary Peltola becoming the first Alaska Native in Congress in 2022.[10] Hispanic in-migration is transforming rural landscapes, with the nonmetro Hispanic population having nearly doubled in size between 1990 and 2019.[11]

As of the 2020 census, "Hispanics represent[ed] the largest share of the rural minority population," at about nine percent of the national rural population.[12] Non-Hispanic Black people represented 7.7 percent. Non-Hispanic multiracial people constituted 3.9 percent. Native Americans constituted 2.5 percent. And Asians comprised one percent.[13] Regional demographics vary substantially, however. For example, in rural New Mexico, more than half of the population identifies as Hispanic or Latino and 10 percent identifies as Native American.[14] In certain rural South Carolina counties, 37 percent of residents are Black, 15.6 percent identify as Hispanic or Latino, and 4.9 percent are Native American.[15]

---

[8] Kenneth Johnson and Daniel Lichter, *Growing Racial Diversity in Rural America: Results from the 2020 Census*, CARSEY RESEARCH NATIONAL ISSUE BRIEF #163 (2022); Maybell Romero, *Viewing Access to Justice for Rural Mainers of Color through a Prosecution Lens*, 71 ME. L. REV. 227, 229 (2019); *Racial and ethnic minorities made up about 22 percent of the rural population in 2018, compared to 43 percent in urban areas*, U.S. DEPT. OF AGRIC. ECON. RESEARCH SERVICE (2018), www.ers.usda.gov/data-products/chart-gallery/gallery/chart-detail/?chartId=99538 [https://perma.cc/N334-PB9S].

[9] RURAL POVERTY IN THE UNITED STATES (Ann R. Tickamyer et al. eds., 2017).

[10] Sam Gringlas, *Georgia's Rural Black Voters Helped Propel Democrats Before. Will They Do It Again?* WUSF (Sept. 12, 2022), https://wusfnews.wusf.usf.edu/2022-09-12/georgias-rural-black-voters-helped-propel-democrats-before-will-they-do-it-again; Anna V. Smith, *How Indigenous Voters Swung the 2020 Election*, HIGH COUNTRY NEWS (Nov. 6, 2020), www.hcn.org/articles/indigenous-affairs-how-indigenous-voters-swung-the-2020-election; Grace Segers, *Native American Voters Critical to Biden's Success in Arizona*, CBS NEWS (Nov. 20, 2020), www.cbsnews.com/news/native-american-voters-critical-to-bidens-success-in-arizona/; Azi Paybarah, *Who Is Mary Peltola, the First Alaska Native in Congress?*, THE WASHINGTON POST (Sept. 1, 2022), www.washingtonpost.com/politics/2022/08/31/mary-peltola-alaska-special-election-palin/.

[11] Daniel T. Lichter and Kenneth M. Johnson, *A Demographic Lifeline to Rural America: Latino Population Growth in New Destinations, 1990–2019*, Federal Reserve Bank of St. Louis, at 69.

[12] Kenneth Johnson and Daniel Lichter, *Growing Racial Diversity in Rural America: Results from the 2020 Census*, UNH Carsey School of Public Policy (May 25, 2022).

[13] *Id.*

[14] Elizabeth Dwyer Sandlin, *Transforming Health Care in Rural New Mexico*, UNM HEALTH SCIENCES NEWSROOM (Sept. 7, 2023), https://hsc.unm.edu/news/2023/09/transforming-health-care-rural-nm.html [https://perma.cc/D22C-JHLK].

[15] Surekha Carpenter & Sonya Ravindranath Waddell, *Analysis: The Connection between Race and Opportunity in Rural Parts of the 5th Federal Reserve District*, DAILY YONDER (Apr. 1, 2021), https://dailyyonder.com/analysis-the-connection-between-race-and-opportunity-in-rural-parts-of-the-5th-federal-reserve-district/2021/04/01/ (rural South Carolina 37 percent Black); *Population Estimates:*

This chapter does not take on the logic, ethical assumptions, or practical implications behind the argument that white, conservative voters deserve to be neglected or punished for their voting patterns. But in any event, that logic, questionable as it may be, does not serve the populations of non-white people (and political liberals or the politically inactive) who get lost in the reasoning.[16] What's more, accepting the rural-as-white trope also clouds the reasons *why* rural regions have often ended up overrepresenting and over-empowering white people (and white conservatives in particular). It is not just something in the water.

This chapter contemplates that rural populations of color are very much present, and deserve attention as an integral part of the conversation on rural marginalization and pathways to rural prosperity. Indeed, it is not possible to understand the role rural environmental injustice plays in our broader societal structures without understanding the potent, combined forces of market supremacy, white supremacy, and urbanormativity operating together. As the "minority of the minority," rural populations of color are among the country's most vulnerable to egregious exploitation because of the ever-present factors of remoteness, distance, and the limited political power that comes with poverty and relatively small volumes of population numbers.

The call in Chapter 2 to incorporate an intersectional lens on rural experiences can help illuminate how populations' experiences overlap and diverge. Where rural regions do overrepresent and over-empower white populations, to accept rural whiteness as natural and inevitable overlooks law's role in systematically making rural regions livable only for certain people. Understanding the role structural racism has played in shaping modern rural America is an important part of holding institutions and policymakers accountable. Such understanding can also help illuminate the role restorative racial justice and forward-looking racial equity must play in any rural revitalization scheme, as explored in Chapter 8.

LAW'S HISTORICAL AND ONGOING ROLE IN MAKING RURAL REGIONS DISPROPORTIONATELY WHITE

Some major historical factors are well known for contributing to the whitening and racial stratification of rural regions. The South, which is predominantly rural, saw more than half the Black population leave for northern urban life during the Great Migration.[17] The explicitly racist laws of the Jim Crow era – including a regime of laws and norms in Southern states and municipalities in place from 1877 to 1965 that

---

Percent Distribution by Race, S.C. REVENUE & FISCAL AFF. OFF. (2020), https://rfa.sc.gov/data-research/population-demographics/census-state-data-center/population-data/population-estimates-percent-race-2020 (Saluda County, SC 15.6 percent Hispanic or Latino; Marlboro County, SC 4.9 percent Native American).

16 *Cf.* Ann Eisenberg, *Deconstructing Dangerous "Hurricane Karma" Rhetoric about the South*, ENV'T NARRATIVES PROJECT (Nov. 1, 2018), https://envnarratives.com/2018/11/01/deconstructing-dangerous-hurricane-karma-rhetoric-about-the-south/.

17 Michael J. Klarman, *Race and the Court in the Progressive Era*, 51 VAND. L. REV. 881, 898 (1998).

legalized an elaborate system of racial segregation and behavior regulation[18] – were a major catalyst for this population shift.

Nineteenth-century Homestead Laws were another substantial force in rural whitening, violently redistributing land from Native Americans to European settlers.[19] According to historian Paul Frymer, legislators of the Homestead Act and related measures

> clearly intended that these land policies could change the racial demographics of a specific geographical terrain; they designed statutes such as the Armed Occupation Act, the Land Donation Act, the Preemption Act, and the Homestead Act to move as many settlers as possible on to contested lands to overwhelm and numerically dominate the pre-existing populations. Only after this successful rush and push created a majority of whites residing in the territory would Congress vote to formally incorporate the land as a state.[20]

In addition to displacing Indigenous populations, congressional machinations through the early twentieth century gave white populations an economic leg up that was not afforded to non-white populations. Dr. King once said of the Homestead Laws:

> at the same time that America refused to give the Negro any land, by Act of Congress, she was giving away millions of acres of land in the West and the Midwest, which meant that America was willing to undergird her white peasants from Europe with an economic floor. Not only did the nation give the land, it built land-grant colleges to teach these people how to farm. It provided county agents to further their expertise in farming. It provided low interest rates so that they could mechanize their farms. And today many of these people are being paid through federal subsidies *not* to farm. These are the very people who, in many instances, are saying to the Negro that he should lift himself by his own boot straps.[21]

In many ways, the story of the evolution of the United States is the story of white people extracting land and labor from non-white people, often through law as much as through conquest or other forms of violence, then ensuring (through law) that this white resource-hoarding has been able to persist. Thus, even though formerly enslaved people did indeed acquire thousands of acres of land in the South,[22]

---

[18] Margaret Hu, *Algorithmic Jim Crow*, 86 FORDHAM L. REV. 633, 652 (2017) (internal quotations omitted).

[19] Act of May 20, 1862, ch. 75, 12 Stat. 392.

[20] Paul Frymer, *"A Rush and a Push and the Land Is Ours": Territorial Expansion, Land Policy, and U.S. State Formation*, 12 PERSP. ON POLITICS 1, 121 (2014), https://pfrymer.scholar.princeton.edu/sites/g/files/toruqf4721/files/pfrymer/files/pop2014.pdf.

[21] Martin Luther King, Jr., *The Future of Integration*, in ISSUES 1968 (William W. Boyer ed., 1968), https://perma.cc/B39Y-FETW; Jessica A. Shoemaker, *Fee Simple Failures: Rural Landscapes and Race*, 119 MICH. L. REV. 1695, 1731 (2021) (observing that farm policies distort farmland values, increasing them artificially).

[22] *Id.* at 1717.

over time, much of that land has been taken through tax foreclosure, partition suits, discriminatory tactics by agents of the USDA, and other legally enabled paths to dispossession.[23]

Property law itself is at the heart of rural whitening. Jessica Shoemaker's *Fee Simple Failures* provides a scathing indictment of property law as a servant of white supremacy, with one section of her article aptly titled, "How Rural Landscapes Got So White." As Shoemaker explains, "All real property titles in this country ultimately trace back to European colonization of this country" and the diminishment and displacement of Indigenous people.[24] When the Supreme Court affirmed and enabled the superior rights of European-owned titles to U.S. land and recognized a mere "right of occupancy" for Native Americans, it also established that Indigenous owners could only transfer their land to the federal government – a limitation which continues today under tribal lands' federal trust status.[25]

Shoemaker assesses how the fee simple absolute's endlessness – the robust grant of perpetuity it affords its holder – has served to entrench racial disparities in land ownership by locking in racialized patterns of intergenerational wealth. The grift that property law plays, though, is a tricky one. The fee simple absolute estate, the most robust property ownership that one can have in the United States, has a history in common law rooted in rhetoric about stewardship, freedom, mutual responsibility, and productivity. The United States purportedly rejected Europe's system of feudalism, lords, and serfs. Yet, Shoemaker highlights how those nominal principles mask features of the fee simple absolute estate that have served to concentrate an astounding 98 percent of agricultural land in the hands of white owners.[26] Shoemaker explains:

> Although perpetual property rights were originally intended to encourage owner investment, security, and place-based attachment, in practice, the fee simple's endlessness has entrenched familial and generational wealth. Endlessness, exacerbated by recent reforms to make dynastic ownership and control easier to achieve, has entrenched historic racial disparities and now further facilitates continued white landownership – including in more concentrated and even absentee forms. As a result, minority farmers who are already less likely to inherit farmlands because their ancestors were excluded from agricultural landownership also face steep competition for increasingly valuable farmland assets. In this competition for new land, minority farmers are also less likely to come to the table with generational wealth (in part because of this same ancestral exclusion) and more likely to face private discrimination in the transaction.[27]

---

[23] Shoemaker, *supra* note 21, at 1718.
[24] *Id.* at 1713.
[25] *Id.* at 1714.
[26] *Id.* at 1699.
[27] *Id.* at 1702.

Thus, while the origins of U.S. property law are rooted in rhetoric about free-dom, egalitarianism, stewardship, and democracy, the historical and modern realities are quite far from these ideals. While 98 percent of agricultural land is white-owned, "as many as 80 percent of farm laborers are Hispanic."[28] Most of those laborers are immigrants, "vulnerable in immigration status" and under con-stant threat of deportation.[29] The ever-present fear of retaliation means workers feel constrained from speaking out about grueling working conditions – involving abuses such as very low wages, wage theft, unaddressed injuries, toxic exposures, and sexual assault.[30]

Shoemaker points to the law's commodification of property as central to the stratification of rural society along racial lines. She critiques "the fee simple's ever-increasing construction as an abstract set of profit rights" and how this conception "facilitates a commodified form of ownership separate and apart from the physical experience of the land itself," in turn "allowing for the fracturing and scattering of profit rights for investment and wealth accumulation apart from the (increas-ingly marginalized) day-to-day work of farming."[31] Thus, modern rural landscapes are very much characterized by a system of feudalism: White landlords lock in their increasingly consolidated property ownership – forever – while vulnerable, predom-inantly Hispanic laborers "move to rural places for low-wage agricultural work that keeps them poor."[32]

In West Virginia and South Carolina, I have often heard about a unique property scenario that poses an ongoing challenge for Black and Appalachian rural commu-nities: "heirs' property." Heirs' property is also a substantial challenge for Indigenous populations and Hispanic colonias at the U.S.–Mexico border.[33] Although "there is no national data regarding the amount of land held as heirs' property," some estimate that proportions may be as high as 60 percent of land owned by Black

---

[28]　*Id.* at 1706–07.

[29]　*Id.*

[30]　Jill Lindsey Harrison, Pesticide Drift and the Pursuit of Environmental Justice 125 (2011); Daniel Costa, *The Farmworker Wage Gap Continued in 2020*, Working Economics Blog (July 20, 2021), www.epi.org/blog/the-farmworker-wage-gap-continued-in-2020-farmworkers-and-h-2a-workers-earned-very-low-wages-during-the-pandemic-even-compared-with-other-low-wage-workers/; Kathleen Sexsmith, Francisco Alfredo Reyes, & Megan A.M. Griffin, *Sexual Violence Is a Pervasive Threat for Female Farm Workers – Here's How the US Could Reduce Their Risk*, The Conversation (July 31, 2023), https://theconversation.com/sexual-violence-is-a-pervasive-threat-for-female-farm-workers-heres-how-the-us-could-reduce-their-risk-204871.

[31]　Shoemaker, *supra* note 21, at 1702.

[32]　*Id.* at 1709.

[33]　Sarah Farmer, *Knowledge of 'Heirs Properties' Issues Help Families Keep, Sustain Land*, U.S. Dept. of Agriculture (Oct. 8, 2021), www.fs.usda.gov/features/knowledge-heirs-properties-issues-help-families-keep-sustain-land [https://perma.cc/RM67-FV2B]. Colonias may be defined as "residential subdivisions usually in unincorporated areas of a county, lacking all or some of the basic services, such as water and sewer, paved roads, electricity, drainage. etc." *The TCEQ and Colonias*, Texas Commission on Environmental Quality, www.tceq.texas.gov/border/colonias.html [https://perma .cc/7LA5-9YRL].

Americans, as much as 25 percent of land in some Appalachian counties, and as high as 31 percent in the regions known as Indian Country.[34]

Heirs' property refers to land that has been passed down through a family over the course of generations without the use of wills or formal estate planning. Default intestacy rules pass the land down in the ownership structure of a tenancy in common. This means that if a widow dies and her property passes automatically to her four children, each child owns a 25 percent stake in the property, but with an equal right to possess and use the whole property as the other cotenants. When those children die, their interests do not automatically consolidate, but pass in similar fashion to their respective children or next of kin in the absence of wills.

This means that after just a few generations, an acre of land might be owned by dozens, if not hundreds of people. Those people may or may not live near the land or even know of each other's existence. The land's limited formal documentation traps it in a sense, making it less useful to the family than a typical ownership structure. Whoever does live on it or try to use it will face barriers to mortgages and repair loans, aid relief, and other public programs.

For individual families, heirs' property is a major issue. The land may be a source of deep familial attachment and community, a connection to longstanding traditions and meaning. Or it may simply be an asset, but an illiquid one that needs to be unlocked to help the marginalized owners take advantage of the intergenerational wealth that so many white families take for granted.[35] Wealthier, white families' land has faced less risk of becoming heirs' property because of easier access to attorneys and other estate planning resources.

Most egregiously, heirs' property has historically been lost with relative ease. All it would take is one of forty unacquainted heirs to sign a document selling a share to a developer, making the developer a tenant in common with the other heirs. The developer could sue for partition, demanding that the land either be physically divided up among the heirs, or that the court order a sale of the land. Given the correlation with heirs' property and poverty, and the high number of heirs often making physical division impractical, the developer could then buy the property at a discount at auction and profit heavily from the family's insecure land tenure. This is part of the story of Hilton Head, which was 98 percent Black as of 1880, and where "the total acreage of Gullah Geechee-owned land has decreased by an estimated 70 percent since 1995."[36]

34   *Amount of Land Owns as Heirs' Property*, Center for Agriculture & Food Systems, https://farmlandaccess.org/heirs-property/#amountoflandowned [https://perma.cc/8VGP-CCYY]; *Fractionation*, U.S. Department of the Interior, www.doi.gov/buybackprogram/fractionation [https://perma.cc/SD6X-G78Z].

35   Jesse J. Richardson Jr., *Land Tenure and Sustainable Agriculture*, 3 Tex. A&M L. Rev. 799, 808 (2016).

36   Carol Motsinger & Daniel J. Gross, *His Ancestors Fought for Their Freedom in the Civil War. Now, He Fights to Preserve What They Left Him*, Greenville News (July 20, 2021), www.greenvilleonline.com/story/news/local/south-carolina/2021/07/20/hilton-head-island-south-carolina-fight-past-future-complicated-alex-brown-tourism-travel/7058921002/.

Recently, in large part due to the advocacy of law professor Thomas Mitchell, states have been adopting variations of the Uniform Partition of Heirs Property Act, which offers heirs some protections. South Carolina's version of the statute, adopted in 2017, bears the name of state Senator Clementa Carlos Pinckney, who was tragically murdered at age forty-one on June 17, 2015, when a white man opened fire as Senator Pinckney was conducting services at the Mother Emanuel AME Church in Charleston.

The law protects heirs' property owners in a few ways.[37] It creates processes for heirs to buy out other heirs who want to sell. In this way, heirs who want the land may be able to retain it. The law also establishes sales processes that will better afford heirs a return on the land's wealth in the event of sale. And it forces courts to take into account the unique and vulnerable status of heirs' property, creating an approach to partition suits that is more contextually sensitive than past approaches, which so often resulted in dispossession.

The proliferation of heirs' property acts, as well as the attention to the matter of land dispossession, is an important development for rural minorities' land retention. These acts are a rare instance of reform offering property protections to the vulnerable. Yet, the broader conversation on solving heirs' property puzzles sometimes feels like it's missing the big picture. The acres owned as heirs' property, and which do indeed need forward-looking protections, are overshadowed by the sheer volume of Black and Brown land claims and titles that have been snuffed out altogether over the past decades and centuries.

Emily Prifogle demonstrates how immigration law, agricultural law, labor law, property law, and public welfare programs can all operate together to entrench racial stratification in rural communities. At the heart of this stratification is the contradictory position of migrant workers. Migrant labor is considered an "economic necessity" to agriculture, while at the same time, migrant laborers are excluded from secure status within the country, certain social safety nets, and the prospect of integrating into the communities where they work.[38]

Prifogle documents this phenomenon in a case study of relationships among rural white women and migrant worker communities in Michigan in the mid century.[39] From the 1960s to today, there have been concerted efforts for public and nonprofit aid workers and organizers to reach and assist farm laborers, who often live in isolation on farmers' private property.[40] Farmers' property rights have offered a rare instance of rural legal issues gaining prominence as nationally

---

[37] *See generally* Thomas W. Mitchell, *Reforming Property Law to Address Devastating Land Loss*, 66 ALA. L. REV. 1, 1 (2014).

[38] Emily A. Prifogle, *Rural Social Safety Nets for Migrant Farmworkers in Michigan, 1942–1971*, L. Soc. INQUIRY (2021), https://repository.law.umich.edu/cgi/viewcontent.cgi?article=3265&context =articles at 2.

[39] *Id.* at 1

[40] *Id.*

relevant, as with the oft-taught case of *State v. Shack* and the Supreme Court's shocking holding in *Cedar Point Nursery v. Hassid* that a California law allowing union organizers to enter farms to speak to workers was an unconstitutional taking of private land.[41]

In the two decades prior to the 1960s, that formal aid to farmworkers did not exist, and efforts by farmworker organizers like Cesar Chavez had not yet gained momentum. Labor and welfare laws during that period "excluded rural agricultural laborers, focusing instead on forms of work more common in urban areas."[42] The absence of the state in meeting farmworkers' even basic needs meant that the predominantly white farm communities needed to "make the contradiction ... sustainable in ad hoc ways."[43]

Those strategies included the creation of "informal safety nets," which involved "public displays of charity, supported by both local churches and businesses, to uplift workers and reform their lives toward a white, middle-class, Protestant ideal."[44] Women in these Michigan communities "distributed resources and services such as food, clothing, and childcare to migrant workers who lived in poverty, often without decent shelter or clean water. The resulting informal safety nets were vital to local economic structures and migrant well-being."[45] While these informal social safety nets were motivated by "a moral and paternalistic obligation" and "good intentions," the evolution of these charitable interventions served to "sustain[] exploitative legal structures" and ultimately "help[ed] maintain a reliable and subordinated workforce."[46] Thus, these safety nets had "equally important functions for the settled white rural residents: policing migrant morality, maintaining rural segregation, and performing surveillance of community outsiders."[47]

Prifogle concludes that the result of relationships between formal law – which excluded migrant laborers from labor protections and formal social safety nets – and informal safety nets on the other hand "was a façade of family farms that concealed the industrial-scale migrant labor force required to sustain Michigan's agricultural economy."[48] This case study illustrates how rural stereotypes – such as wholesomeness, neighborliness, and family orientations – can not only work to subordinate rural communities to urban domination, but can shield inequality, exploitation, and sustained efforts to maintain homogeneity and white supremacy within rural communities.

---

[41] State v. Shack, 58 N.J. 297, 277 A.2d 369 (1971); Cedar Point Nursery v. Hassid, 141 S. Ct. 2063, 210 L. Ed. 2d 369 (2021).

[42] *Id.* at 2. The Social Security Act, the 1935 National Labor Relations Act, and the Fair Labor Standards Act all excluded farm agricultural workers from their respective benefits and protections. *Id.* at 6.

[43] *Id.* at 2.

[44] *Id.*

[45] *Id.*

[46] *Id.*

[47] *Id.*

[48] *Id.* at 3.

Law's role in facilitating unique forms of white supremacy in the countryside is not merely a relic of history. Property law, immigration law, labor law, agricultural law, Native American law, zoning law, and other institutions supporting rural racial stratification endure. Shocking stories of environmental injustice in rural communities of color abound, even if they do not receive enough attention to trigger national interventions. West Virginia's "Chemical Valley."[49] Louisiana's exurban "Cancer Alley."[50] North Carolina's hog waste crises.[51] Uranium mine wastes in Indian Country.[52] Ashwood and MacTavish attribute these phenomena to "the tyranny of the majority" and "utilitarian logic" justifying minority sacrifice in the name of democracy – and profit.[53]

However, as with geographic inequality more broadly, there is no reason to accept these conditions as natural or inevitable.[54] As to property law, Shoemaker asserts, "It is important to recognize these features of property law as what they are: choices."[55] Thus, "It is possible to imagine a different set of ownership institutions that produce more just, equitable, and sustainable rural outcomes."[56] She asks, "What if at least some rural property rights were instead tied to actual possession and use? What if property access were framed more deeply as a relationship to community, combined with responsibilities to tread gently on the land as a citizen of place? What if we reimagined rural property altogether?"[57] Such a radical reimagination of rural landscapes is revisited in the next chapter.

AN INTERSECTIONAL LENS FOR THE RURAL FUTURE

It might be tempting to conclude that the experiences of rural populations are entirely different based on those populations' respective races or ethnicities. But there is overlap across communities. Chapter 6 discussed two common themes among rural populations' views of the regulatory state: (1) a perception that agency

---

[49] Ken Ward, Jr., *How Black Communities Became 'Sacrifice Zones' for Industrial Air Pollution*, MOUNTAIN STATE SPOTLIGHT (Dec. 21, 2021), https://mountainstatespotlight.org/2021/12/21/black-communities-industrial-air-pollution/.

[50] Lisa Song & Lylla Younes, *EPA Calls Out Environmental Racism in Louisiana's Cancer Alley*, PROPUBLICA (Oct. 19, 2022), www.propublica.org/article/cancer-alley-louisiana-epa-environmental-racism.

[51] Jamie Berger, *How Black North Carolinians Pay the Price for the World's Cheap Bacon*, VOX (April 1, 2022), www.vox.com/future-perfect/23003487/north-carolina-hog-pork-bacon-farms-environmental-racism-black-residents-pollution-meat-industry.

[52] Jana L. Walker, Jennifer L. Bradley, & Timothy J. Humphrey, *A Closer Look at Environmental Injustice in Indian Country*, 1 SEATTLE J. FOR SOCIAL JUSTICE 379 (2002).

[53] Loka Ashwood and Kate MacTavish, *Tyranny of the Majority and Rural Environmental Injustice*, 47 J. OF RURAL STUD. 271 (2016).

[54] *Id.*

[55] Shoemaker, *supra* note 21, at 1701.

[56] *Id.*

[57] *Id.* at 1702.

outcomes make it harder to make a living; and (2) a perception that agency out-comes fail to protect rural residents from environmental threats. The first view tends to be associated with white rural cultures and politics, while the second more with rural racial minorities.

But there is more cross-pollination of these and related ideas among diverse racial groups than tends to be appreciated. That cross-pollination has been illustrated in mul-tiracial uprisings against oppression in the coalfields, and ongoing reliance on coal across diverse landscapes;[58] in disillusionment and despair about public health crises in rural regions that are alternately majority-white, Black, Native, and Hispanic, including the indiscriminate nature of the opioid epidemic;[59] and in the high proportion of rural people just trying to get by, and not seeing government as helpful to that task.[60] Thus, while this chapter is meant to illuminate how very much race matters to these analyses of marginalization, it still insists that place and class do, too, and at the same time.

In a similar vein, some criticize racial justice advocates as inadequately taking class and a diversity of suffering into consideration. However, Dr. King and other socialist thinkers have been quite explicit in recognizing white, rural suffering. For instance, King included in his speech on "The Other America," "millions of ... Appalachian whites" along with Mexican-Americans, Puerto Ricans, Indians, and other "people of various backgrounds" who live in "an arena of blasted hopes and shattered dreams."[61] More recently, progressive drafters of the proposed Green New Deal were similarly inclusive of rural suffering and white suffering, noting "depopu-lated rural communities" multiple times, among many others, as warranting inter-ventions "to promote justice and equity."[62]

The myth of rural whiteness forces the conversation on rural challenges into an artificially narrow box. Either non-white rural populations are addressed standing alone as an anomalous curiosity, or they are not included at all. Centrally, conversa-tions on rural whiteness should be called to account for *why* some rural regions are disproportionately white.

Racism within rural communities is tempting to grab at as the low-hanging fruit explaining rural minorities' displacement and disenfranchisement. This prejudice does, of course, exist, and political actors try their best to exploit racial fears and animosities, to convince rural white populations that their enemy is at the gate. But this chapter has also explored the overwhelming structural forces that have driven rural whitening and racial stratification. Law itself seems to drive rural populations

---

[58] Judah Schept, Coal, Cages, Crisis: The Rise of the Prison Economy in Central Appalachia 76, 87 (2022).

[59] *See* Chapter 6, *supra*.

[60] *See* Michael Chameides et al., *The Emerging Movement to Build Multi-Racial Power in Rural Communities*, Barn Raiser (Aug. 1, 2023), https://barnraisingmedia.com/rural-america-is-growing-more-diverse-and-building-political-power/.

[61] *The Other America Speech Transcript – Martin Luther King Jr.*, Rev, www.rev.com/blog/transcripts/the-other-america-speech-transcript-martin-luther-king-jr (last visited May 9, 2023).

[62] H.R. Res. 109, 116th Cong. (2019–2020), www.congress.gov/bill/116th-congress/house-resolution/109/text.

of color either out of rural regions, or to the bottom of their socioeconomic hierarchies. These laws are stacked against rural populations of color due to the powerful, oppressive combination of white supremacy, market supremacy, and urbanormativity intertwined.

Conversations on rural whiteness should also do more to account for racial and ethnic diversity across rural landscapes. Non-white rural residents do warrant their own sustained attention, and deserve such attention in standalone inquiries. But non-white rural residents must also be foregrounded as an integral part of the broader fabric of rural society. It is impossible to understand the rural United States, or even the United States itself – the provision of the very food we eat – without understanding the experiences of rural populations of color and the structural forces that affect their lives.

RACISM IN THE RURAL ELECTRIFICATION ACT

The Rural Electrification Act of 1936 (REA) played its own role in the racial stratification of rural regions. It echoed themes of so many other laws and programs that advantaged whites, contributing to non-whites' displacement or subjugation. Centrally, enjoying electrification meant owning property. This chapter has reviewed the many barriers to property ownership by non-white rural populations. But the REA and related programs went beyond disparities in property ownership in their racist approaches to the distribution of resources across populations and landscapes.

Significantly, the text of the REA itself makes no mention of race, racism, segregation, or apparent bases on which to discriminate other than the criteria discussed in previous chapters targeting critical masses of interested farmers (and nonfarm populations) and the requirement that the REA's loans be dispersed only when they could be self-liquidating. The *invisibility* of racism in the text and legislative history of the REA speaks to the importance of piercing through law as it is written to investigate law's implementation on the ground – a task for which the Law and Political Economy (LPE) Project and critical lenses prove helpful to examine law through its many dimensions.

Geographer Conor Harrison documents one story of state-driven racial discrimination enmeshed into the project of rural electrification. In the summer of 1934, Harrison explains, the Rural Electrification Administration undertook to survey North Carolina's seventy-seven counties "in an effort to better plan and guide what appeared to be imminent rural electrification," which had grown locally and nationally politically popular by that point.[63] As of 1932, "only 3.2 percent of North Carolina farms had electricity."[64] This survey involved interviews with 25,508 households,

---

[63] Conor Harrison, *Race, Space, and Electric Power: Jim Crow and the 1934 North Carolina Rural Electrification Survey*, 106 ANNALS OF THE AM. ASS'N OF GEOGRAPHERS, 909, 911 (2016).

[64] *Id.* at 916.

which were grouped around proposed electrification lines. The administrators then ranked the proposed lines based on their projected profitability.

Rural North Carolina, at that time, included counties that were predominantly white or predominantly Black.[65] Both white and Black populations were often tenant farmers.[66] Harrison explains how the REA administrators approached these differences:

> [A]bsent from any of the final reporting, unexplained in the instructions to the field surveyors, and largely taken as self-evident throughout the survey process, was the use of one variable to negatively adjust the projected electricity consumption of certain households at a rate much higher than any other variable – race.[67]

This so-called "correction factor" reflected officials' "total agreement," as revealed in a survey of the officials, "that African Americans were inferior" and that "the negro" needed to be kept "in his place."[68] On its face, the correction factor directed surveyors to assess the sincerity of the homeowner and the condition of the homeowner's premises in order to ensure successful profitability of electrification lines. However, the subjectivity of the variables within the factor allowed discriminatory attitudes to shape them.

Even more egregiously, an explicit component of the correction factor involved discounted household ratings based on the resident's race. This factor interacted with projected household energy usage. Harrison explains:

> For example, a household might receive both an A for the condition of the premises and an A for the rating of the interview …. [I]f the respondent were a white homeowner, the correction factor would be 1.000. This means that if the respondent were projected to use 100 kWh of electricity a month, that amount would be multiplied by 1.000, and the electricity use attributed to that particular house would remain the same. If the respondent were a white tenant with the same housing and interview grades, the correction factor would be 0.900, thus decreasing the electricity assigned to the home to 90 kWh. For an African American homeowner with two A grades, the correction factor was 0.850, and for an African American tenant the correction factor was 0.800. This means that race directly affected projections of electricity use not only at the household level but also more broadly, as such projections were used to determine those areas in the county that would be electrified and those that would not. African American householders, just by virtue of their race, received at least a 15 or 20 percent "markdown" in their projected electricity use. Although the instructions to field surveyors contain vast explanations for nearly every category of data collected, the instructions have no written justification for the correction factor.[69]

---

[65] *Id.* at 914. Only "one in ten counties (out of 100 in North Carolina) [had] a majority African American population." *Id.*

[66] *Id.* at 914.

[67] *Id.* at 911.

[68] *Id.* at 915–16.

[69] *Id.* at 920.

The correction factor, therefore, was there "to 'correct' for any resulting racial equality that might have slipped through" based on the relative objectivity of the remaining factors present in the survey.[70] Unsurprisingly, then, "the most desirable line in the eyes of the survey directors would be one densely settled exclusively by white homeowners," even in the counties that were predominantly Black.[71]

It is not clear, Harrison notes, how much this survey affected deployment of rural electrification in North Carolina. The survey data was first used by a state agency, the North Carolina Rural Electrification Authority (NCREA), which sought to pursue rural electrification but clashed with the federal Rural Electricity Administration. The federal REA "preferred to work directly with newly organized rural electric cooperatives rather than through state agencies or private utilities."[72] The federal REA was also the entity with access to actual funding. After its tense relationship with the NCREA, the federal REA "won out," and Edgecombe County, a majority-Black community, "was the first to receive federal rural electrification funds and to build lines in North Carolina."[73] In the following years, much of the state was electrified relatively quickly.

The exercise of federal authority to (potentially) circumvent the racist motivations of the North Carolina-based surveyors may sound like a victory of a progressive national government over a provincial regional one. But the REA and the New Deal were rife with racial inequities, the ramifications of which last to this day. As of 2014, 14 percent of households on Native American reservations still lacked electricity, a rate ten times greater than the national average.[74] This is in large part because the REA excluded many tribal nations, declining to make them eligible to apply for loans on equal footing with other entities.[75]

Rural populations of color continue to fight for a better future. On that April day in 2019, the room at Penn Center was full for the students' presentation. Many of the women present wore colorful head wraps and other garments reminiscent of West African traditions – some of the cultural heritage preservation the Gullah Geechee are famous for. The students did a great job. They walked through how heirs' property and tax delinquency are highly correlated because the presence of a large numbers of heirs creates a lack of clarity about who is responsible for paying taxes. They explained the multi-year process of real property assessment by the county auditor,

---

[70] *Id.*

[71] *Id.* at 921.

[72] *Id.* at 927.

[73] *Id.*

[74] Laurie Stone, *Native Energy: Rural Electrification on Tribal Lands*, RMI (June 24, 2014), https://rmi .org/blog_2014_06_24_native_energy_rural_electrification_on_tribal_lands/.

[75] Joseph Lee, *Living in the Dark: Native Reservations Struggle with Power Shortages in Pandemic*, THE GUARDIAN (Aug. 12, 2020), www.theguardian.com/environment/2020/aug/12/native-americans-energy-inequality-electricity; Catherine J. K. Sandoval, *Energy Access is Energy Justice: The Yurok Tribe's Trailblazing Work to Close the Native American Reservation Electricity Gap*, in ENERGY JUSTICE, INTERNATIONAL AND U.S. PERSPECTIVES (EDWARD ELGAR 2018), at 2.

procedures for paying taxes and late fees, notice the county must provide to delinquent taxpayers, the ultimate potential sale of tax-delinquent properties at public auction, and the property owner's right to redeem the property for one year after sale by paying the delinquent taxes. But an employee of the county clerk's office in the audience knew these processes more intimately than we did. She jumped in to save us when we didn't have answers to questions. And the discussion was quite lively. The community, it was clear, had been dealing with this issue for a *long* time.

I have grappled, though not enough, with how racial inequality within rural communities interacts with the urban majority's exploitation of the extractive rural economy. Place-based interventions, it seems clear, are necessary. But they are not enough. When interventions to improve rural fates lack safeguards to ensure that those interventions will target and dismantle intra-rural hierarchies, they risk funneling resources to rural elites, white populations, and other powerful stakeholders, as has been shown time and again with federal policies such as the REA. Yes, it is easy to vilify the individual officials who absorbed and reinforced the racist milieu in which they came up. But where the REA or similar programs did funnel resources into a system of racial stratification, it was as much a failure of federal governance as anything else.

It seems clear that the question of localism versus oversight rests at the heart of modern rural questions, posing perhaps the most difficult challenge to how to approach questions of rural revitalization. "Community-driven initiatives," "regional self-determination," and "local control" all hold intuitive appeal as themes for approaching rural interventions, especially when viewed in light of the first several chapters of this book highlighting the real risk of urban domination and exploitation of a rural underclass. Yet, subjugation within rural communities complicates these visions, pointing toward a more nuanced path of federalism – a joint national–local project that empowers and protects the most vulnerable. This book's conclusion in the subsequent chapter contemplates what a proactively anti-racist approach to rural revitalization and restorative rural racial justice can and should look like.

8

The Myth of Rural Obsolescence

I spent December 2022 in Manhattan, living in an Airbnb in Hell's Kitchen to be closer to my family for a bit.[1] I was also attempting to make progress on my book manuscript during the break between classes. From New York, I took Amtrak to attend a conference in DC, then my mom took the bus down from Ithaca for a few days before I did a stint Upstate. The "tripledemic" was ramping up, and we were hoping no one would get COVID, the flu, or RSV, especially right before Christmas.

Once again, I was tallying up months in big cities. It seemed ironic that during 2022, the year I was trying to make substantial headway on this book, I spent so much time in major urban centers – more than I ever had previously. Some might expect that a book on rural resilience should be written in West Virginia, or Ithaca, or the South Carolina coast. But my 2022 urban immersion felt like the right opportunity to ask myself: Am I getting everything completely wrong?

After a semester back in South Carolina, staying in Manhattan did feel like I was in the future. It's easy to be vegan there. The ease and affordability of walking or taking the subway or Amtrak is thrilling. Recycling seems to be taken seriously. People can be who they want to be. My father's side of the family is Jewish, and it felt nice to be surrounded by Jewish people and Menorah displays during Hannukah.

But the cost of living, even for a transient month, felt untenable. I joked about a bonfire that I was throwing money on daily just to exist there. The Airbnb cost more than three times my mortgage in South Carolina. Just like in DC, there were unhoused people everywhere, looking very cold.

I enjoyed my temporary urban life. I am, indeed, just as in love with New York City as anyone else who grew up on Broadway shows and Carrie Bradshaw. And I felt the temptation to say, "This is it. This is the future." I was tempted to forget what life is like outside those urban borders. Being in the city feels like getting high on something. You literally can't see past the skyscrapers. The longer you stay

---

[1] Portions of this chapter were excerpted from Ann M. Eisenberg, *Rural America as a Commons*, 57 U. RICH. L. REV. 769 (2023).

in Oz, you can start to forget Kansas – and to convince yourself you don't need it. Being there during the season of clichéd Hallmark movies, I did understand why people chafe at the suggested "need" for the proverbial Kansas. Cities are so often lambasted as furnishing a life of shallow ambition and consumerism. Rural regions are portrayed as the "real" America to which everyone must return no matter how it may have abused them.

The city has its own underclass and working class. Those workers have varying levels of visibility and vulnerability as they make the city run – walking the dogs of the wealthy, delivering a seemingly infinite array of restaurant delivery orders in a frenetic network of bikes and scooters, trying to coax tourists into rickshaws. As unequal as New York may be, I wonder if it is preferable to be a present, visible urban laborer than an invisible, distant rural laborer. Of course, I'm sure there were invisible urban laborers there, too – I just couldn't see them.

When I would go to a Manhattan Shake Shack or to a new building made of beautiful materials, or when I threw something away, or when I turned the lights on, or lit the Airbnb's gas stove, I reminded myself: All of these materials came from or are going somewhere; all of them are touched by human hands, whether in the United States or beyond. Beef. Salmon. Milk. Lettuce. Coffee. Chocolate. Gas. Rubber. Steel. Cotton. Water. My New York trash may have well ended up back in South Carolina.[2] My Manhattan light switch may have been powered by a plant or windmill Upstate.[3] Maybe New York City will be self-reliant – apart from rural contributions to its operations – one day. But I have trouble seeing it.

It turned out that I would be going back to West Virginia in 2023. Between my urban stints in DC and New York in 2022, Kat forwarded a job posting, and I interviewed for and accepted a position at WVU Law, this time as a tenured member of the faculty. I was told that the bakery in Morgantown with the best scones in the world survived the pandemic. I did not know then that I would arrive to WVU at a time when West Virginia would be making national headlines again: for firing faculty in historic numbers, eliminating entire humanities departments, and ignoring student protests. It would be the latest painful chapter in the longer story of regional extraction.

My hope in returning to West Virginia was to continue to push the conversation on the so-called urban–rural divide toward a fuller truth. A truth that includes the sordid history and faulty assumptions behind the extractive rural economy, the displacement and subjugation of non-white rural populations, and the ongoing necessity of recognizing and strengthening complex systems of urban–rural interdependence. A fuller truth that can help orient future interventions away from market

---

[2]   Gabrielle Komorowski, *Trash from NYC, New Jersey Sent to South Carolina* WYFF (Nov. 20, 2013), www.wyff4.com/article/trash-from-nyc-new-jersey-sent-to-south-carolina-1/7006437.

[3]   Emily S. Rueb, *How New York City Gets Its Electricity*, N.Y. TIMES, www.nytimes.com/interactive/2017/02/10/nyregion/how-new-york-city-gets-its-electricity-power-grid.html (last visited November 19, 2023).

supremacy and urbanormativity, and toward geographic equity, ecological steward-ship, and a more resilient society overall.

With many ready to dismiss nonurban life as a relic of history, rural America's place in the future is in question. The rural role in the American past is under-standably more apparent. As the story of urbanization goes in the United States and elsewhere, the majority of the population used to live in rural places, includ-ing small towns and sparsely populated counties.[4] A substantial proportion of those people worked in agriculture, manufacturing, or extractive industries.[5] But trends associated with modernity – mechanization, automation, globalization, and envi-ronmental conservation, for instance – have reduced the perceived need for a rural workforce.[6]

Roughly since the industrial revolution of the nineteenth century, rural depop-ulation has continued with some consistency. In 1940, the U.S. rural population peaked at 57 percent of the total population.[7] Today, that proportion is 14 percent.[8] This narrative and these figures, I posit, fuel a widespread embrace of the myth of rural obsolescence. This myth refers to the idea that rural communities, in this age of modernity, are no longer needed.

Ample commentary associates urbanization with societal evolution and a general idea of progress or inevitability.[9] Livelihoods in agriculture and extractive industries, in particular, are a difficult way of life. Some rural legacy industries, such as coal mining, are understood as no longer necessary, if not actively harmful.[10] It is a desir-able thing that fewer people should be compelled to engage in that work. Larger cities also offer sustainability benefits by some metrics. Concentrating populations

---

[4] Kenneth M. Johnson & Daniel T. Lichter, *Rural Depopulation: Growth and Decline Processes over the Past Century*, 84 RURAL SOC. 3 (2019).

[5] CAROLYN DIMITRI ET AL., U.S. DEP'T OF AGRIC. THE 20TH CENTURY TRANSFORMATION OF U.S. AGRICULTURE AND FARM POLICY (June 2005), www.ers.usda.gov/webdocs/publications/44197/13566_eib3_1_.pdf (In 1900, 41 percent of total workforce employed in agriculture, compared to 1–2 percent today). In 1840, almost 70 percent of the labor force worked in agriculture. That figure dropped to 2 percent in 2000. Ezra Klein & Susannah Locke, *40 Maps that Explain Food in America*, VOX (June 9, 2014), www.vox.com/a/explain-food-america.

[6] Rick Su, *Democracy in Rural America*, 98 N.C. L. REV. 837, 844 (2020); Steven M. Virgil, *Community Economic Development and Rural America: Strategies for Community-Based Collaborative Development*, 20 J. AFFORDABLE HOUS. & CMTY. DEV. L. 9 (Fall 2010); Christopher D. Merrett & Cynthia Struthers, *Globalization and the Future of Rural Communities in the American Midwest*, 12 TRANSNAT'L L. & CONTEMP. PROBS. 33, 64 (2002).

[7] Johnson & Lichter, *supra* note 4.

[8] ELIZABETH A. DOBIS ET AL., USDA ECON. RSCH. SERV., RURAL AMERICAN AT A GLANCE (2021), www.ers.usda.gov/webdocs/publications/102576/eib-230.pdf?v=4409

[9] *See, e.g.*, William McGreevey et. al., *Propinquity Matters: How Better Health, Urbanization, and Income Grew Together, 1870–2008*, 15 GEO. J. ON POVERTY L. & POL'Y 605, 615 (2008).

[10] *See* Michelle W. Anderson, *The Western, Rural Rustbelt: Learning from Local Fiscal Crisis in Oregon*, 50 WILLAMETTE L. REV. 465 (2014); Patrick McGinley, *Collateral Damage: Turning a Blind Eye to Environmental and Social Injustice in the Coalfields*, 19 J. ENVTL. & SUSTAINABILITY L. 305, 403 (2013).

in denser localities can help concentrate public and private resources and make use of those resources more efficiently.[11] Rural populations' presence in distressed regions borne of fading industries raises questions of whether it is a beneficial use of scarce public resources to support rural regions, and whether the rural way of life is consistent with modern needs.[12] And thus, the fate of the 14 percent and their communities, at least in the most struggling regions, is in question.[13]

However, the severe and numerous modern crises we face as a society offer good reason to question the sanguine assumptions underlying the urbanization-as-progress narrative. The coasts where the majority of the population is concentrated are becoming increasingly hazardous as climate change fuels sea level rise and more extreme weather patterns.[14] Domestic and international climate displacement and migration will increase.[15] Meanwhile, the food system whose abundance and reliability we are told to value is killing us with obesity, heart disease, diabetes, cancer, and environmental degradation.[16] Figures on wealth and income inequality are staggering.[17] The modernized cities rural residents are told

[11] *See* John R. Nolon, *Changes Spark Interest in Sustainable Urban Places: But How Do We Identify and Support Them?* 40 Fordham Urb. L.J. 1697, 1700 (2013).

[12] *Cf.* Matthew Yglesias, *The Inefficiency of Rural Living*, Slate (June 6, 2012), https://slate.com/business/2012/06/the-inefficiency-of-rural-living.html.

[13] *Cf.* Sheila R. Foster & Christian Iaione, *The City as a Commons*, 34 Yale L. & Pol'y Rev. 281, 297 (2016); Jim Chen, *Filburn's Legacy*, 52 Emory L.J. 1719, 1766 (2003) (characterizing rural depopulation as consequence of economic growth and asking "a most embarrassing question: 'Is North Dakota necessary?'").

[14] IPCC, Intergovernmental Panel on Climate Change, Sixth Assessment Report, Climate Change 2022: Impacts, Adaptation and Vulnerability (2022), www.ipcc.ch/report/ar6/wg2/; *cf.* Elizabeth A. Andrews & Jesse Reiblich, *Reflections on Rural Resilience: As the Climate Changes, Will Rural Areas Become the Urban Backyard?* 44 Wm. & Mary Env't L. & Pol'y Rev. 745, 747 (2020) ("Will rural localities become the receiving communities for climate change refugees retreating from flooding urban areas?"); Michelle Wilde Anderson, *Losing the War of Attrition: Mobility, Chronic Decline, and Infrastructure*, 127 Yale L.J. F. 522, 541 (2017) (advocating reinvesting in distressed regions due to likely need for populations to relocate there from coasts and deserts in coming decades).

[15] Stephanie M. Stern, *Climate Transition Relief: Federal Buyouts for Underwater Homes*, 72 Duke L.J. 161 (2022); E. Tendayi Achiume, *Empire, Borders, and Refugee Responsibility Sharing*, 110 Calif. L. Rev. 1011, 1038 (2022).

[16] *See generally* Katherine L. Oaks, *The Public Value of Ecological Agriculture*, 21 Vt. J. Env't L. 544, 545 (2020); Mary Jane Angelo, *Corn, Carbon, and Conservation: Rethinking U.S. Agricultural Policy in a Changing Global Environment*, 17 Geo. Mason L. Rev. 593 (2010); William S. Eubanks II, *A Rotten System: Subsidizing Environmental Degradation and Poor Public Health with Our Nation's Tax Dollars*, 28 Stan. Env't L.J. 213 (2009).

[17] According to the Pew Research Center, from 1983 to 2016, upper-income families accumulated 79 percent of aggregate national wealth, compared to 17 percent for middle-income families and 4 percent to lower-income families. In 2018, even before the COVID-19 pandemic, the income of the top 10 percent of earners was 12.6 times that of the bottom 10 percent. Juliana Menasce Horowitz et al., Pew Rsch. Ctr., Most Americans Say There Is Too Much Economic Inequality in the U.S., but Fewer than Half Call It a Top Priority (Jan. 9, 2020), www.pewresearch.org/social-trends/2020/01/09/trends-in-income-and-wealth-inequality/. *See also* Jedediah Britton-Purdy et al., *Building a Law-and-Political-Economy Framework: Beyond the Twentieth-Century Synthesis*, 129 Yale L.J. 1784 (2020) (connecting socioeconomic inequality to other crises).

they can "just move" to often actively combat affordable housing development.[18] Racial stratification remains entrenched in most aspects of American life.[19] Only the radical even dare fantasize about infrastructure other wealthy countries take for granted, such as a functioning and accessible national passenger rail transportation system.[20]

While many urbanites are quick to dismiss rural issues as niche issues, geographic inequality, rurality, and rural livelihoods are implicated in one way or another in virtually all of these crises. Framing the countryside as obsolescent or superfluous overlooks fundamental aspects of the often invisible urban–rural interdependence that undergirds American life.[21] As discussed in Chapter 4, cities still rely heavily on rural resources and workers, and will need to do so even more in the face of climate change.[22] As such, rural resources, workers, and localities need to be taken more seriously as a critical component of an interdependent national system.

Rural America has received some attention as the locus of important collective resources, such as waterways, wildlife, forests, and public lands, and relatedly, as the site of often severe political contestation.[23] However, these conversations have not quite captured how rural America as a holistic entity within broader society is

---

[18] Bethany Y. Li, *Now Is the Time!: Challenging Resegregation and Displacement in the Age of Hypergentrification*, 85 FORDHAM L. REV. 1189, 1203 (2016).

[19] *See generally* Angela P. Harris & Aysha Pamukcu, *The Civil Rights of Health: A New Approach to Challenging Structural Inequality*, 67 UCLA L. REV. 758 (2020); Deborah N. Archer, *"White Men's Roads through Black Men's Homes": Advancing Racial Equity through Highway Reconstruction*, 73 VAND. L. REV. 1259 (2020); Dorothy E. Roberts, *Foreword: Abolition Constitutionalism*, 133 HARV. L. REV. 1, 3 (2019).

[20] *See* Adam P. Wald, *Planes, Trains & Automobiles: Regulating the Transportation Technologies of Tomorrow*, 26 B.U. J. SCI. & TECH. L. 379, 380 (2020).

[21] *See* J. B. Ruhl & Robin Kundis Craig, 4°C, 106 MINN. L. REV. 191, 201 (2021) (advocating "redesign" of population distribution, infrastructure, agriculture, and other social-ecological system components to pursue transformational adaptation to climate change); Junjie Wu et al., *Rural-Urban Interdependence: A Framework for Integrating Regional, Urban, and Environmental Economic Insights*, 99 AM. J. AGRIC. ECON. 464 (2017).

[22] *See* Laurie Ristino, *Surviving Climate Change in America: Toward a Rural Resilience Framework*, 41 W. NEW ENG. L. REV. 521 (2019); GREG FULKERSON & ALEXANDER R. THOMAS, URBAN DEPENDENCY: THE INESCAPABLE REALITY OF THE ENERGY ECONOMY (2020); Ruhl & Craig, *supra* note 21, at 195–203.

[23] *See generally* Camille Pannu, *Drinking Water and Exclusion: A Case Study from California's Central Valley*, 100 CALIF. L. REV. 223 (2012); Anthony B. Schutz, *Toward a More Multi-Functional Rural Landscape: Community Approaches to Rural Land Stewardship*, 22 FORDHAM ENV'T L. REV. 633 (2011); Erin Morrow, *The Environmental Front: Cultural Warfare in the West*, 25 J. LAND RES. & ENV'T L. 183 (2005); Christopher S. Elmendorf, *Ideas, Incentives, Gifts, and Governance: Toward Conservation Stewardship of Private Land, in Cultural and Psychological Perspective*, 2003 U. ILL. L. REV. 423 (2003); Sandra B. Zellmer, *Sustaining Geographies of Hope: Cultural Resources on Public Lands*, 73 U. COLO. L. REV. 413, 417 (2002); James R. Rasband, *The Rise of Urban Archipelagoes in the American West: A New Reservation Policy?*, 31 ENV'T L. 1 (2001).

itself collectively important. The physical resources that sit in rural places and the necessary goods produced in rural regions cannot be protected and produced without workers engaging in that work. Those workers – whose numbers need to grow if rural resources are to be conserved, developed, and used sustainably[24] – cannot fully pursue these important public and quasi-public activities without infrastructure to support them and their activities.[25]

I increasingly think of rural America as an essential resource that policymakers have wasted, to our collective detriment. "Waste" can be defined as "expended carelessly," "discarded," or "frittered away." In the legal context, waste is understood as a form of destruction, whether through willful initiative or passive neglect. Even setting aside questions of morality and political destabilization, given the collective importance of rural resources, workers, and infrastructure, extracting value from rural America to the point of depletion over the past several decades has been a collective mistake. The prior chapters of this book have established how policymakers have facilitated those extractive dynamics, enabled rural isolation, and undermined rural vitality in the name of collective benefits that remain elusive.

This final chapter seeks to complicate narratives of urbanization as progress and rural neglect as benign. The chapter proposes that rural America itself – not just the bulk of the country's natural resources that lie within it – can and should be understood as a commons. A commons is a collective resource that we all need and use. Understanding rural America as a commons yields surprisingly challenging implications. Yet, those implications can help make sense of some aspects of modern urban–rural tensions. They can also offer a broad normative framework for making better governance decisions going forward, moving away from market-supremacist principles and toward principles centered on the pursuit of national resilience and the avoidance of further waste and injustice.

Centrally, it makes sense that varying levels of embeddedness in, entitlement to, proximity to, and cost-bearing of a commons would affect different populations' perceptions of the commons and how to govern it. As an illustrative analogy, I have been told more than once by coastal urbanites that Western public lands "belong to all of us." The suggestion behind the claim is that locals living near those lands should feel no greater sense of ownership or entitlement to them

---

[24] *See* Bruce R. Huber, *The Durability of Private Claims to Public Property*, 102 GEO. L. J. 991, 1034–35, 1039 (2014) (observing constraints in federal land management agencies' enforcement power of conservation priorities with constrained budgets misaligned with task of monitoring millions of acres of land); Olivier De Schutter, *The Green Rush: The Global Race for Farmland and the Rights of Land Users*, 52 HARV. INT'L L. J. 503, 541, 554 (2011) (discussing more labor-intensive nature of sustainable agroecological practices as compared to highly industrialized agriculture); Erin Dewey, *Sundown and You Better Take Care: Why Sunset Provisions Harm the Renewable Energy Industry and Violate Tax Principles*, 52 B.C. L. REV. 1105, 1110 (2011) (discussing connections among renewable energy production, labor needs, and facilities siting in rural areas).

[25] *Id.*

than anyone else and should stop complaining about federal agencies' governance decisions.

Yet, that urbanite does not bear the costs of public lands governance as directly as the resident nearby does. The resident nearby may have a greater formal right of access to those public lands in some fashion than the urbanite, or they may have the same formal rights. These variations suggest that, while the urbanite is technically entitled to some form of relationship with public lands governance by virtue of the lands' public nature, it would be undemocratic and unfair for the resident nearby to have the exact same relationship in terms of avenues for input or deriving value from the lands. Yet, it would also be undemocratic and unfair for the local resident to dominate the lands or deny the urbanite's relationship.

If we consider the entirety of rural America as analogous to public lands, the commons characterization points toward finding a delicate balance between recognizing the urban majority's entitlement to rural resources on the one hand, while accounting for higher and more varied levels of rural embeddedness, entitlement, proximity, and cost-bearing in commons governance.[26] Understanding rural America as a commons does not mean that the urban majority is entitled to dominate rural regions. As Joseph Sax said decades ago while contemplating the balance between local and national interests, "[W]e should be reluctant to require people to arrange their lives to serve the demands of some larger, external community ... for what we think comprises 'our benefit.'"[27]

Perhaps most importantly, recognizing that the urban majority has some level of entitlement to rural America also implies that the urban majority bears responsibility for rural America. If we accept the premise that rural resources belong to everyone, in a sense – which I argue that we should – we necessarily imply that everyone has an obligation to take care of, or steward, rural resources. And to characterize those resources worthy of protection only as the trees, wildlife, rivers, and lakes, when people live near and among those resources, needlessly diminishes the import of a holistic, populated rural America as a public amenity.

The commons characterization of rural America offers a more hopeful path than the de facto national policy of wasting rural places and populations over the past several decades. No matter the ideal governance balance among competing entitlements, a commons warrants stewardship. The past 150 years of national policy treating rural places and people as loci merely for extracting value until depletion can evolve into a policy of treating rural resources like shared amenities. And this holistic commons characterization underscores that commons governance cannot

---

[26] Cf. Joseph Sax, *Do Communities Have Rights – The National Parks as a Laboratory of New Ideas*, 45 U. PITT. L. REV. 499 (1984) (discussing tensions between national governance priorities and local interests for communities located in national parks).

[27] *Id.* at 509.

simply prioritize physical resources. People and places warrant stewardship for the collective benefit, too.[28]

The discussion that follows briefly reviews commons literature. It then turns to three under-discussed rural amenities – agricultural land, energy production, and infrastructure – and argues that each of these rural puzzle pieces can be understood as (1) amenities or activities with serious collective import for rural and urban populations and (2) amenities or activities characterized by hoarding, abuse, or waste at the hands of the private sector enabled by a legal system that fails to account for that collective import.

Putting these pieces together, the chapter argues that understanding rural America itself as a commons can help inform an approach to governance that better reflects rural America's collective import. The discussion concludes with thoughts about governing rural America as a commons, including the often unspoken task of balancing differentiated urban and rural stakes in, and entitlements to, the rural commons. An embrace of a stewardship approach will entail interventions that are both more robust and more thoughtful than measures commonly discussed for addressing rural challenges.

The chapter proposes five principles that can guide diverse interventions into rural regions at any level of government in order to better govern rural America as a commons. These principles can steer policies away from market supremacy and toward making the commons of rural America more resilient for everyone's benefit. Those principles are: (1) accounting for more rural work as work in the public interest (i.e., recognizing the collective import of the rural commons); (2) building capacity to avoid boom-bust cycles in rural communities (to help steward the rural commons); (3) democratizing rural resources (to strike a better balance in sharing the rural commons); (4) pursuing racial justice as central to resilience (to counter the deleterious effects of racial stratification in the rural commons); and (5) recognizing that investing in rural infrastructure benefits society as a whole (because that infrastructure stabilizes, supports, protects, and connects the rural commons). These principles are introduced at a high level of generality. They would benefit from further research, and most importantly, from the input of rural residents who stand to be affected by governance decisions.

CHARACTERISTICS OF A COMMONS

What is a commons? The concept is much discussed and even, some might argue, overplayed. According to scholarship across diverse disciplines, virtually anything

---

[28] *Cf.* Lisa R. Pruitt & Linda Sobczynski, *Protecting People, Protecting Places: What Environmental Litigation Conceals and Reveals about Rurality*, 47 J. OF RURAL STUD. 326 (2016) (discussing environmental advocates' exclusion of rural environmental justice communities in advocacy); Joseph Sax, *Do Communities Have Rights? The National Parks as a Laboratory of New Ideas*, 45 U. PITT. L. REV. 499 (1984) (discussing how legal doctrines and national priorities fail to value communities facing displacement, and how viewing rural populations' presence among natural resources as a question of "community" rather than "natural resource management" affects governance considerations).

with public import or collective usage is a commons: Natural resources, public lands, "parking spots, knowledge and culture, intellectual property, medical care, tax rights, marketing, the allocation of criminal defense, government budgets, the presidential nomination process, and credit default swap markets" have all been characterized as commons.[29]

The classic example of a "common pool resource" is that it is vulnerable to "rivalry, overexploitation, and degradation."[30] As Brigham Daniels explains, "The script of the tragedy of the commons is simple. We have a commons resource; we fail to limit access to the resource adequately, and the result is a free-for-all that threatens collective interests."[31] Commons resources become exhausted when "we see a rush to satisfy narrow self-interests work[ing] to the detriment of broader interests – individually rational decisions leading to collective catastrophes."[32] Strained fish populations, scarce grazing land, and vulnerable forests all illustrate classic commons examples of shared resources that risk exhaustion through competitive overuse. In sum, a commons is some sort of collectively important resource that is (1) consumed in some fashion and (2) challenged by competing users.[33]

But characterizing a commons is often simply a question of scale, and a commons does not need to be an explicitly public or actively shared resource. The entire earth, for instance, has been portrayed as a commons.[34] Eric Freyfogle argues that "a commons exists in any setting characterized by interconnection and interdependence, whether ecological or social, which is to say essentially everywhere."[35]

In their 2016 article, *The City as a Commons*, Sheila Foster and Christian Iaione advanced the idea that the commons concept could be helpfully applied to geographic spaces whose mix of public and private resources were used collectively by inhabitants. They used the framework to ask "how [urban] space is used and for whose benefit" in the face of increasing pressures of privatization and commodification.[36] The commons argument weighs against the threat of economic elites' enclosure of urban resources "which might otherwise be more widely shared by a broader class of city inhabitants."[37] The authors asked whether the commons concept might

---

[29] Sheldon Bernard Lyke, *Diversity as Commons*, 88 Tul. L. Rev. 317, 324 (2013); *see also* Brigham Daniels, *Governing the Presidential Nomination Commons*, 84 Tul. L. Rev. 899, 907 (2010) (characterizing groundwater aquifers, beaches, air sheds, polar ice caps, parking spots, sidewalk vending, government budgets, silence, and e-mail inboxes as commons).

[30] Foster & Iaione, *supra* note 13, at 288.

[31] Daniels, *supra* note 29, at 901.

[32] *Id.* at 902.

[33] *Id.* at 906.

[34] Eric T. Freyfogle, *Naming the Tragedy*, 2014 B.Y.U. L. Rev. 1415, 1420 (2014).

[35] *Id.*

[36] Foster & Iaione, *supra* note 13, at 282.

[37] *Id.* at 284.

"provide a framework and set of tools to open up the possibility of more inclusive and equitable forms of 'city-making.'"[38]

Foster and Iaione observed that characterizing something as a commons has implications well beyond the act of labeling. They argued that a commons characterization can be "less a *description* of the resource and its characteristics and more of a *normative claim* to the resource."[39] That claim may be "to open up (or to re-open) access to a good – i.e., to recognize the community's right to access and to use a resource which might otherwise be under exclusive private or public control – on account of the social value or utility that such access would generate or produce for the community."[40]

Many of Foster's and Iaione's observations apply to rural America writ large as well, which I define as the smaller towns and more remote regions of the country, in addition to the non-coastal portions of the nation often dismissed as "flyover country."[41] Important questions loom as to how rural space is used and for whose benefit in the face of increasing pressures of depopulation, privatization, commodification, and ownership concentration.[42] Economic elites' enclosure of rural resources impede broader sharing, locally and nationally, of the benefits of those resources. Tools to approach the possibility of more inclusive, equitable, and sustainable "rural-making" have eluded modern commentators outside certain social science fields. Thus, these same factors warrant asking whether rural America is a commons and, if so, how it might be better governed as such.

RURAL AMERICA AS A COMMONS

Portions of rural America have already received attention as the locus of certain commons resources.[43] Setting aside more oft-discussed rural natural resources and public lands, the discussion that follows contemplates agricultural land, rural energy, and rural infrastructure as resources with commons characteristics. Put together, these pieces paint a picture of rural America itself as a holistic commons that warrants more strategic intervention.

To illustrate these resources as part of the rural commons as a whole, the discussion focuses on their collective implications beyond the classic example of

---

[38] *Id.* at 285.

[39] *Id.* at 288 (emphasis in original).

[40] *Id.*

[41] *See* Lisa R. Pruitt, *Rural Rhetoric*, 39 CONN. L. REV. 159, 177 (2006) (discussing competing definitions of rural).

[42] *Cf.* Vanessa Casado Pérez, *Ownership Concentration: Lessons from Natural Resources*, 117 NW. U. L. REV. 37 (2022); Marcello De Maria, *Understanding Land in the Context of Large-Scale Land Acquisitions: A Brief History of Land in Economics*, 8 LAND 1 (2019), https://doi.org/10.3390/land8010015.

[43] *See, e.g.*, Ristino, *supra* note 22.

exhaustion of natural resources. Specifically, this discussion focuses on each of these rural puzzle pieces as (1) activities or amenities with serious collective import for rural and urban populations and (2) activities or amenities historically and currently characterized by hoarding, abuse, or waste at the hands of the private sector enabled by a legal system that fails to account for that collective import.

AGRICULTURAL LAND AS A COMMON RESOURCE

Despite the physical distance of agricultural land from the majority of the population, decisions about how agricultural land is used have far-reaching impacts on U.S. society, including intimate effects on Americans' bodies. Scholars generally agree that the crops U.S. farmers produce end up in American food whether those products are healthy or not.[44] Michael Pollan drew public attention to these connections in his 2007 book *Omnivore's Dilemma*, in which he illustrated how large-scale monoculture production of corn in the "Corn Belt" contributes to corn's presence in "virtually every processed food in our grocery stores," including animal products.[45]

The consequences of modern agricultural land uses include an obesity rate of 42 percent,[46] heightened rates of diabetes among minority populations,[47] and the persistence of widespread food insecurity.[48] Although some might attribute these trends to individuals' lifestyle choices, obesity rates are rising globally with increased industrial agriculture, and "no national success stories" exist for efforts to curb any country's obesity pandemic.[49] Certainly, other factors, such as car-centric urban design and food deserts, also influence these trends.[50] However, it would be difficult

---

[44] Lawrence F. Dempsey, *Feeding the Racial Disparity in Disease: How Federal Agricultural Subsidies Contribute to a Racial Disparity in the Prevalence of Diet Related Illness*, 7 BIOTECHNOLOGY & PHARMACEUTICAL L. REV. 109, 130 (2014); David V. Fazzino II, *Whose Food Security? Confronting Expanding Commodity Production and the Obesity and Diabetes Epidemics*, 15 DRAKE J. AGRIC. L. 393, 403 (2010).

[45] MICHAEL POLLAN, OMNIVORE'S DILEMMA (2007); Angelo, *supra* note 16, at 595.

[46] *Adult Obesity Facts*, CDC, www.cdc.gov/obesity/data/adult.html (last visited May 9, 2023); Patricia L. Farnese, *Remembering the Farmer in the Agriculture Policy and Obesity Debate*, 65 FOOD & DRUG L.J. 391 (2010).

[47] Dempsey, *supra* note 44, at 130; Fazzino, *supra* note 44, at 403.

[48] Agriculture's causal role in these conditions is the object of debate. Farnese, *supra* note 46. *See generally* Emily M. Broad Leib & Margot J. Pollans, *The New Food Safety*, 107 CALIF. L. REV. 1173 (2019); Emily Broad Leib, *The Forgotten Half of Food System Reform: Using Food and Agricultural Law to Foster Healthy Food Production*, 9 J. FOOD L. & POL'Y 17 (2013).

[49] Olga Khazan, *The Paradox of Obesity and Produce*, ATLANTIC (June 2, 2014), www.theatlantic.com/health/archive/2014/06/eating-more-fruits-and-vegetables-wont-stop-obesity/371992/.

[50] *See, e.g.*, Mark J. Nieuwenhuijsen, *Influence of Urban and Transport Planning and the City Environment on Cariovascular Disease*, 15 NATURE REV. CARDIOLOGY 432 (2018), www.nature.com/articles/s41569-018-0003-2; Dianna M. Smith & Steven Cummins, *Obese Cities: How Our Environment Shapes Overweight*, 3 GEOGRAPHY COMPASS 518 (Jan. 2009).

to credibly dispute that agricultural land uses and the policies that enable them are playing a role in a "toxic food culture" that contributes to overconsumption of unhealthy foods at the center of several public health crises.[51]

Agriculture is also a major industry with other impacts on the economy, the environment, and public health. Industrialized agriculture – an industry worth tens of billions of dollars per year[52] – remains a central source of carbon emissions, water pollution, water waste, and soil depletion.[53] Agricultural activities' effects extend far beyond the farm. In short, even though agricultural production is invisible to most of the population, agricultural land and business operations have serious ramifications for far-reaching aspects of society.

Despite agricultural land uses' collective import, property law, agricultural policy, and environmental regulations have enabled hoarding, abuse, and waste of agricultural land and resources by private operations. To begin with the property problem, agricultural land tenure has received increasing attention of late as a thorny problem with privatized contours and collective implications.[54] In *Fee Simple Failures*, discussed in Chapter 7, Jessica Shoemaker argues persuasively that distribution and management of agricultural land has reached crisis levels.[55] Ninety-eight percent of agricultural land is "owned and controlled by people who are White."[56] Ownership of agricultural land also grows ever more concentrated in the hands of a shrinking number of powerful absentee landlords.[57]

Shoemaker observes that the very rationale for private property law in the early United States embraced a vision of agricultural labor and stewardship, rewarding white, male Europeans for working the land as part of interconnected communities.[58] Yet today, even that limited vision of (relatively) diversified

---

[51] Debra L. Donahue, *Livestock Production, Climate Change, and Human Health: Closing the Awareness Gap*, 45 ENV'T L. REP. NEWS & ANALYSIS 11112, 11119 (2015) (although U.S. Department of Agriculture disagrees, "most commentators concur that current agricultural policies are unsustainable" and "promote unhealthy eating and environmental problems ranging from water pollution to soil erosion to weed proliferation"); Andrea Freeman, *Transparency for Food Consumers: Nutrition Labeling and Food Oppression*, 41 AM. J. L. & MED. 315, 327 (2015); Farnese, *supra* note 46, at 392.

[52] Farming and Farm Income, USDA ECON. RSCH. SERV. (Mar. 14, 2023), www.ers.usda.gov/data-products/ag-and-food-statistics-charting-the-essentials/farming-and-farm-income/#:~:text=Crop%20cash%20receipts%20totaled%20%20%24237.8,50.3%20percent)%20of%20the%20total.

[53] Keith E. Sealing, *Attack of the Balloon People: How America's Food Culture and Agricultural Policies Threaten the Food Security of the Poor, Farmers, and Indigenous Peoples of the World*, 40 VAND. J. TRANSNAT'L L. 1015, 1027 (2007).

[54] *See, e.g.*, Pérez, *supra* note 42; Jesse J. Richardson Jr., *Land Tenure and Sustainable Agriculture*, 3 TEX. A&M L. REV. 799 (2016).

[55] Jessica A. Shoemaker, *Fee Simple Failures: Rural Landscapes and Race*, 119 MICH. L. REV. 1695 (2021); Leib, *supra* note 48, at 18 (characterizing entire food system as in crisis).

[56] Shoemaker, *supra* note 55, at 1699.

[57] *Id.* at 1700; Sealing, *supra* note 53, at 1025 (describing high level of concentration of industrialized agriculture industries).

[58] Shoemaker, *supra* note 55, at 1698.

ownership and local investment by enfranchised landowners has largely been lost. Property law, particularly the everlasting nature of the fee simple absolute, has contributed to "dynastic" agricultural land tenure that far more closely resembles the medieval English feudal systems that early Americans purported to reform.[59] The proliferation of state "right-to-farm" laws protecting agribusinesses from nuisance suits has further cemented their dynastic position within rural communities and society more broadly.[60]

Property law is not the only culprit enabling unsustainable modern agriculture. Federal and state subsidies for, and regulations of, agriculture have largely discounted nutrition, public health, and climate change, which many attribute to lobbying efforts by powerful industry interest groups.[61] For similar reasons, weak federal and state regulatory frameworks and enforcement allow pollution and industry consolidation to remain relatively unchecked.[62] The esoteric and technical nature of agricultural law acts as a barrier to greater scrutiny and democratization.[63] The fact that most law schools do not offer even one agricultural law course points to a concession of this area to only the highly specialized practitioner and expert, despite the area's collective import.

The implications of these conditions in agricultural land tenure are multifold. The racialized, corporatized concentration of agricultural land corresponds with heavy agricultural industrialization. That strict commodification of land, crops, and animals harms the public by way of the crises described earlier. In turn, the commodification, privatization, and concentration of agricultural land fuels hierarchical and abusive approaches to labor, livestock, and competition, harming people, animals, and places at local and national scales.[64] While some would characterize this food system as efficient and productive, and certainly many farmers are pushing back against these trends, the evidence of the overall system's structural brutality and unsustainability is overwhelming.

---

[59] *Id.* at 1700; Daniel B. Rosenbaum, *Reforming Local Property for an Era of National Decline*, 70 BUFF. L. REV. 1115, 1116 (2022).

[60] Danielle Diamond et al., *Agricultural Exceptionalism, Environmental Injustice, and U.S. Right-to-Farm Laws*, 52 ENV'T L. REP. (ELI) 10727 (2022).

[61] MacKenzie Thurman, *Climate-Smart Agriculture Certification: A Call for Federal Action*, 122 COLUM. L. REV. F. 37, 56 (2022).

[62] *See* Margot J. Pollans & Matthew F. Watson, *FDA as Food System Steward*, 46 HARV. ENV'T L. REV. 1 (2022); Margot J. Pollans, *Eaters, Powerless by Design*, 120 MICH. L. REV. 643, 659 (2022); Laura Killalea, *"Horrible Outcomes for Pigs and Humans Alike": North Carolina's Right to Farm Law as an Unconstitutional Taking of Property near Pork Production Facilities*, 13 GEO. WASH. J. ENERGY & ENV'T L. 68 (2022).

[63] Joshua Ulan Galperin, *Legitimacy, Legality, Legacy, and the Life of Democracy*, 45 VT. L. REV. 563, 569 (2021) (acknowledging potential to dismiss agricultural decisionmaking structures as esoteric despite their being "broadly important as they govern the ground floor of food policy in this country."); Joshua Ulan Galperin, *The Death of Administrative Democracy*, 82 U. PITT. L. REV. 1, 3 (2020) (arguing that USDA decisionmaking structures are not "too esoteric to be meaningful").

[64] *See* Courtney G. Lee, *Racist Animal Agriculture*, 25 CUNY L. REV. 199 (2022); Thurman, *supra* note 61.

The collective implications of agricultural land and activities alongside the concentration of this resource in the hands of the few raises questions about who is entitled to benefit from agricultural land, and who is entitled to input over its governance. Do urban majorities have a right, obligation, or impetus to intervene to better manage this common good, even to wrest this resource away from the increasingly small segment of society that controls it? And if so, how might that be done?

RURAL ENERGY AS A COMMON RESOURCE

U.S. prosperity over the past century has largely been fueled, quite literally, by rural energy production. For instance, Nick Stump has addressed how "Appalachia, with its vast deposits of coal and oil and gas, has been absolutely central in the United States" to economic growth.[65] Appalachia has "been pillaged as a 'national sacrifice zone' or an 'energy sacrifice zone' because both the land and the people have been exploited in order to keep energy prices lower for the nation … to drive economic growth and ultimately … to facilitate capital accumulation among elite energy interests."[66]

Appalachia has not been alone as a site of rural energy production fueling regional and national needs. Conditions surrounding Western coal production have often mirrored the Appalachian experience, particularly in proximity to Indigenous communities.[67] Over the past two decades, most of the country's sites of shale gas extraction through hydraulic fracturing have been concentrated in "poorer, rural areas" in diverse regions.[68] Poor rural and Indigenous communities in the South have borne the greatest burdens of nuclear energy production.[69]

Certainly, urban communities, particularly communities of color, experience disproportionate burdens of energy production as well, particularly with the siting of power plants run on fossil fuels.[70] But environmental justice conversations often overlook how the extraction and production processes of the fossil fuel economy to

---

[65] Priya Baskaran, *Remaking Appalachia: Ecosocialism, Ecofeminism, and Law: A Conversation with Author Nicholas F. Stump and Professor Priya Baskaran*, 69 UCLA L. REV. DISCOURSE 106, 113 (2021).

[66] *Id.*

[67] *See* Ezra Rosser, *Ahistorical Indians and Reservation Resources*, 40 ENV'T L. 437 (2010).

[68] Matthew Castelli, *Fracking and the Rural Poor: Negative Externalities, Failing Remedies, and Federal Legislation*, 3 IND. J. L. & SO. EQUAL. 281 (2015); Jeanne Marie, Zokovitch Paben, *Green Power & Environmental Justice – Does Green Discriminate?* 46 Tex. Tech L. Rev. 1067, 1079 (2014).

[69] Kylie M. Allen, *Indigenous Nuclear Injuries and the Radiation Exposure Compensation Act (RECA): Reframing Compensation toward Indigenous-Led Environmental Reparations*, 10 ARIZ. J. ENV'T L. & POL'Y 264, 266 (2020); LOKA ASHWOOD, FOR-PROFIT DEMOCRACY: WHY THE GOVERNMENT IS LOSING THE TRUST OF RURAL AMERICA (2018).

[70] *See generally* Lara J. Cushing, Shiwen Li, Benjamin B. Steiger & Joan A. Casey, *Historical Redlining is Associated with Fossil Fuel Power Plant Siting and Present-day Inequalities in Air Pollutant Emissions*, 8 NATURE 52 (2022).

date have fundamentally involved the exploitation of rural resources, workers, and localities.[71] Energy, as we see each day when we charge our phones and cool and heat our homes and workplaces, is everywhere. But a substantial proportion of it comes from far-off places invisible to the average energy consumer.

Yet, rural regions' historical contributions to energy production are only half the story. Looking forward, rural energy production has a key role to play in decarbonizing the economy to ward off the worst effects of climate change.[72] Rural land, resources, and workers are essential, scholars largely agree, in order to transition away from fossil fuels.[73]

Naumann and Rudolph observe that a lack of mainstream attention to energy transitions as a rural phenomenon is "surprising" because "materializations of energy transition discourses are intimately entwined with, and shaped by, rural conditions, which likewise shape rural areas."[74] Rural regions have gained "new importance" in how they are "utilized, perceived and governed" because of their necessity to large-scale renewable energy generation "and as sites for adapting to and mitigating climate change."[75]

Energy law scholars recognize that "deep decarbonization will require a massive build-out of utility-scale wind and solar farms. This, in turn, will necessitate the construction of a large, nationally connected system of transmission lines to deliver electricity from remote, rural areas to 'load centers' – high-population areas that consume a greater amount of electricity."[76] In sum, rural energy production has brought collective gains in the past and is collectively needed now and in the future. Yet, much like with agricultural land uses, rural energy production is largely invisible to the urban majority.

The legal history of rural energy production exhibits some overlapping and divergent themes with agricultural land governance. A similar combination of private property regimes and passive state and federal regulation has enabled fossil fuel companies to accumulate concentrated land ownership, exploit workers and localities, and pollute landscapes with minimal consequences.[77] Historically, rural energy production has been characterized by exaggerated domination by a small amount of industry players, who have in turn greatly exacerbated global vulnerability to climate change.

Despite the public import of energy production, federal law and regulations have simply never reined in the fossil fuel sector to the extent necessary to counteract

---

[71] *Cf.* Ashwood, *supra* note 69.

[72] Matthias Naumann & David Rudolph, *Conceptualizing Rural Energy Transitions: Energizing Rural Studies, Ruralizing Energy Research*, 73 J. Rural Stud. 97 (2020).

[73] Shelley Welton, *The Bounds of Energy Law*, 62 B.C. L. Rev. 2339, 2379 (2021).

[74] Naumann & Rudolph, *supra* note 72.

[75] *Id.*

[76] Alexandra Klass et al., *Grid Reliability through Clean Energy*, 74 Stan. L. Rev. 969, 988 (2022).

[77] *See, e.g.,* Glynis Board, *Who Owns West Virginia?* WV Pub. Broad. (Dec. 11, 2013), https://wvpublic.org/who-owns-west-virginia/. *See also* Steven Stoll, Ramp Hollow: The Ordeal of Appalachia (2017).

the sector's many harms or to distribute the sector's gains equitably. To date, federal policymakers and regulators have adopted a laissez-faire approach to shale gas extraction, allowing the industry to hoard its economic benefits while imposing burdens on land, workers, and infrastructure in rural communities and beyond, although of course some workers, landowners, and localities have seen some economic benefits.[78] The friendly federal approach to fracking reflects a continuation of its traditions with coal, an industry which abused workers, communities, and landscapes with minimal oversight, some of which continues today. Yet, when federal law has intervened into fossil fuel development, it has often done so ineffectually. For instance, many agree that the Surface Mining Coal and Reclamation Act of 1977 actually facilitated the rise of mountaintop removal coal mining rather than curtail or mitigate it.[79]

Emergent trends in the rural renewable energy sector already indicate ripeness for similar risks of hoarding and abuse. "Carbon supremacists" advocate reducing carbon emissions as swiftly as possible with little regard to distributional considerations, which promotes the risk of a private sector free-for-all to exploit rural energy.[80] Sociologist Loka Ashwood has extensively documented how the Nuclear Regulatory Commission and a nuclear plant in rural Georgia have coordinated to subjugate the local community for value extraction driven by profit motives and the "tyranny of the majority."[81] The proliferation of wind farms in rural regions has caused local agitation. Rural necessity means rural residents and workers remain vulnerable to the collective imposing clean energy production on them in the name of the greater good, as has played out over decades of fossil fuel production.[82]

In short, we continue to need rural energy as a collective good, but without an approach to rural energy as a common resource, the energy sector may hoard, abuse, and waste this collective amenity as well. The collective implications of rural energy alongside the history of abuses by the hands of the few again raises questions about the appropriate balance between local, national, private, and public considerations. Do urban majorities have a right, obligation, or impetus to ensure effective governance of this common good, and to keep the benefits of rural energy production from being hoarded? And if so, how can that be done while accounting for different

---

[78] Ann M. Eisenberg, *Beyond Science and Hysteria: Reality and Perceptions of Environmental Justice Concerns Surrounding Marcellus and Utica Shale Gas Development*, 77 U. PITT. L. REV 183 (2015) (discussing federal exemptions of shale gas extraction from all major environmental statutes).

[79] JUDAH SCHEPT, COAL, CAGES, CRISIS: THE RISE OF THE PRISON ECONOMY IN CENTRAL APPALACHIA 87 (2022); McGinley, *supra* note 10.

[80] *See* SHALANDA M. BAKER, REVOLUTIONARY POWER: AN ACTIVIST'S GUIDE TO THE ENERGY TRANSITION (2021).

[81] *See* ASHWOOD, *supra* note 69.

[82] Welton, *supra* note 73, at 2379 (noting risk that transformation to renewable energy may exacerbate longstanding inequalities, continuing to shunt burdens of large renewable energy infrastructure onto marginalized rural communities); Shalanda H. Baker, *Anti-Resilience: A Roadmap for Transformational Justice within the Energy System*, 54 HARV. C.R.-C.L. L. REV. 1, 19 (2019).

levels of rural embeddedness, entitlement, and cost-bearing in relation to the shared resource of rural energy?

RURAL INFRASTRUCTURE AS A COMMON RESOURCE

Rural infrastructure as a collectively important good can be understood on two scales. The most prominent scale is the national one. Much of the existing on-the-ground national transportation infrastructure runs through rural regions. Traveling great distances on the ground necessitates travel over highways and railroads hosted by more population-sparse localities. Both people and resources rely on this transportation network to move around the country. Other national networks, such as energy and telecommunications infrastructure, are also largely woven together across rural regions.[83] That rural-hosted infrastructure plays a key role in the national economy.[84]

The pursuit of national resilience involves the pursuit of better national infrastructure and regional systems, including in transportation, energy transmission, broadband deployment, and other sectors.[85] A national network of high-speed, low-emissions passenger trains, for instance, far beyond Amtrak's currently limited reach, would substantially reduce national greenhouse gas emissions contributing to climate change.[86] Building out and enhancing these systems throughout the country, even in relatively population-sparse regions, would not just benefit rural regions by helping make them more prosperous. Better national infrastructure reduces costs and eases barriers to travel, the shipping of goods, disaster recovery, and other aspects of a thriving society.

Rural infrastructure is also collectively important on more localized scales. The collective importance of local rural infrastructure can be understood in two ways. First, the political and social upheaval of the past decade illustrates that regional deterioration yields negative sociopolitical effects, beyond the moral problems associated with letting entire regions decay. The widespread attention to rural anger and resentment, and those feelings' manifestations in support for authoritarianism, suggest that national policies allowing rural regions to unravel have not, in fact, worked out well for the nation.[87]

---

[83] *See generally* TRIP, RURAL CONNECTIONS: CHALLENGES AND OPPORTUNITIES IN AMERICA'S HEARTLAND (2020), https://tripnet.org/wp-content/uploads/2020/05/TRIP_Rural_Roads_Report_2020.pdf.

[84] *Id.*

[85] *Cf.* David Schaper, *Potholes, Grid Failures, Aging Tunnels and Bridges: Infrastructure Gets a C-Minus*, NPR (Mar. 3, 2021), www.npr.org/2021/03/03/973054080/potholes-grid-failures-aging-tunnels-and-bridges-nations-infrastructure-gets-a-c.

[86] *See* David Konarske Jr, *Amtrak: The Failure of Passenger Preference and Politics of Nonenforcement*, 53 LOY. U. CHI. L. J. 583, 585 (2022); Darren A. Prum & Sarah L. Catz, *High-Speed Rail in America: An Evaluation of the Regulatory, Real Property, and Environmental Obstacles a Project Will Encounter*, 13 N.C. J. L. & TECH. 247, 284 (2012).

[87] *Cf.* Ian Scoones et al., *Emancipatory Rural Politics: Confronting Authoritarian Populism*, 45 J. PEASANT STUD. 1, 7–9 (2018).

The second way in which local rural infrastructure is collectively important is that society is likely going to use and rely on local rural infrastructure more heavily in the face of current and oncoming crises. The COVID-19 pandemic has already cast a new light on the desirability of population-sparse life, with many urban downtowns suffering from population outflow. Coastal retreat, other forms of climate migration, freshwater scarcity, and sea-level rise all suggest that the interior and more remote regions of the country will gain new desirability as places to live in the near future.[88] Once again putting aside questions of moral obligations to distressed localities, rural regions acting as the geographic safety net raises the question of whether the urban majority that may need to use that safety net should wait until the crises worsen to ensure that the rural refuge has adequate broadband, schools, streets, drinking water, wastewater treatment, and other essentials of civic life.[89]

Rural regions used to enjoy more robust public protections in their access to infrastructure, at both national and local scales. As discussed in Chapter 5, at the scale of national interconnectedness, with the era of congressional deregulation from the 1970s and forward, public oversight of infrastructure industries gave way to greater private discretion as to which localities would be served.[90] Following deregulation, the private sector has often abandoned rural infrastructure, contributing to many rural regions' downward socioeconomic spirals.[91]

The legal history of transportation infrastructure illustrates how the private sector has been deputized to shape an essential rural good despite that infrastructure's collective import, and how the private sector has unsurprisingly failed to steward rural infrastructure. Rural communities used to enjoy more or less satisfactory levels of access to passenger trains, passenger buses, and air travel. Subsequent to the withdrawal of federal oversight through measures such as the Airline Deregulation Act of 1978 and the Bus Regulatory Reform Act of 1982, rural transportation infrastructure shrank, isolating rural regions from the rest of the country.[92]

At the local level, rural infrastructural decay has been spurred by a variety of factors.[93] But much like at the national level, the inadequacy of localities' public amenities can largely be attributed to the retreat of federal and state actors from protecting and supporting those amenities, and the inadequacy of the private

---

[88] *See* Michelle Wilde Anderson, The Fight to Save the Town: Reimagining Discarded America (2022); *Michelle Wilde Anderson on America's Cities: Free Range with Mike Livermore*, Soundcloud (Nov. 2022), https://soundcloud.com/user-311970225/michelle-wilde-anderson-on-americas-cities.

[89] *Cf.* Anderson, *supra* note 88, at 243 (articulating vision of resident-centered governance for distressed local governments).

[90] Ganesh Sitaraman et al., *Regulation and the Geography of Inequality*, 70 Duke L.J. 1763 (2021).

[91] *Id.*

[92] *See* Dempsey, *supra* note 44.

[93] *See* Lisa R. Pruitt & Bradley E. Showman, *Law Stretched Thin: Access to Justice in Rural America*, 59 S.D. L. Rev. 466, 483 (2014).

sector to maintain them.[94] Rural local governments are experiencing the same fiscal crises, service provision gaps, and privatization pressures as local governments of diverse sizes throughout the country.[95] Rural difference, however – including remoteness, population sparseness, and limited economies of scale – means that while cities are able to somewhat overcome this shifting governance regime through mechanisms such as public–private partnerships and philanthropic activities, these privately driven compensatory measures are often unavailable to protect rural infrastructure.[96]

Critically, characterizing rural infrastructure as a common good raises different questions than those posed earlier for agricultural land and rural energy. Rural infrastructure does not necessarily warrant the urban majority reclaiming entitlement, unlike the hoarded and abused goods of agriculture and energy. In one sense, the urban majority is *already* entitled to rural infrastructure; infrastructure is an example of a common good that is non-rivalrous, or shared without depletion.[97] However, just as property rights entail property responsibilities,[98] entitlement to infrastructure suggests an obligation to take care of that infrastructure. Viewed holistically, rural infrastructure belongs to all of us, whether to facilitate national interconnectedness, to support the rural workers we need, or as a resource we might want to take direct advantage of in the future. So if rural infrastructure is a common good, that characterization implies that the urban majority needs to demand and facilitate better stewardship of it.

Put altogether, agricultural land, rural energy, and rural infrastructure begin to paint a fuller picture of how rural America itself is a common resource. Additional puzzle pieces include rural America's vast natural resources and millions of acres of federally owned lands. A synthesized view of these resources suggests that rural America is greater than the sum of its parts. It is a holistic entity, central to the broader national system of geographic interdependence. This portrayal challenges the myth of rural obsolescence, instead illustrating a dynamic and critical component that is central to a better national future.

Yet, the hoarding and waste described earlier, along with overall rural deterioration, suggests that society as a whole is not taking care of the resource that is rural America. Karl Marx's "metabolic rift" offers substantial explanatory power to clarify the disconnect between ongoing rural necessity and urban ignorance about

---

[94] *See* ALICIA ALVAREZ & PAUL R. TREMBLAY, INTRODUCTION TO TRANSACTIONAL LAWYERING PRACTICE (2022) (detailing drop in federal support for local government activities since 1980s).

[95] *See generally* ANDERSON, *supra* note 88; Ellen Dannin, *Crumbling Infrastructure, Crumbling Democracy: Infrastructure Privatization Contracts and Their Effects on State and Local Governance*, 6 NW. J. L. & SOC. POL'Y 47 (2011).

[96] *See* Ann M. Eisenberg, *Rural Blight*, 13 HARV. L. & POL'Y REV. 187 (2018); Ann M. Eisenberg, *Economic Regulation and Rural America*, 98 WASH. U. L. REV. 737 (2021).

[97] *See* Brett M. Frischmann, *An Economic Theory of Infrastructure and Commons Management*, 89 MINN. L. REV. 917, 942 (2005).

[98] *See* Kristen A. Carpenter et al., *In Defense of Property*, 118 YALE L. J. 1022, 1065 (2009).

that necessity.[99] The metabolic rift refers to the divergence over time between the places where food and fiber are produced, and the increasingly distant places where they are consumed, alongside populations' increasing distance from nature.[100] The metabolic rift reveals urbanization – at least dramatic agglomeration urbanization associated with the rise of modern megacities – as yielding inherent justice and sustainability concerns.

In any case, the hoarding, abuse, and waste of the rural commons indicates that a substantially different governance regime is warranted to better account for the collective import of the commons that is rural America.

GOVERNING RURAL AMERICA AS A COMMONS

The question of how to govern rural America as a commons touches on questions surrounding the so-called urban–rural divide that have already received some scholarly and political attention, such as classic questions of "jobs versus environment" trade-offs. However, the overarching commons framework – recognizing that rural America is, in fact, a commons – can help facilitate an enhanced approach with more meaningful normative guidance than the market-supremacist instincts that have guided so many interventions, or failures to intervene, in much of recent history.

Centrally, governing rural America as a commons necessitates recognizing different levels of entitlement to, embeddedness in, proximity to, and cost-bearing of commons governance, and seeking to reconcile these competing relationships. That reconciliation must happen under a broader umbrella of the ultimate goal for governing a commons: stewardship, with a view to sustaining those common resources for future generations and fostering resilience, meaning the ability to recover in the face of changed conditions.

Varied levels of entitlements to the rural commons are reflected in legal claims, most particularly property law, and moral claims, such that the urban majority might assert due to rural resources' collective import, or that an Indigenous tribe might assert for longstanding cultural rights not currently recognized by law. Differing levels of proximity, embeddedness, and cost-bearing of the commons are reflected in the fact that any majoritarian decisions that affect the rural commons have more diffuse effects on the urban majority with more immediate, yet still varied, effects on local rural stakeholders.

Despite the urban majority's normative claim to the rural commons, a central problem with the urban majority seeking to govern the rural commons is that the urban majority has historically often sought input and control over certain resources without offering concomitant stewardship for those more deeply embedded in the

---

[99] *See* ASHWOOD, *supra* note 69.
[100] Geoffrey Garver, *Confronting Remote Ownership Problems with Ecological Law*, 43 VT. L. REV. 425, 444 (2019).

commons. Literature on urbanormativity demonstrates trends in urban majorities imposing poorly tailored laws that assume urban conditions on rural communities, often in the name of the greater good, to rural communities' detriment – failing to take into account rural embeddedness, proximity, and cost-bearing, for instance, or using rural resources for short-term extractive purposes without regard for the eventual depletion of resources, people, and places.[101]

Agricultural land tenure offers an example where it is tempting to advocate greater urban intervention into the rural commons. By facilitating rural depopulation and agricultural concentration, the urban majority has ceded rural regions to increasingly small groups of economic elites who abuse agricultural land, and in turn, the public's health, often with apparent impunity.[102] The urban majority might shy away from instincts to intervene in the face of agricultural producers highlighting their greater entitlements to, embeddedness in, and cost-bearing of the rural commons, as well as their current contributions to the national food system. However, as Shoemaker articulates, "[A]gricultural lands are public goods with important public functions, and it warrants asking whether our systems for managing and allocating these resources are still serving the public good."[103]

Even in this sphere, urban acknowledgment of rural importance risks missing the mark on different interventions with resources largely located in rural regions. For example, scholars have proposed that farmers currently being compensated to leave land fallow could similarly be compensated to host renewable energy production facilities.[104] While this proposal would address one collective need – expediting emissions reductions – it would arguably betray other collective and local needs, namely, the need to not further entrench and reward current hierarchies of inequitable and unsustainable agricultural land ownership.

This is an instance where urban education, assertions of entitlement, and contestation might strike a better balance for taking care of the common good that is agricultural land rather than acquiescing to "a rural landscape that benefits only a chosen few."[105] Given the extreme conditions reflected in agricultural land tenure, alongside the vulnerability and lack of political power of non-elite local groups subject to the consequences of that land tenure, it would seem to behoove the urban majority to consider intervention through redistributive policies that democratize and improve the agricultural sector.

The prospect of achieving the right balance in governing the rural commons can understandably seem overwhelming in light of the complexity of the task.

---

[101] *See* STUDIES IN URBANORMATIVITY: RURAL COMMUNITY IN URBAN SOCIETY 7 (Gregory M. Fulkerson & Alexander R. Thomas eds. 2006); Ashwood & MacTavish, *supra* note 53.

[102] *See* Rosenbaum, *supra* note 59, at 1116.

[103] Shoemaker, *supra* note 55, at 1739.

[104] *See, e.g.*, Hannah J. Wiseman, Samuel R. Wiseman, & Chris Wright, *Farming Solar on the Margins*, 103 B.U. L. REV. 525 (2023).

[105] *Id.* at 1703.

This discussion now turns to five principles that any intervention into rural regions should prioritize. These principles seek to capture the normative implications of the commons framework in five concrete guidelines that can be incorporated into governance decisions. The principles' overarching theme is the need to steward the commons for future generations, in the interest of a more resilient society. While each principle is treated in isolation, their most powerful iteration involves recognizing them as circular and interdependent: Each is in part premised on acceptance of the others.

These principles often do already make appearances in various policies and frameworks. It is worth noting that the writing of this book has coincided with substantial changes in federal interventions that offer some promise for a different path forward. The combined investments and incentives through the American Rescue Plan Act of 2021, Infrastructure Investment and Jobs Act of 2021, Inflation Reduction Act of 2022, and other major legislative initiatives have been likened to the War on Poverty or the New Deal.[106] People working in the rural development space have acknowledged that new resources may be flowing to rural communities and workers; some of these interventions may be moving the needle in ways rural advocates have long called for. While it is too soon to assess these interventions' full effects on rural communities, the discussion references some of these laws' provisions as potential approaches to rural commons governance.

PRINCIPLE 1: TREATING MORE RURAL WORK AS WORK IN THE PUBLIC INTEREST

Throughout this book, I have referred to the important public contributions and sacrifices made by rural workers and residents, whether in food production, energy production, ecological stewardship, or beyond. The commons framework helps capture the public import of this uniquely rural work. Instead of repeatedly insisting that this rural work is important, or "quasi-public," the commons framework helps normalize the conceptualization of certain rural labor as public interest labor, whether it is through public employment or not.

This principle helps shed light on new possibilities and a better path forward for rural work. It is both unjust and unsustainable, for example, for agricultural workers to toil in obscurity, under such great threats and so little pay and security. Recognizing farmworkers as workers in the public interest necessitates that they are entitled to strengthened job security, greater pay, and improved working conditions, as well as

---

[106] *See generally* Nadia Ahmad, Uma Outka, Danielle Stokes, & Hannah Wiseman, *Synthesizing Energy Transitions*, 39 GA. ST. U. L. REV. 1087, 1121 (2023); Malcolm M. Gilbert & Aspen B. Ward, *What the Trust? Overcoming Barriers to Renewable Energy Development in Indian Country*, 46 PUB. LAND & RESOURCES L. REV. 133, 153 (2023); Lance Gable, *Pursuing Climate Justice: Learning the Lessons of the Covid-19 Response*, 16 ST. LOUIS U.J. HEALTH L. & POL'Y 5, 32 (2022).

stronger avenues for enforcing existing protective laws.[107] While the exploitation of rural workers has so often been justified in the name of the greater good, the commons framework helps reorient that lens: Rural workers should be robustly protected and compensated because of their important contributions to the greater good.

This discussion has emphasized agriculture, energy, and conservation, but there is room to consider what kinds of rural work ought to be treated as work in the public interest. Hannah Haksgaard as argued, for example, that rural lawyers, even in private practice, should be considered engaged in public interest work.[108] Haksgaard's definition of public interest centers on how even private practitioners in rural areas mitigate widespread rural lawyer shortages, expand access to services for low-income populations, and have positive impacts on their communities. While this argument differs somewhat from the conceptualization of work stewarding the rural commons as work for the greater good, the underlying principles of our analyses are the same: Certain rural work remains underappreciated as work for the greater good, and recognizing those contributions implies that policies should treat that work as more valuable than they currently do.

Recognizing rural work as work in the public interest can also refer to other types of rural burdens. As discussed earlier, rural communities are going to be asked more and more to bear the burden of hosting clean energy in the name of the greater good. The commons framework suggests that asking rural communities to bear this burden is not necessarily a bad thing. However, that burden should be recognized as borne in the public interest, and adequately facilitated and compensated as such.[109]

How can rural work, and rural burden more broadly, be adequately recognized, protected, and compensated when it is work in the public interest? Interventions into rural communities should ask these questions in the interest of better governing rural America as a commons.

PRINCIPLE 2: BUILDING CAPACITY TO AVOID BOOM-BUST CYCLES

The company town associated with so many extractive rural industries was never a sustainable model of development. Building up a locality or region around one

---

[107] *US Labor Law for Farmworkers*, FARMWORKER JUSTICE, www.farmworkerjustice.org/advocacy_program/us-labor-law-for-farmworkers/ [https://perma.cc/Y6ZL-UALW] ("[F]arm work is not covered by many important labor protections enjoyed by most other workers in this country ... [although] farmworkers do rely on some provisions of the federal Fair Labor Standards Act ("FLSA") and the Migrant and Seasonal Agricultural Worker Protection Act ("AWPA") to provide minimum levels of worker protections.").

[108] Hannah Haksgaard, *Rural Practice as Public Interest Work*, 71 ME. L. REV. 209 (2019).

[109] *Cf.* Sarah Mills, *Michigan's System to Approve Green Energy Projects Is Broken*, BRIDGE MICHIGAN (Sept. 25, 2023) www.bridgemi.com/guest-commentary/opinion-michigans-system-approve-green-energy-projects-broken [https://perma.cc/6GXY-ZGE4] (discussing rural concerns about bearing clean energy burden alone).

industry is an extractive task in and of itself. This model is designed to do one thing: extract value from the land and the workers for profit to be funneled elsewhere, until depletion. As much as the extractive process may bring its own harms, the point of depletion brings the company town or single-industry region to the point of collapse. As we have seen, those collapses fuel regional and national destabilization, effectuating harms far beyond the localities most hurt.

The commons governance model demands that, where unique rural work is pursued, boom-bust cycles must be avoided in the name of stewarding the rural commons for the long term. The formula for avoiding boom-bust cycles is simple in theory, but requires thoughtful, collaborative, and resource-intensive approaches to effectuate.[110] First, localities should be supported to pursue economic diversification. An economy not reliant on a single industry is more resilient when one industry contracts or fades out altogether. Interventions in the pursuit of rural economic activity should consider whether such disproportionate reliance on a single industry will result, and should in turn take steps to avoid this dependency.

The second ingredient for avoiding boom-bust cycles is the strengthening of capacity-building institutions. Another feature of the company town is the weakness of such a town's institutions. The industry wields influence over local schools, stores, and governing structures, and uses that power to keep the local population subjugated to be funneled toward its labor and resource needs. Interventions into rural regions can avoid the creation of new company towns by pursuing the opposite model. Investing in and planning for well-funded, transparent local governance institutions, educational institutions, civic organizations, and collaborative local visioning processes all make communities more resilient, in contrast to merely furnishing single-industry dependencies.

Of course, recognizing the importance of such investments requires a relinquishment of market supremacy and industry profit as the primary goal of rural–industry–government relations. Clean energy provides an example of how this principle might be implemented in policy. While federal and state institutions may establish frameworks for how clean energy manufacturing or siting should be pursued in rural localities, this commons principle necessitates that those frameworks should extend their considerations beyond the narrow questions related solely to the clean energy industry, not leaving rural local governments to navigate development on their own.

Frameworks should establish baselines for Community Benefits Agreements and Project Labor Agreements that help reduce the risk of community dependency and open pathways to community capacity and diversified development. While one could argue that such a pursuit should not fall on the shoulders of the individual clean energy developers, placing this burden on those developers is indeed essential to commons governance. Even if clean energy development

---

[110] *See* Gwen Arnold et al., *Boom, Bust, Action! How Communities Can Cope with Boom-Bust Cycles in Unconventional Oil and Gas Development,* 39 REV. OF POL'Y RESEARCH 541 (2022).

is pursued by the private sector, it is typically enabled in the name of the greater good – and pursued within the rural commons. As such, the opportunity to profit from the rural commons in the name of collective benefit should come with requirements to help steward the rural commons for the future.

The "energy communities" provision of the Inflation Reduction Act illustrates the potential and peril of seeking to balance national interests and rural ones when it comes to community capacity-building. Several provisions of the IRA facilitate a 10 percent tax credit for locating new clean energy facilities in an "energy community." An "energy community" is defined as:

(i)   a brownfield site [as defined under the Comprehensive Environmental Response, Compensation, and Liability Act],

(ii)   a metropolitan statistical area or nonmetropolitan statistical area which –
    (I)   has (or, at any time during the period beginning after December 31, 2009, had) 0.17 percent or greater direct employment or 25 percent or greater local tax revenues related to the extraction, processing, transport, or storage of coal, oil, or natural gas … and
    (II) has an unemployment rate at or above the national average unemployment rate for the previous year … or

(iii) a census tract –
    (I)   in which –
        (aa) after December 31, 1999, a coal mine has closed, or
        (bb) after December 31, 2009, a coal-fired electric generating unit has been retired, or
    (II) which is directly adjoining to any census tract described in subclause (I).

On the one hand, this provision looks promising. It seems wise for federal law to incentivize locating renewable energy facilities in localities that are currently burdened with brownfields, the loss of coal, oil, and natural gas revenues and employment, and coal mine or plant closures. Such incentives might help offset the losses borne by fossil fuel communities in transition, while also pursuing the important national policy goal of renewable energy production. These communities will undoubtedly be found across a variety of landscapes, but many communities falling into this category are likely to be rural – contributing to the rural common good of energy production.

However, this provision also raises questions about how the siting will be pursued. Will the community have an avenue to request such a facility? Or might such a facility be imposed upon them? Will the facility's siting require a Community Benefits Agreement such that the community's contributions to collective needs will be reflected in equitably distributed local benefits? Will such community benefits be funneled into capacity-building enterprises, such as schools and telecommunications infrastructure? If there were an application process to solicit facilities, would communities with the greatest needs be afforded support in order to access and effectively leverage those resources?

In other words, thrusting renewable energy production onto rural communities would not constitute stewardship of the rural commons, but merely continued patterns of extraction and exploitation that risk continuing to facilitate hoarding and waste of the rural commons. Stewardship of the rural commons while maximizing its collective benefits entails taking care of the workers, localities, and infrastructures that facilitate production of the collective's goods. Taking steps to avoid boom-bust cycles in the frameworks that govern community economic development is essential to that stewardship.

PRINCIPLE 3: DEMOCRATIZING RURAL RESOURCES

Legal frameworks that facilitate hoarding and waste of rural resources are inimical to the commons framework. As such, commons governance should facilitate the democratization of rural resources, especially where those resources have been unduly concentrated and privatized for the benefit of a few.

Rural property, and agricultural land in particular, offer important examples where democratizing principles should be incorporated into governance frameworks. The prospect of land reform tends to be a nonstarter in the United States, in part due to cultural attachment to the ideology of market supremacy. However, Shoemaker's analysis gives us permission, indeed the impetus, to consider land reform seriously.[111] Observing that property design "is much more dynamic and pluralistic than our intuitions may first suggest,"[112] Shoemaker proposes her own three guiding principles for rural property reform.

These include, first, that property frameworks should reconnect ownership and active stewardship, as opposed to continuing to facilitate the commodification of land that enables absentee ownership. Shoemaker notes a variety of law and policy tools that could be used to pursue this specific aim, including connecting ownership to residency requirements and limiting absentee corporate ownership of farmland.[113] Second, "opportunities to access agricultural land must be fair and equitable."[114] And third, Shoemaker proposes we recognize that "property change is possible but practically difficult."[115] As "a creature of state law ... some reforms are slow to proceed or may not happen at all."[116] Importantly, however, there is the room for federal leadership, as when the Farm Bill encouraged states to pass the Uniform Partition of Heirs Property Act, offering more protection for owners of heirs' property.[117]

---

[111] Shoemaker, *supra* note 55, at 1746.
[112] *Id.* at 1740.
[113] *Id.* at 1748
[114] *Id.*
[115] *Id.* at 1749.
[116] *Id.*
[117] *Id.*

Shoemaker's proposals for considering rural property reform can be applied to other contexts where resources with collective import have been subject to inordinate concentration and abuse. And so, too, can past and current models that have effectively deployed or managed rural resources through more broadly shared ownership and management – like the Rural Electrification Act and rural electric cooperatives.

What does democratized rural clean energy look like? What does democratized rural natural resource management look like? How do we balance local interests with regional and national ones, and avenues for input for all who are entitled to the rural commons, but experience it at varied distances? The commons framework insists that these questions be considered in approaches to rural governance.

PRINCIPLE 4: PURSUING RACIAL JUSTICE AS CENTRAL TO RESILIENCE

Extreme racial stratification in some rural regions is another illustration of improperly concentrated ownership or domination of the rural commons. A commons is meant to be shared, and shared fairly. Even without considering the clear moral need for restorative racial justice in rural communities explored in Chapters 6 and 7, the disproportionate shares of white land ownership illustrate an imbalance facilitated by misguided governance of the commons.

The pursuit of racial justice is central to the pursuit of resilient stewardship of the rural commons. In addition to being morally wrong, racial stratification is destabilizing, unsustainable, and wasteful.[118] Racial stratification and segregation diminish the importance of the public sphere and motivate retreat to private corners, just when investments in shared public amenities, such as infrastructure, become critical to collective survival.

Another reason racial justice is central to resilience is that pluralistic perspectives and practices tend to be more effective perspectives and practices, especially in a diverse society. In other words, allowing one demographic to dominate rural regions also narrows the cultural knowledge and values that are brought to bear on the stewardship activities that affect the rural commons, such as agricultural land ownership.

As a central example, ample commentary has observed common differences underlying Indigenous perspectives on approaches to land stewardship, as compared to white ones. Rebecca Tsosie contrasts the "Indigenous land ethic" with the European "ethic of opportunity."[119] The former refers to "a world in which Native

---

[118] *Cf. US: Boldly Act on Racism, Poverty, Voting*, HUMAN RIGHTS WATCH (Jan. 12, 2023), www.hrw .org/news/2023/01/12/us-boldly-act-racism-poverty-voting (characterizing entrenched racism in United States as existential threat to US democracy).

[119] Rebecca Tsosie, *Indigenous Sustainability and Resilience to Climate Extremes: Traditional Knowledge and the Systems of Survival*, 51 CONN. L. REV. 1009, 1017 (2019).

people, their lands, and their resources, interact under a Divine plan created for a particular place on earth … [as] a set of laws and instructions [that] is designed to provide order, balance, and abundance, securing the ability of future generations to also live on these lands."[120] Tsotsie notes that this perspective might be associated in essence "with environmental sustainability."[121] The European perspective, by contrast, refers to "utilitarian norms" and the justification of corporations' exploitative practices on U.S. soil.[122]

The Inflation Reduction Act pursues some interventions that seek to counteract rural racial stratification. Its provision entitled, "Support for Underserved Farmers, Ranchers, and Foresters" provides for appropriations for technical support for underserved farmers; for "improv[ing] land access (including heirs' property and fractionated land issues) for underserved farmers, ranchers, and forest landowners"; for equity commissions to "address racial equity issues within the Department of Agriculture"; and to provide financial support for victims of the Department of Agriculture's history of racial discrimination.[123] This measure seems poised to help counteract the harms of racialized land concentration in agriculture by democratizing access to agriculture, helping remedy some past harms, and pursuing the greater resilience that is innately tied to fairer racial dynamics.

But one wonders what measures that go even further would look like. The proposed Justice for Black Farmers Act,[124] the Land Back movement,[125] and initiatives to "take seriously the plight of Latinxs" in rural regions[126] all offer important considerations for strengthening governance of the rural commons through the pursuit of racial equity.

PRINCIPLE 5: RECOGNIZING THAT INVESTING IN RURAL INFRASTRUCTURE IS IN THE PUBLIC INTEREST

Once one debunks the myths of rural irrelevance, rural unsustainability, organic rural decline, rural radicalism, rural whiteness, and rural obsolescence, and once one establishes that much of rural work is public interest work, that long-term planning for rural economies is possible, that access to rural resources can be democratized, and that rural racial justice is conceivable, the fifth guiding principle for governing the rural commons follows. Investing in rural infrastructure is not a waste

---

[120] *Id.*

[121] *Id.*

[122] *Id.*

[123] Inflation Reduction Act of 2022, Pub. L. No. 117-169, § 22007, 136 Stat. 1818, 2021–23 (2022).

[124] Justice for Black Farmers Act, S. 300, 117th Cong. §§ 202-03, 401-04, 522 (2021).

[125] Mel Neal, *Between A Rock and A Hard Place: The Current Situation of the #landback Movement and Indigenous-Imagined Futures*, 13 Ariz. J. Envtl. L. & Pol'y 47 (2022).

[126] Luz E. Herrera & Pilar Margarita Hernández Escontrías, Ph.D., *Latinxs Reshaping Law & Policy in the U.S. South*, 31 S. Cal. Rev. L. & Soc. Just. 1, 66 (2022).

of money or a lost cause. Investing in rural infrastructure does not need to involve unfairly distributing benefits to one particular demographic. Investing in rural infrastructure is not merely an act of charity, as it is so often portrayed in conversations on rural subsidies.

Instead, investing in rural infrastructure is necessary to sharing and stewarding the rural commons. The rural workers pursuing their work in the public interest can do that work sustainably in towns and counties – localities designed and supported to avoid boom-bust cycles – that are well connected to national transportation, telecommunications, and energy networks. Those workers can do their jobs all the more effectively, for the long term, in communities with good roads, drinking water, housing stock, and schools. Well-invested rural infrastructure can be positioned to receive climate migrants in a resilient fashion, rather than as a destabilizing shock. National and local rural infrastructure is infrastructure for everyone, and our policies should treat it as such.

The "unprecedented" new funding streams available through the legislation listed earlier offer promise for a new era of rural infrastructure investments.[127] However, questions remain about the bridges that need to be built for this era to be realized. "As has been documented repeatedly, the nonprofits and other civic agencies that comprise the leaner and overburdened civic infrastructure of rural places are at a disadvantage when navigating complex bureaucracies and applying for federal funds…. Even when funds are earmarked for rural places, they often still fail to reach their intended beneficiaries."[128]

And thus, this story comes full circle. We need more people like Kat, and WVU's Land Use Clinic, helping bridge those gaps.

CONCLUSION

A more prosperous and equitable future for rural America is possible. The first step toward that realization is recognizing that rural marginalization results from choices. Those choices have so often been made in the name of market supremacy. We can make different choices rooted in sustainability, justice, and the need for collective action to survive climate change. Rural communities are so far from being a vestige of the past: They are an integral part of the nation's future, and it behooves us all to claim entitlement to imagine them as such.

---

[127] Kathleen Flanagan & Jerry Neal Kenney, *Rural-to-Rural Partnerships: Leveling the Playing Field to Secure Federal Funding*, THE DAILY YONDER (May 23, 2023), https://dailyyonder.com/rural-to-rural-partnerships-leveling-the-playing-field-to-secure-federal-funding/2023/05/23/ [https://perma.cc/3928-6JDR].

[128] *Id.*

Index